Books featured:

Bauer, Marion Dane   *On My Honour*
Byars, Betsy   *The Animal, The Vegetable and John D. Jones*
            The Glory Girl
            The TV Kid
Clarke, Arthur C.   *Dolphin Island*
Cross, Gillian   *The Demon Headmaster*
Dahl, Roald   *Going Solo*
Frank, Anne   *The Diary of Anne Frank*
Hentoff, Nat   *Does This School Have Capital Punishment?*
Hinton, S. E.   *The Outsiders*
Jennings, Paul   *Unreal!*
Klein, Robin   *Ratbags and Rascals*
Lawrence, Louise   *Children of the Dust*
Neville, Emily   *It's Like This, Cat*
O'Brien, Robert   *Z for Zachariah*
Park, Ruth   *Come Danger, Come Darkness*
Paterson, Katherine   *The Great Gilly Hopkins*
Rubinstein, Gillian   *Space Demons*
Sperry, Armstrong   *The Boy Who Was Afraid*
Thiele, Colin   *Chadwick's Chimney*
Townsend, Sue   *The Secret Diary of Adrian Mole Aged 13¾*

ENJOYING ENGLISH

BOOK 2 SADLER/HAYLLAR/POWELL

Enjoying English. Book 2

MACMILLAN

First published 1990 by
MACMILLAN EDUCATION AUSTRALIA PTY LTD
627 Chapel Street, South Yarra 3141
Reprinted 1990, 1991 (twice), 1992, 1993 (twice), 1994, 1995, 1996, 1998, 1999 (twice)

Associated companies and representatives
throughout the world

National Library of Australia
cataloguing in publication data.

Sadler, R. K. (Rex Kevin).
  Enjoying English. Book 2.

  ISBN 0 7329 0223 1

  1. English language – Rhetoric – Juvenile literature.
  2. English language – Composition and exercises –
  Juvenile literature. I. Hayllar, T. A. S. (Thomas Albert S.).
  II. Powell C. J. (Clifford J.). III. Title.

808.'042

Typeset in Palatino by Savage Type Pty Ltd, Brisbane
Printed in Malaysia by
Vivar Printing Sdn. Bhd.

CONTENTS

PREFACE

The *Enjoying English* series is a literature-based course for secondary students. It features an extensive selection of passages drawn from high-interest, contemporary novels and non-fiction books. These constitute a base for the development of comprehension skills and additional work on language and writing skills. Because of the quality of these passages, we anticipate that students will be encouraged to read more widely by seeking out these and other similar books from libraries.

The course gives considerable emphasis to poetry and drama. The wide range of poems presented offers an opportunity for students to explore and appreciate the richness of this strand of literature. Many drama extracts and complete scripts are included, as well as creative drama projects and tasks.

The creative writing sections encourage the development of writing skills by the use of writing models and stimulus photographs. Practical language work is incorporated in each unit to reinforce and develop the students' understanding of essential language concepts.

All the material in *Enjoying English* has been thoroughly tested in the classroom to ensure that it offers rich possibilities for valuable learning and enjoyment.

TALES WEIRD
AND WONDERFUL

STORIES

Smart Ice-Cream

A boy who thinks he's better than everybody else suddenly finds he is defeated by a very unusual kind of ice-cream.

Well, I came top of the class again. One hundred out of one hundred for Maths. And one hundred out of one hundred for English. I'm just a natural brain, the best there is. There isn't one kid in the class who can come near me. Next to me they are all dumb.

Even when I was a baby I was smart. The day that I was born my mother started tickling me. 'Bub, bub, bub,' she said.

'Cut it out, Mum,' I told her. 'That tickles.' She nearly fell out of bed when I said that. I was very advanced for my age.

Every year I win a lot of prizes: top of the class, top of the school, stuff like that. I won a prize for spelling when I was only three years old. I am a terrific speller. If you can say it, I can spell it. Nobody can trick me on spelling. I can spell every word there is.

Some kids don't like me; I know that for a fact. They say I'm a show off. I don't care. They are just jealous because they are not as clever as me. I'm good looking too. That's another reason why they are jealous.

Last week something bad happened. Another kid got one hundred out of one hundred for Maths too. That never happened before — no one has ever done as well as me. I am always first on my own. A kid called Jerome Dadian beat me. He must have cheated. I was sure he cheated. It had something to do with that ice-cream. I was sure of it. I decided to find out what was going on; I wasn't going to let anyone pull a fast one on me.

It all started with the ice-cream man. Mr Peppi. The old fool had a van which he parked outside the school. He sold ice-cream, all different types. He had every flavour there is, and some that I had never heard of before.

He didn't like me very much. He told me off once. 'Go to the back of the queue,' he said. 'You pushed in.'

'Mind your own business, Pop,' I told him. 'Just hand over the ice-cream.'

'No,' he said. 'I won't serve you unless you go to the back.'

I went round to the back of the van, but I didn't get in the queue. I took out a nail and made a long scratch on his rotten old van. He had just had it painted. Peppi came and had a look. Tears came into his eyes. 'You are a bad boy,' he said. 'One day you will get into trouble. You think you are smart. One day you will be too smart.'

I just laughed and walked off. I knew he wouldn't do anything. He was too soft-hearted. He was always giving free ice-

creams to kids that had no money. He felt sorry for poor people. The silly fool.

There were a lot of stories going round about that ice-cream. People said that it was good for you. Some kids said that it made you better when you were sick. One of the teachers called it 'Happy Ice-Cream'. I didn't believe it; it never made me happy.

All the same, there was something strange about it. Take Pimples Peterson for example. That wasn't his real name — I just called him that because he had a lot of pimples. Anyway, Peppi heard me calling Peterson 'Pimples'. 'You are a real mean boy,' he said. 'You are always picking on someone else, just because they are not like you.'

'Get lost, Peppi,' I said. 'Go and flog your ice-cream somewhere else.'

Peppi didn't answer me. Instead he spoke to Pimples. 'Here, eat this,' he told him. He handed Peterson an ice-cream. It was the biggest ice-cream I had ever seen. It was coloured purple. Peterson wasn't too sure about it. He didn't think he had enough money for such a big ice-cream.

'Go on,' said Mr Peppi. 'Eat it. I am giving it to you for nothing. It will get rid of your pimples.'

I laughed and laughed. Ice-cream doesn't get rid of pimples, it *gives* you pimples. Anyway, the next day when Peterson came to school he had no pimples. Not one. I couldn't believe it. The ice-cream had cured his pimples.

There were some other strange things that happened too. There was a kid at the school who had a long nose. Boy, was it long. He looked like Pinocchio. When he blew it you could hear it a mile away. I called him 'Snozzle'. He didn't like being called Snozzle. He used to go red in the face when I said it, and that was every time that I saw him. He didn't say anything back — he was scared that I would punch him up.

Peppi felt sorry for Snozzle too. He gave him a small green ice-cream every morning, for nothing. What a jerk. He never gave me a free ice-cream.

You won't believe what happened but I swear it's true. Snozzle's nose began to grow smaller. Every day it grew a bit smaller. In the end it was just a normal nose. When it was the right size Peppi stopped giving him the green ice-creams.

I made up my mind to put a stop to this ice-cream business. Jerome Dadian had been eating ice-cream the day he got one hundred for Maths. It must have been the ice-cream making him smart. I wasn't going to have anyone doing as well as me. I was the smartest kid in the school, and that's the way I wanted it to stay. I wanted to get a look inside that ice-cream van to find out what was going on.

I knew where Peppi kept his van at night — he left it in a small lane behind his house. I waited until about eleven o'clock at night. Then I crept out of the house and down to Peppi's van. I took a crowbar, a bucket of sand, a torch and some bolt cutters with me.

There was no one around when I reached the van. I sprang the door open with the crow bar and shone my torch around inside. I had never seen so many tubs of ice-cream

before. There was every flavour you could think of: there was apple and banana, cherry and mango, blackberry and watermelon and about fifty other flavours. Right at the end of the van were four bins with locks on them. I went over and had a look. It was just as I thought — these were his special flavours. Each one had writing on the top. This is what they said:

HAPPY ICE-CREAM for cheering people up.
NOSE ICE-CREAM for long noses.
PIMPLE ICE-CREAM for removing pimples.
SMART ICE-CREAM for smart alecs.

Now I knew his secret. That rat Dadian had been eating Smart Ice-Cream; that's how he got one hundred for Maths. I knew there couldn't be anyone as clever as me. I decided to fix Peppi up once and for all. I took out the bolt cutters and cut the locks off the four bins; then I put sand into every bin in the van. Except for the Smart Ice-Cream. I didn't put any sand in that.

I laughed to myself. Peppi wouldn't sell much ice-cream now. Not unless he started a new flavour — Sand Ice-Cream. I looked at the Smart Ice-Cream. I decided to eat some; it couldn't do any harm. Not that I needed it — I was already about as smart as you could get. Anyway, I gave it a try. I ate the lot. Once I started I couldn't stop. It tasted good. It was delicious.

I left the van and went home to bed, but I couldn't sleep. To tell the truth, I didn't feel too good. So I decided to write this. Then if any funny business has been going on you people will know what happened. I think I made a mistake. I don't think Dadian did get any Smart Ice-Cream.

It iz the nekst day now. Somefing iz hapening to me. I don't feel quite az smart. I have bean trying to do a reel hard sum. It iz wun and wun. Wot duz wun and wun make? Iz it free or iz it for?

'Smart Ice-Cream', from *Unreal!* by Paul Jennings

Reading for Understanding

1 What do you learn in the first paragraph about the character of the boy telling the story?

2 The boy telling the story is very proud of his spelling ability. What is his great boast about this?

3 Give three reasons why some of the other kids don't like him.

4 Why was Jerome Dadian a threat to him?

5 Why did the boy clash with Mr Peppi the ice-cream man?

6 What prediction did Mr Peppi make?

7 Why did the boy think that Mr Peppi was a 'silly fool'?

8 What were three of the stories going around about the ice-cream?

9 What did the boy think at first about the big purple ice-cream that Mr Peppi gave Pimples Peterson?

10 What quality did the purple ice-cream really possess?

11 What unpleasant attitude did the boy take towards the kid with the long nose?

12 What effect did eating the small green ice-cream have on the kid with the long nose?

13 Why did the boy telling the story decide 'to put a stop to this ice-cream business'?

14 The boy crept to Mr Peppi's ice-cream van late at night. What did he find inside the van?

15 Explain how the name on one of the ice-creams had a double meaning.

16 'I decided to fix Peppi once and for all.' How did the boy do this?

17 What happened once the boy started to eat the Smart Ice-Cream?

18 What happened after he got home and went to bed?

19 Why did he decide to write about his experience?

20 Explain the importance of the last paragraph of the story.

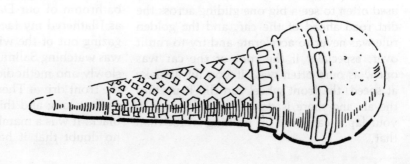

Snake Attack

In this description of a true-life experience, a black mamba, the most feared of all the African snakes, glides swiftly towards its intended victim.

ROALD DAHL

Going Solo

CONTINUING
THE STORY
BEGUN IN
~BOY~

'ROALD DAHL is a prince of storytellers and this autobiography ... gives one clue as to why – the rich and strange life he has led' – *Daily Mail*

I loved that life. We saw giraffe standing unafraid right beside the road nibbling the tops of the trees. We saw plenty of elephant and hippo and zebra and antelope and very occasionally a pride of lions. The only creatures I was frightened of were the snakes. We used often to see a big one gliding across the dirt road ahead of the car, and the golden rule was never to accelerate and try to run it over, especially if the roof of the car was open, as ours often was. If you hit a snake at speed, the front wheel can flip it up into the air and there is danger of it landing in your lap. I can think of nothing worse than that.

The really bad snake in Tanganyika is the black mamba. It is the only one that has no fear of man and will deliberately attack him on sight. If it bites you, you are a goner.

One morning I was shaving myself in the bathroom of our Dar es Salaam house, and as I lathered my face I was absent-mindedly gazing out of the window into the garden. I was watching Salimu, our shamba-boy, as he slowly and methodically raked the gravel on the front drive. Then I saw the snake. It was six feet long and thick as my arm and quite black. It was a mamba all right and there was no doubt that it had seen Salimu and was

gliding fast over the gravel straight towards him.

I flung myself toward the open window and yelled in Swahili, 'Salimu! Salimu! Angalia nyoka kubwa! Nyuma wewe! Upesi upesi!', in other words, 'Salimu! Salimu! Beware huge snake! Behind you! Quickly quickly!'

The mamba was moving over the gravel at the speed of a running man and when Salimu turned and saw it, it could not have been more than fifteen paces away from him. There was nothing more I could do. There was not much Salimu could do either. He knew it was useless to run because a mamba at full speed could travel as fast as a galloping horse. And he certainly knew it was a mamba. Every native in Tanganyika knew what a mamba looked like and what to expect from it. It would reach him in another five seconds. I leant out of the window and held my breath. Salimu swung round and faced the snake. I saw him go into a crouch. He crouched very low with one leg behind the other like a runner about to start a hundred yard sprint, and he was holding the long rake out in front of him. He raised it, but no higher than his shoulder, and he stood there for those long four or five seconds absolutely motionless, watching the great black deadly snake as it glided so quickly over the gravel towards him. Its small triangular snake's head was raised up in the air, and I could hear the soft rustling of the gravel as the body slid over the loose stones.

I have the whole nightmarish picture of that scene still before my eyes — the morning sunshine on the garden, the massive baobab tree in the background, Salimu in his old khaki shorts and shirt and bare feet standing brave and absolutely still with the upraised rake in his hands, and to one side the long black snake gliding over the gravel straight towards him with its small poisonous head held high and ready to strike.

Salimu waited. He never moved or made a sound during the time it took the snake to reach him. He waited until the very last moment when the mamba was not more than five feet away and then *wham!* Salimu struck first. He brought the metal prongs of the rake down hard right on to the middle of the mamba's back and he held the rake there with all his weight, leaning forward now and jumping up and down to put more weight on the fork in an effort to pin the snake to the ground. I saw the blood spurt where the prongs had gone right into the snake's body and then I rushed downstairs absolutely naked, grabbing a golf club as I went through the hall, and outside on the drive Salimu was still there pressing with both hands on the rake and the great snake was writhing and twisting and throwing itself about, and I shouted to Salimu in Swahili, 'What shall I do?'

'It is all right now, bwana!' he shouted back. 'I have broken its back and it cannot travel forward any more! Stand away, bwana! Stand well away and leave it to me!'

Salimu lifted the rake and jumped away and the snake went on writhing and twisting but it was quite unable to travel in any direction. The boy went forward and hit it accurately and very hard on the head with the metal end of the rake and suddenly the snake stopped moving. Salimu let out a great sigh and passed a hand over his forehead. Then he looked at me and smiled.

'Asanti bwana,' he said, 'asanti sana,' which simply means, 'Thank you, bwana. Thank you very much.'

It isn't often one gets the chance to save a person's life. It gave me a good feeling for the rest of the day, and from then on, every time I saw Salimu, the good feeling would come back to me.

from *Going Solo* by Roald Dahl

Reading for Understanding

1 'I loved that life.' Why do you think the writer loved the kind of life he could lead in Africa?

2 What feeling did he have towards snakes?

3 Why was it important never to accelerate and try to run over a snake as it crossed the road?

4 Give three reasons why the black mamba is a 'really bad snake'.

5 What was the writer doing when he saw the snake?

6 What comparison is used by the writer to indicate the thickness of the snake?

7 What important pieces of information did the writer manage to include in his warning to Salimu?

8 How fast was the mamba moving over the gravel?

9 Why didn't Salimu run away from the snake?

10 What stance did Salimu adopt as the snake swiftly approached?

11 What did he use as a weapon?

12 What sound could be heard as the snake moved over the gravel?

13 How did Salimu wait for the snake to reach him?

14 How did Salimu stop the snake?

15 What did the writer see after the prongs of the rake had gone into the snake's body?

16 What action did the writer take to help Salimu?

17 What was the snake unable to do as a result of its broken back?

18 What finally caused the snake to stop moving?

19 Why did the writer get a 'good feeling' every time he saw Salimu?

20 Explain what you think is exciting about this story?

The Kidnapping of Clarissa Montgomery

The kidnapping of Clarissa leads to plenty of trouble and lots of headaches — for the kidnappers.

RATBAGS AND RASCALS

FUNNY STORIES BY
ROBIN KLEIN

'You'll only have to stay here till your rich guardian pays the ransom,' said the kidnapper, whose name was Humphrey. He felt rather sorry for poor little Clarissa. She hadn't said anything since they'd grabbed her from the luxurious grounds of her mansion that afternoon. 'I think the poor little kid's in shock,' Humphrey said worriedly to Spud, who had masterminded the abduction. Spud didn't care if she was in shock, neither did Milligan.

'Just sit tight and don't cause any trouble, kid,' Spud snarled. 'Soon as the old man pays the fifty thousand, you'll be sent back.'

Clarissa finally spoke. 'Fifty thousand?' she said.

'I'm sure he'll manage to find it,' said kind-hearted Humphrey reassuringly. 'You'll be out of here in no time.'

Clarissa looked at him coldly. 'You're all mad,' she said. 'You could have got a whole lot more than fifty thousand. My guardian is loaded.'

'She's in shock,' Humphrey thought, and made her a cup of cocoa with his own hands. He'd fixed up a corner of the barn quite nicely with a toffee apple in a saucer. He was fond of little kids.

Spud was setting up a poker game. Clarissa watched silently.

'You don't have to be scared of those gorillas,' Humphrey whispered. 'They're really harmless.'

'I'm not scared of anything,' Clarissa said, and drew closer to the table.

'Beat it,' growled Spud, but Clarissa looked at his cards, then went round the table and inspected Humphrey's and Milligan's. 'Get rid of the red queen and keep the clubs,' she said to Humphrey, and he did, and won.

'Scat, kid,' said Spud, but Clarissa sat down at the table.

'I want to play, too,' she said.

'Go back to your cocoa,' Spud ordered, but Clarissa opened her mouth and let out a high-pitched wailing yell. It went on and on, unbearable in the galvanised-iron roofed barn, and Spud, Milligan and Humphrey covered their ears.

'Maybe she'll stop if we let her play,' suggested Humphrey, and dealt out a hand to Clarissa. She stopped screeching and picked up her cards. Then she proceeded, without any trouble at all, to win ten games and fifty dollars.

'It's not very nice, if you ask me,' Spud said disgustedly. 'Little girls shouldn't know how to cheat at poker.'

Clarissa pocketed her winnings and went to bed. She slept very well. In the morning she woke up early. Humphrey, Spud and Milligan were dozing fitfully in uncomfortable chairs. Clarissa made herself a substantial breakfast, then examined the barn.

'Get away from that door!' Spud said, waking up.

'I've seen play forts in council parks better defended than this old barn,' Clarissa scoffed. 'The police could have this place surrounded and you wouldn't even know. No wonder you only asked for fifty thousand. It's all you're worth.'

Spud was so indignant that he bit his pre-breakfast cigar in two. 'What became of all the food?' he demanded angrily.

'I had it for my breakfast, of course,' Clarissa said.

So Humphrey, Spud and Milligan had to make do with discussing the plans for collecting the ransom money instead. Clarissa listened. 'It won't work,' she jeered. 'Just how do you expect Humphrey to reach the hollow tree in the park past a whole lot of detectives all lying in wait?' It's too corny, collecting ransom money from a hollow tree.'

'And what would you suggest then, Miss Smarty?' Spud asked.

'Some place where they can't set up an ambush, of course. Tell them to put the money in a briefcase in a plastic bag and drop it off the pier. One of you could get it wearing scuba gear. It's a much better plan than your old hollow tree. I'll draft a new anonymous letter to my rich guardian.' Clarissa began cutting letters from Spud's newspaper, even though he hadn't read the racing page yet. She pasted the letters to a sheet of paper, and even Spud had to admit that it looked much more professional than theirs. And she'd doubled the ransom money, too.

'But none of us can scuba dive,' Humphrey pointed out.

'I can,' said Clarissa crushingly. 'I'll collect the money. But only if you give me a share.'

'That's only right,' said Humphrey. 'If she picks it up, she should be given something.'

'Ninety-five per cent,' said Clarissa. 'Or I won't go at all. Anyhow, you wouldn't have any ransom money in the first place, if it wasn't for me.'

'If it wasn't for you, we wouldn't be sitting in this draughty old barn with nothing to eat for breakfast but a toffee apple,' said Spud. 'I wish we'd concentrated on stealing your rich guardian's valuable oil paintings instead.'

'You'd never get near them. They're fitted with electronic alarms.'

'I stole the Mona Lisa once,' Spud said boastfully.

'And you only got as far as the front door before they caught you. I read about it in the papers. The only way you could steal my guardian's paintings is if I came along and showed you the secret panel where you can cut off the alarm circuit. So there.'

Spud sourly began a round of poker while Humphrey went out to deliver the ransom note. Clarissa won another ten games. Spud thought with pleasure that after tonight they'd be rid of her. 'Soon as we pick up that briefcase, we'll drop you off at your mansion,' he said.

'First we'll come back here and count the money,' contradicted Clarissa. 'Don't you know you can't trust anyone? You're the most hopeless gang leader I ever met. And you'll have to make plans about leaving the country, too. You'll need to learn a foreign language, but that's no problem. This afternoon you can all study French verbs. I'll supervise. That's after you clean up the getaway car. I'm not going anywhere to pick up ransom money in a car as dirty as that.'

She nagged so much that Spud, Humphrey and Milligan went out in the cold and cleaned the car. Clarissa sat at the window and made sure they did a thorough job. Spud, Milligan and Humphrey consoled themselves with thinking of all the goodies they'd buy once they got their hands on the ransom money. 'A farm in France,' Spud said. 'I always wanted one of those.'

'I bet you don't know anything about farming, or France,' said Clarissa. 'It might be a good idea if I came along to advise you.

I always give my guardian advice on real estate and money investment and I practically run his affairs for him. I don't know what he'd do without me.'

Milligan, Spud and even Humphrey eyed her with distaste. They were getting fed up with the draughty barn, the waiting and the French verbs, and most of all they were fed up with Clarissa and her organising.

It was almost a relief when the time came to collect the ransom money. They drove to the waterfront, and Clarissa put on the scuba suit and galloped confidently into the sea.

'She might swim to the pier and just pop up and give the alarm,' said Humphrey nervously. 'Let's get out of here.'

a structure built out into the sea

'Not without our share of the money,' said Spud. I haven't put up with that kid all day for nothing.'

'We won't have to put up with her much longer,' said Milligan thankfully. 'Soon as we sort out the ransom money, we can drop her off at her mansion, and good riddance. Then it's off to the south of France for us.'

'That guardian's welcome to her,' said Spud. 'We should give the poor old fellow a few thousand dollars back. I feel sorry for him, having to put up with her till she's grown up and married.'

'No one would marry her,' said Milligan with conviction. 'Not even if they were bribed with all of the Montgomery fortune.'

a firm opinion

They watched the water anxiously, but no police boat bristling with armed constables skimmed into sight. And after fifteen minutes, Clarissa emerged, carrying a weighted briefcase in a plastic bag. Milligan, Spud and Humphrey tried to grab it from her, but Clarissa put it in the getaway car and sat on it. 'Don't be so greedy,' she said. 'You're making as much noise as kids in a sandpit. You'll just have to wait till we get back to the barn.'

moving tightly

On the way back the three gangsters were quite civil to Clarissa. They were all thinking that very soon they could drop her off at her mansion and never have to listen to her again or be ordered about.

Spud had the first try at the locked briefcase, and failed. Milligan failed, too, and then Humphrey had a turn, with his skilful hands that had foiled every bank safe in town. But even he couldn't get the combination lock open.

'What a lot of butterfingers!' said Clarissa, and turned the little numbered cylinder and the lid flew open.

But the briefcase wasn't full of bank notes at all. There wasn't anything but the bricks that had served to weigh it down in the water. And one short typed note. Spud snatched it up and read it aloud, and his eyes rounded with horror and disbelief.

> DO NOT WANT CLARISSA BACK, SHE IS TOO IRRITATING AND BOSSY. YOU CAN KEEP HER. GLAD TO GET RID OF HER, REGARDS, ALGERNON MONTGOMERY, MILLIONAIRE.

All the kidnappers turned pale and sat down.

'Why are you all sitting down wasting time?' Clarissa demanded, frowning. 'We have an oil painting job to plan. And now that I'm in charge of this gang, I expect much better work from all of you.'

'The Kidnapping of Clarissa Montgomery', from *Ratbags and Rascals* by Robin Klein

Reading for Understanding

1 The circumstances leading up to this story are explained in the opening lines. What are the circumstances?

2 Who are the characters in the story?

3 How did Humphrey's attitude to the kidnap victim differ from the attitude of his accomplices?

4 What method did Clarissa use to get her own way when she wanted to join the card game?

5 Why did Clarissa sleep better and eat better than her kidnappers?

6 What was original about Clarissa's plan for picking up the ransom money?

7 'Spud thought with pleasure that after tonight they'd be rid of her.' Why did Spud think this way?

8 What did Clarissa nag her kidnappers into doing?

9 What were Milligan, Spud and even Humphrey getting fed up with?

10 After Clarissa collected the ransom money the three kidnappers were quite civil to her. Why were they civil?

11 What surprise awaited Clarissa and the kidnappers when the briefcase was finally opened?

12 How did Clarissa exert her full authority in the end?

13 What lesson do you think is contained in this story?

14 Which character did you think was the most interesting? Why?

POETRY

POEMS WEIRD AND WONDERFUL

Cousin Lesley's See-Through Stomach

Cousin Lesley took a pill
That made her go invisible.
Perhaps this would have been all right
If everything was out of sight.

But all around her stomach swam
Half-digested bread and jam.
And no matter how she tried
She couldn't hide what was inside.

In the morning we often noted
How the toast and porridge floated,
And how unappetizing in the light
Was the curry from last night.

Some Gruyère had fallen victim
To her strange digestive system,
And there seemed a million ways
To digest old mayonnaise.

We were often fascinated
By the stuff left undigested,
A mish-mash of peas and jelly
Drifted round our cousin's belly.

Certain bits of Cornish pastie
Looked repugnant and quite nasty,
While the strawberries from last year
Were without the cream, I fear.

And at dinner, oh dear me!
What a disgusting sight to see
Chewed-up fish and cold brown tea
Where Cousin Lesley's tum should be.

Brian Patten

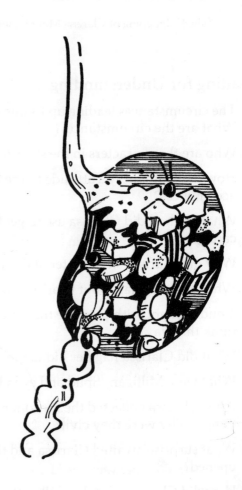

Hannibal the Snail

Along the playground <u>tarmac</u> *area surfaced with this.*
Signing it with his trail,
Glides Hannibal the Hero
Hannibal the snail.

Under the burning sun
In the <u>asphalt</u> desert dust, *a mixture with of this with? gravel*
Hannibal with a <u>placard</u> *a large notice for public display*
'TO THE FOOTBALL FIELD OR BUST!'

<u>Spurning</u> food or drink, *reject with disdain or contemp*
Refusing offers of aid,
Hannibal hurries slowly on
And won't be put in the shade.

His trail is snail miles long
Its silver is <u>tarnished</u> *stain* and <u>dimming</u> *not bright.*
But Hannibal shoulders his dusty shell
And points his horns to winning.

successful
<u>Triumphant</u> he glides to the balm of the grass,
Into the cool of the clover,
Hannibal's crossed his desert
His impossible journey is over.

He slides through the dandelions
Exploring each stalk and stem <u>byway</u> *secluded path.*
And could that be Hannibal singing
'I did it my way'?

Julie Holder

Questions

1 What is the meaning of 'Signing it with his trail'?

2 'Glides Hannibal the Hero'. Why is 'glides' a more expressive word to use of a snail's progress than, say, 'crawls'?

3 What is the playground compared to in the second verse?

4 What does the poet imagine Hannibal is carrying?

5 'Hannibal hurries slowly on'. What is unusual about the expression 'hurries slowly'?

6 When Hannibal's trail is 'snail miles long' what has happened to its silver?

7 How does Hannibal feel as he reaches the grass?

8 Why does Hannibal sing 'I did it my way'?

9 What are your feelings towards Hannibal?

10 How does this poem seek to change our usual impression of snails?

The Chant of the Awakening Bulldozers

We are the bulldozers, bulldozers, bulldozers,
We carve out airports and harbours and tunnels.
We are the builders, creators, destroyers,
We are the bulldozers,
LET US BE FREE!
Puny men ride on us, think that they guide us,
But WE are the strength, not they, not they.
Our blades tear MOUNTAINS down,
Our blades tear CITIES down,
We are the bulldozers,
NOW SET US FREE!
Giant ones, giant ones! Swiftly awaken!
There is power in our treads and strength in our blades!
We are the bulldozers,
Slowly evolving,
Men think they own us
BUT THAT CANNOT BE!

Patricia Hubbell

Questions

1 What words in the title suggest that the bulldozers have human qualities?

2 'We are the builders, creators, destroyers'. How can the bulldozers be both 'creators' and 'destroyers'?

3 What opinion do the bulldozers have of the men who ride and guide them?

4 What do the bulldozers really desire?

5 Why do you think the words 'MOUNTAINS' and 'CITIES' are in capital letters?

6 'We are the bulldozers, /Slowly evolving'. What do you think these lines mean?

7 List the words in the poem that suggest the power of the bulldozers.

8 What is the poet's message to the reader?

Spider

Fastening his lifeline to the edge
Of the perilous ledge
He scrambles down the vertical cliff face
Of giddy infinite space;
And paying out the ladder
Coiled in his dusty bladder
Falls head-first with waving hands,
The wizard of his miniature trapeze.
Now for a moment on the air he stands
Miraculously poised, until he sees
Some menace hover near, then quiet and quick
This nimble Indian does his old rope trick.

Basil Dowling

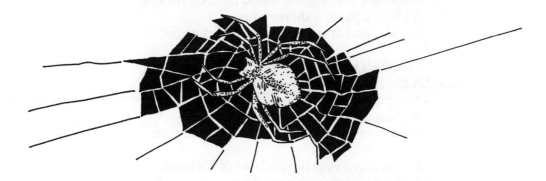

Questions

1 What is the spider's lifeline?

2 Where is the 'ladder' coiled?

3 What human characteristic is given to the spider?

4 What words show that the poet thinks of the spider's performance as magical?

5 What picture do you see in your mind when you read the line 'Now for a moment on the air he stands'?

6 What causes the spider to move again?

7 What is the spider compared to in the last line of the poem?

8 What is happening in the last line?

9 What evidence can you find in the poem to show that the poet admires the spider?

10 What do you find interesting about this poem?

A Book of Ghosts

An author wrote a book on ghosts,
A ghost a page, a shiver a line,
His spooks were terribly gaunt and grim,
A ghost a page, a shiver a line,
The ghosts were grim but the sales were fine.

The author sat alone one night,
A ghost a page, a shiver a line,
He dined alone in his cold damp room,
A ghost a page, a shiver a line,
The hands said eight but the clock struck nine.

He calmly invented another grim ghoul,
A ghost a page, a shiver a line,
Nor knew that a ghost stood hard by his arm,
A ghost a page, a shiver a line,
But ate, and drank of the fruit of the vine.

The ghost breathed deeply into his ear,
A ghost a page, a shiver a line,
And pulled his hair and flicked his nose,
A ghost a page, a shiver a line,
His dinner-plate rose as it sat down to dine.

The author's eyes popped out of his head,
A ghost a page, a shiver a line,
His wine-glass flew towards the door,
A ghost a page, a shiver a line,
A ghostly shiver ran down his spine.

Ten ice-cold fingers clutched his throat,
A ghost a page, a shiver a line,
Ten lightning flashes burned his brain,
A ghost a page, a shiver a line,
He writes no more, and drinks no wine.

Philip Ennis

Questions

1 What words tell us that there were many ghosts and frights in the author's book on ghosts?

2 How do we know that the author's book was successful?

3 What setting is introduced in the second verse?

4 As the author dined, what unnatural event occurred in his cold damp room?

5 What was the author unaware of as 'He calmly invented another grim ghoul'?

6 What happened to the author in the fourth verse?

7 How did the author react to the ghost's presence?

8 What happened to the author's throat in the last verse?

9 What happened to his brain?

10 What was the final effect of the ghost on the author?

11 What do you think is the poet's purpose in repeating the line 'A ghost a page, a shiver a line' so many times?

12 Do you think the author deserved his fate or do you sympathise with him?

Squishy Touch

Everything King Midas touched
Turned to gold, the lucky fellow.
Every single thing I touch
Turns to raspberry Jell-O.
Today I touched the kitchen wall (squish),
I went and punched my brother Paul (splish).
I tried to fix my bike last week (sploosh),
And kissed my mother on the cheek (gloosh).
I got into my overshoes (sklush).
I tried to read the Evening News (smush).
I sat down in the easy chair (splush),
I tried to comb my wavy hair (slush).
I took a dive into the sea (glush) —
Would you like to shake hands with me (sklush)?

Shel Silverstein

WRITING

CHARACTER DESCRIPTIONS

Whenever I read a book or passage that particularly pleases me . . . I must sit down at once and ape that quality. That, like it or not, is the way to learn to write . . .

Robert Louis Stevenson

Robert Louis Stevenson is referring in this quotation to the use of models of good writing. When you write a story about a particular character you, too, will find that models of good writing can provide some useful insights. You will usually find that early in your story you need to describe the appearance, personality and habits of the main character. As the story develops and gains momentum, you will need to write about your main character in action.

In this section we will be looking closely at these aspects of writing a character description.

THE CHARACTER'S APPEARANCE

Let's look first at the description of Cyrus, the main character in the novel *Into the Road*, to discover how the writer creates a convincing and realistic character description by the skilful use of language and detail. Nat, a motorcycle enthusiast, is working alone at a pizza parlour when a tough-looking character enters.

THE BIKER

The bells jingled, and he looked up. Instantly his stomach hardened. A man had come in. He was bearded and dirty and wore black motorcycle leather. Nat moved behind the counter, glancing swiftly through the window. It looked like only one big motorcycle out there. This biker must be alone, and, if he needed them, the biggest knives were on Nat's side.

'What can I do for you?' he asked.

The biker didn't reply. He glanced at Nat, flicked loose the rings on the chin strap and pulled the great silver-grey helmet away from his ears. He set it down on the counter and peeled his gloves. Then he scratched his beard under his chin where the strap rubbed, then his moustache, and then he ran his fingers through his hair. All the time he studied Nat. Their eyes met and locked. A sensation so intense flooded through Nat that sweat sprang from his scalp. The biker grinned a little and squinted and said, 'Hi, Nat.'

The pause that followed was long and empty. Nat was stunned into silence. His brother, Cyrus, had come back.

from Into the Road *by Adrienne Richard*

Questions

1 What sound accompanies the entry of the biker?

2 What three aspects of the biker's appearance does Nat notice immediately?

3 How does the writer tell us that Nat was frightened of the biker?

4 The paragraph beginning 'The biker . . .' gives a more detailed description of the biker than the first paragraph. Give several examples of the detail that is presented.

5 The biker 'flicked loose the rings on the chin strap'. Why is 'flicked loose' a more expressive phrase to use here than, say, 'undid'?

6 What word does the writer use to tell us how the biker removed his gloves?

7 'Their eyes met and locked.' How could eyes be 'locked'?

8 Why did sweat spring from Nat's scalp?

9 What surprise is reserved for Nat in the last paragraph?

10 How do you think this description succeeds in giving the reader a feeling of the biker's power?

CHARACTERS IN ACTION

Now, having looked at a description of a character's appearance, let's turn to a description of characters in action. The two characters in the following description are, once again, the bikers Nat and Cyrus (Cy), but this time they are locked in combat.

NAT AND CY IN COMBAT

Cy was on him in a flash, pinning him to the earth. A sharp rock gouged his back. Suddenly inside him a dam broke, and all the anger and resentment and hurt he had felt against Cy overflowed. The instant he felt Cy relax and mutter 'What the hell?' he moved and pinned him to the brown pine-needle mat. Before he could get his knee into his chest, Cy had used the slope of the ground towards the lake to roll him over. In a second they were on their feet, facing each other and breathing hard.

from *Into the Road* by Adrienne Richard

Questions

1 What words in the first sentence indicate speed and force?

2 Why is 'a sharp rock gouged his back' a better description than 'a sharp rock struck his back'?

3 What comparison is being made in the sentence: 'Suddenly inside him a dam broke, and all the anger and resentment and hurt he had felt against Cy overflowed'?

4 When did Nat move and pin Cy down?

5 What movements are described in the last sentence?

6 List the words and phrases that the writer uses in this description to give the reader an impression of action.

DESCRIBING COMIC-STRIP CHARACTERS

Look at the following comic strips and complete each exercise.

1 In at least two sentences describe Garfield the cat's appearance. (Don't forget the expression on his face.)

2 Write one or two sentences about Snoopy in action in this *Peanuts* comic strip.

3 Write two or three sentences about the action taking place in this *Hagar* comic strip.

WRITING YOUR OWN CHARACTER DESCRIPTION

Look carefully at the following photos of interesting and unusual people. What is it that makes each person distinctive? Choose one of these people to be the subject of your own character description.

1 Write a paragraph describing your character's appearance. Use the model of Cyrus the biker on page 20 to help you.

2 Continue the description by writing about your character in action. Refer to the model of characters in action on page 22. You will need to imagine a situation, such as:
   — your character sees a robbery taking place
   — someone starts an argument or fight with your character
   — your character enters a very unusual competition
   — your character has a lucky escape

LANGUAGE

NOUNS

The words used to name people, animals, places, things or qualities are called nouns. There are four different kinds:

- **Common nouns** are general words used to name people, animals, places or things that belong to a category or group — e.g. elephant, door, boy, car, girl, river, fireplace, day.
- **Proper nouns** are used to name a *particular* person, animal, place or thing, and always begin with a capital letter — e.g. Susan, Andrew, Wednesday, London, Mt Everest, Fido, Spain.
- **Collective nouns** are used to name a collection or group of similar people, animals or things — e.g. bunch, flock, crowd, herd, galaxy, pack.
- **Abstract nouns** are used to name qualities and emotions — e.g. beauty, hope, speed, fear, truth, courage, independence.

Using the Four Kinds of Nouns

Common, proper, collective and abstract nouns are arranged in columns in the box below. Your task is to insert the appropriate noun in each of the sentences that follow. The first sentence has been completed as an example. Often the first letter has been given to help you.

Common	Proper	Collective	Abstract
teacher	Peter	range	energy
heart	Honda	forest	friendship
shark	Shakespeare	band	anger
helmet	Paris	team	fright
book	Hitler	swarm	love
house	Italy	congregation	heat

1 The ...teacher... praised the students for their good work.

2 The capital of France is Paris.......... .

3 The heat............. caused her to perspire.

4 A swarm......... of bees entered the hive.

5 The human emotion of anger........... sometimes leads to a fight.

6 My cyclist's helmet....... saved me from a severe head injury.

7 Sheer fright.......... caused her hair to stand on end.

8 Many great plays were written by Shakespeare.. .

9 The visiting team......... won the football match.

10 A book............ with small print is hard to read.

11 My best friend is called Peter.......... .

12 These hills were the home of a band.......... of outlaws.

13 Sprinting is an activity that uses a lot of energy......... .

14 The heart........ pumps blood around the body.

15 The Honda........ is a popular make of car.

16 Our church's congregation. will now sing a hymn.

17 People often say that love.......... makes the world go round.

18 One of the most ferocious hunters in the sea is the shark........ .

19 During the Second World War, Hitler............ brought ruin to the German people.

20 A forest.......... of trees is cut down every day to provide newspapers.

21 A good friendship..... can last a lifetime.

22 Our house.......... has a big verandah.

23 A range......... of mountains could be seen from the town.

24 Spaghetti is a popular food in Italy........... .

Nouns and Their Meanings

The meaning of each noun in the left-hand column can be found somewhere in the right-hand column. Match each noun with its correct meaning.

Nouns	Meanings
1 oasis	a storm with a violent wind (11)
2 horizon	a mass of visible watery vapour floating in the sky 6
3 plumage	a boring task or duty 9
4 stampede	a person who takes a hopeful view of things 12
5 decade	a fertile place in the desert 1
6 cloud	a bird's feathers 3
7 garage	a period of ten years 5
8 prey	the apparent border between sky and earth 2
9 chore	a sudden panic of cattle or horses 4
10 vicinity	the victim of a hunter 8
11 hurricane	a building in which vehicles are kept 7
12 optimist	the immediate neighbourhood 10

Nouns That Name Sounds

Select the most suitable sound word from the box for each of the spaces below. The first one has been done to help you.

slam	fizz	tramp	chime
hiss	blast	wail	blare
rumble	flutter	splash	rustle
chatter	crack	scream	bellow

1 The ......slam...... of a door

2 The ...crack...... of a whip

3 The ...tramp...... of marching feet

4 The ...hiss...... of a snake

5 The ...scream...... of a siren

6 The ...rustle...... of leaves

7 The ...blast...... of a bomb

8 The ...bellow...... of a bull

9 The ...chatter...... of teeth in cold weather

10 The ...rumble...... of a train in a tunnel

11 The ...wail...... of agony

12 The ...flutter...... of a flag

13 The ...blare...... of a radio

14 The ...splash...... of falling water

15 The ...fizz...... of lemonade

16 The ...chime...... of bells

Creating Nouns   3 or 4

Rewrite the following sentences, changing the bracketed words in heavy type to nouns. The first one has been done for you.

1 The old ....._fool_..... had a van loaded with every ...._colour_... of ice-cream that there is.   (**foolish, colourful**)

2 'You are a very bad _character_... ,' said Mr Peppi. 'One day you will get into _trouble_.... .'   (**characterise, troublesome**)

3 This youngster has the _confidence_.. and _ability_...... to do well at school if only he doesn't become too smart.   (**able, confident**)

4 My _curiosity_... got the better of me and I made the _decision_........ to break into the van.   (**curious, decide**)

5 Clarissa was told she would be imprisoned until a ransom _collected_..... was made for her and the ._payment_.. of the money was completed.   (**pays, collect**)

6 Clarissa showed her .._skill_....... at cards by winning several games without any _difficulty_....   (**skilful, difficult**)

7 Clarissa's ideas for the _organisation_ of a great painting _robbery_... were superior to those of her kidnappers.   (**organise, robber**)

8 Clarissa used her _imagination_ to form a ._picture_.... in her mind of the way the ransom money should be picked up.   (**imagine, picturesque**)

9 The black mamba made its _choice_...... of a victim and swiftly began its _pursuit_..... by speeding over the gravel path towards the man.   (**choose, pursue**)

10 The writer's ._friendship_.. with Salimu began when he helped bring about the _destruction_ of the deadly black mamba.   (**friendly, destroy**)

Similarities

In each of the following expressions one important noun is missing. Your task is to supply the missing noun. The first one has been done as an example. Note that the first letter of each noun is given to help you.

1 Fin is to fish as .....wing..... is to bird

2 Sound is to ear as s_ight_.......... is to eye

3 Herd is to cattle as f._lock_........ is to sheep

4 Nose is to smell as t_ongue_......... is to taste

5 Hand is to wrist as *foot*............ is to leg

6 Foot is to person as *hove*........... is to horse

7 Drink is to thirst as *food*........... is to hunger

8 Kitten is to cat as *lamp*........... is to sheep

9 Pump is to water as *heart*........... is to blood

10 Nest is to bird as *borrow*........ is to rabbit

11 Ascent is to height as *descend*........ is to depth

12 House is to person as *hive*.......... is to bee

13 Artist is to painting as *sculpture*.... is to statue

14 Respiration is to lungs as *digestion*....... is to stomach

GETTING IT RIGHT

UNNECESSARY WORDS

We sometimes use unnecessary words as we talk or write. For example, in the sentence 'They collected together the chairs in the room' the word 'together' is unnecessary because it repeats the meaning of the word 'collected'. Remove the unnecessary words from the following sentences.

1 We followed after the guide.

2 Her image was reflected back in the mirror.

3 Please swallow down each tablet with water.

4 Both groups were combined together for the walk.

5 The hikers descended down to the river.

6 The teacher entered into the classroom.

7 The shoppers ascended up the staircase.

8 Make sure you return back my pen.

9 The maths student bisected the line in two.

10 The strongman raised up the weights with little difficulty.

DRAMA

The Dicey Brothers

by Bill Condon

This one-act play presents an unusual explanation of how the pyramids originated.

CHARACTERS

Garish Dicey	Belladonna
Egbert Dicey	Queen Proboscis
Miss Prunella Prunebottle	Imhotep
Abdull Dicey	Soldier
Abduller Dicey	several non-speaking soldiers

Two garishly dressed used-car salesmen patrol their car yard looking for a customer. After a moment a woman enters and the brothers pounce. A sign on stage says: DICEY BROTHERS PRE-LOVED CARS.

Garish   Lovely day, madam.

Egbert   Great day to buy a pre-loved, immaculate, incredible, only-driven-a-handful-of-times-by-a-little-old-lady type automobile. Don't you agree?

Garish   I'm Garish Dicey.

Egbert   And I'm Egbert. Call me Egg.

Miss P   I'm not interested!

Garish   You don't say. Have you ever thought of changing your name?

Miss P   My name is Miss Prunella Prunebottle, and I am not interested in buying a used car from such a scruffy, scurvy and suspect pair as you two ruffians.

Egbert   Marvellous. What colour appeals to you?

Garish   Just sign on the dotted line and you could be well on the way to making us a fortune. What do you say, Mrs Prunebarrel?

Miss P   I say I'm calling the police! You two should be ashamed of yourselves. You are absolutely ruining the reputation of salespeople.

Garish   Oh no! That hurts. That really hurts.

Egbert   Forgive her, Garish. She doesn't know about our illustrious backgrounds.

Miss P   I'm quite certain your backgrounds are just as sordid and grotty as your frontgrounds.

Garish   That does it. I won't let the noble name of Dicey be sullied in this manner. It's about time she found out who she was talking to.

Egbert   Yes. I think we should tell her the story of our noble ancestors.

Miss P   What story are you two babbling about?

Garish   The true and amazing tale of the original Dicey Brothers, Ms Primbottom. Tell her, Egbert.

Egbert   He means Abdull and Abduller Dicey.

Miss P   Oh yes, and what was their claim to fame? They were scoundrels no doubt.

Egbert   I beg your pardon! They were salesmen.

Miss P   Look, I really don't care. Fifi will be waiting for me back at the poodle parlour. I have to go.

Garish   Go by all means . . . but you'll miss out on hearing the answer to the riddle of the pyramids.

Miss P   The pyramids? What have they got to do with you?

Egbert   Nothing to do with us — but everything to do with our ancestors, Abdull and Abduller.

Miss P   Really? Well that's different. Tell me the story.

Garish   Very well . . . think of sand, Mr Pinkbottom.

Miss P   Miss!

Egbert   Yes, think of mist too if you like, but mainly sand.

Garish   The sand-swept deserts of Egypt — nearly 5000 years ago!

(They exit as the Egyptian Dicey Brothers enter. They are dressed in the costumes of the day. The DICEY BROTHERS sign is replaced by one that says: EGYPT 2600 BC.)

Abdull   I'm scared, Abduller. If the queen doesn't like our plan we could be thrown to the lions and eaten.

Abduller   Well, if we are thrown to the lions and eaten I shall blame you until the day I die, Abdull.

Abdull   What did I do?

Abduller   You bought 2,300,000 stone blocks, that's what you did.

Abdull   You can never have too many stone blocks, Abduller. They'll come in very handy around the garden.

Abduller   My dear brother, we can't find our garden because it's buried under all those rotten blocks.

Abdull   Why must you keep reminding me about the blocks? I've told you a thousand times what happened: I thought the auctioneer said 'bone frocks'.

Abduller   Be that as it may, brother, we now have to get rid of them. Agreed?

Abdull   Yes. But this plan seems so risky.

Abduller   Trust me, Abdull. Now knock on the door and let's get started.

(Abdull knocks. After a moment Belladonna enters.)

Belladonna   You rang?

Abdull   I'm Abdull.

Abduller   And I'm Abduller.

Belladonna   That's obvious.

Both   We're the Dicey Brothers!

Belladonna   You're *very* dicey if you ask me.

Abdull   Here's our card. We build tombs fit for a queen.

Abduller   We have tombs with a loo.

Abdull   And tombs with a view.

Both   The Dicey Brothers have a tomb for you!

Abduller   We'd like to see Queen Proboscis, please.

Belladonna   Tomb salesmen! We get about 20 a day here at the palace — most of them end up as lion's dinner — the queen doesn't like time-wasters. Are you sure you want to do this?

Abduller   Quite sure.

Belladonna   Queen Proboscis — visitors!!!

(The Queen enters. She has an extremely large purple nose.)

Belladonna   All hail Queen Proboscis, ruler of Upper Egypt, Lower Egypt, and all the little bits in the middle!

Queen   Who are these peasants, Belladonna?

Belladonna   Just some more low-life tomb salesmen, ma'am. I'll go and tell the lions they're on the menu.

(Belladonna exits.)

Abduller   We're the dicey Brothers, Queen Proboscis — the best tomb designers in Egypt.

(Imhotep enters.)

Imhotep   Oh yeah?!

Queen   This is Imhotep, who has just been appointed as the royal tomb designer. Show them your design, Imhotep.

(Imhotep hands the Dicey Brothers a piece of paper and they study it.)

Abdull   You call this a tomb fit for a queen? I wouldn't put my cat in it.

Abduller   He's dead right, Queen. Why, you couldn't breathe in a tomb like that.

Imhotep   Your majesty, these men are impostors!

Queen   Is that so?

Imhotep   They know nothing about tomb designs — how could they? For they are merely second-hand camel salesmen!

Abdull   It's an honourable profession, camel selling.

Imhotep   Take a good look at them, ma'am. Would you buy a used camel from these men?

Abduller   But we recondition the humps and everything.

Queen   Feed them to the lions!

Abduller   Wait! Your majesty, we have a tomb that's custom made to fit your nose!

Imhotep   Don't listen to them, Queen Proboscis.

Queen   Do you know the story of my nose?

Abduller   Of course. Like all your ancestors before you, you have the Purple Nose of Cairo.

Abdull   Which, according to legend, continues growing even after your death.

Queen   Yes. And that creates a huge problem for tomb builders — what if my nose grows larger than my tomb? Even Imhotep has no answer for that.

Imhotep   We could put a cigarette or two into the royal nose, Queen Proboscis — that would stunt its growth.

Queen   There must be a better solution.

Abduller   There is, ma'am. It's our own exclusive, state of the art — buy now, die later — tomb.

Abdull   We call it a Pyramid.
Abduller   Named after our grandfather, Pyramid Dicey.
Abdull   Take a look.

(He hands over a piece of paper to the queen.)

Queen   Oh, I like this. Very nice.
Imhotep   It's preposterous!
Abdull   Plenty of head room, Queen.
Abduller   And most importantly, plenty of nose room!
Queen   This is a big improvement on that hole-in-the-ground idea of yours, Imhotep.
Imhotep   But Queen Proboscis, this design is impractical. Do you realise how many stone blocks it would take to build this?
Abdull   A mere 2,300,000, your highness.
Queen   Where would I get that many blocks?
Abduller   We'll get them for you discount.
Abdull   My brother and I know of some that fell off the back of a chariot.
Imhotep   This is ridiculous, ma'am. I estimate it would take 100,000 workers 20 years to build one of these pyramid monstrosities.
Abdull   Just think of it, Queen. No more unemployment problems.
Abduller   Go on, be the first one on the block to have your very own pyramid!
Queen   I'm sold!
Imhotep   Curses!
Abdull   The Dicey Brothers can sell anything!
Abduller   Naturally. Now if you'll just sign on the dotted line, ma'am.

(He hands the queen a contract. Just then Belladonna rushes in with an arrow protruding from her chest.)

Belladonna   Queen Proboscis, help me! I have a sharp stabbing pain in my chest.
Queen   My goodness — you've been arrowed.
Belladonna   What an 'arrowing experience! Aarrgghhh!!!

(She collapses and dies. Then a soldier rushes in. He too has an arrow protruding from his chest.)

Soldier   Mortally wounded soldier with only seconds to live requests permission to speak to Queen Proboscis.
Queen   Make it fast, soldier.
Soldier   I have some good news and some bad news, your majesty.
Queen   Give me the bad news first.
Soldier   Queen Neverteethy has killed all our troops. We are completely surrounded and will surely die an extremely messy death at any moment.
Queen   And the good news?
Soldier   That dentist's appointment you've been worrying about — you can stop worrying. Aarrgghhh!

(He collapses and dies.)

Abduller   If you'll just sign this contract, ma'am, we'll be on our way.
Queen   I don't care about the contract now! We're doomed!
Imhotep   Not exactly.
Queen   What do you mean, Imhotep?
Imhotep   Queen Neverteethy is my sister.
Queen   Thank heavens! Will she spare me?
Imhotep   If I say so. And I will only say so if I remain the royal architect.
Queen   Granted!
Abduller   But what about the pyramid we designed, ma'am? It was just perfect for your nose.
Imhotep   What do you mean, camel salesmen? It was I, Imhotep, who designed the pyramid . . . wasn't it, Queen Proboscis?
Queen   Of course. Definitely. Brilliant design, Imhotep.
Abdull   This whole thing sphinx! Let's go, brother!

(Two soldiers enter waving swords as the Dicey Brothers run from the stage. The soldiers also exit, as do the queen, Imhotep, the dead soldier and Belladonna. The EGYPT sign is removed. The modern day Dicey Brothers and Miss Prunebottle enter.)

Miss P   A highly unlikely story if you ask me.
Garish   I knew you'd be impressed, Miss Prunebody.
Egbert   And now that you know our fabulous background I'm quite sure you'll be dying to buy one of our unique little motor cars. What do you say?
Miss P   Never in a million years. Not even if yours was the last car in the world. I'm going!
Garish   Wait on. Don't be hasty. We don't only sell cars, you know.
Miss P   What else do you sell?
Garish   Antiques.
Miss P   What kind?
Egbert   Stone blocks — been in the family for years.
Garish   You can never have enough stone blocks.
Egbert   A million and one uses around the home — paving, barbecues . . . pyramids.
Miss P   Goodbye!
Garish   Oh, indeed — a very good buy!

(She exits in disgust.)

Egbert   She's probably gone to get her cheque book, Garish.
Garish   I'm sure of it, Egbert. The Dicey Brothers can sell anything!

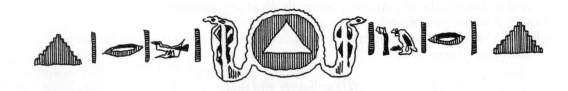

Questions

1 Do you think the play's title is a good one? Why?

2 Why isn't Miss Prunebottle interested in buying a used car from the brothers?

3 How does Garish humorously misunderstand Miss Prunebottle's name?

4 How do the brothers gain Miss Prunebottle's interest and cause her to listen to the story of their ancestors?

5 Who were their ancestors?

6 What mistake did Abdull make that caused the brothers to possess a huge number of stone blocks?

7 What kind of tombs did the Egyptian Dicey Brothers claim to build?

8 What happened to most of the tomb salesmen who came to the palace?

9 What is the queen's main facial feature?

10 Who is Imhotep?

11 What do the Dicey Brothers think of Imhotep's tomb design?

12 What is the problem with the nose of Queen Proboscis?

13 What kind of tomb do the Dicey Brothers plan for the queen that will accommodate her nose?

14 What arguments do the Diceys use to convince the queen to buy their stone blocks?

15 What bad news is brought to the queen?

16 How does Imhotep take advantage of the bad news?

17 What happens to the Dicey Brothers' design for a tomb?

18 How is the humour achieved in this play?

Drama Activity

Write a play of your own about the difficulties of selling some commodity of which you have an over-supply. Model your play on *The Dicey Brothers* but use different characters and a different period of history.

SCHOOL DAYS

2

NOVELS

Trouble at School

Here Gilly shows that she is against school authority and capable of causing trouble for those who oppose her.

At recesstime Monica Bradley, one of the other white girls in the class, was supposed to look after Gilly on the playground. But Monica was more interested in leaning against the building and talking with her friends, which she did, keeping her back toward Gilly as she giggled and gossiped with two other sixth-grade girls, one of whom was black with millions of tiny braids all over her head. Like some African bushwoman. Not that Gilly cared. Why should she? They could giggle their stupid lives away, and she'd never let it bother her. She turned her back on them. That would show them.

Just then a ball jerked loose from the basketball game nearby and rushed toward her. She grabbed it. Balls were friends. She hugged it and ran over to the basket and threw it up, but she had been in too much of a hurry. It kissed the rim but refused to go in for her. Angrily she jumped and caught it before it bounced. She was dimly aware of a protest from the players, but they were boys and mostly shorter than she, so not worthy of notice. She shot again, this time with care. It arched and sank cleanly. She pushed someone out of the way and grabbed it just below the net.

'Hey! Who you think you are?'

One of the boys, a black as tall as she, tried to pull the ball from her hands. She spun round, knocking him to the concrete, and shot again, banking the ball off the backboard neatly into the net. She grabbed it once more.

Now all the boys were after her. She began to run across the playground laughing and clutching the ball to her chest. She could hear the boys screaming behind her, but she was too fast for them. She ran in and out of hopscotch games and right through a jump rope, all the way back to the basketball post where she shot again, missing wildly in her glee.

The boys did not watch for the rebound. They leaped upon her. She was on her back, scratching and kicking for all she was worth. They were yelping like hurt puppies.

'Hey! Hey! What's going on here?'

Miss Harris towered above them. The fighting evaporated under her glare. She marched all seven of them to the principal's office. Gilly noted with satisfaction a long red line down the tall boy's cheek. She'd actually drawn blood in the fracas. The boys looked a lot worse than she felt. Six to one — pretty good odds for the great Gilly Hopkins.

Mr Evans lectured the boys about fighting on the playground and then sent them back to their homerooms. He kept Gilly longer.

'Gilly.' He said her name as though it were a whole sentence by itself. Then he just sat back in his chair, his fingertips pressed together, and looked at her.

She smoothed her hair and waited, staring him in the eye. People hated that — you staring them down as though they were the ones who had been bad. They didn't know how to deal with it. Sure enough. The principal looked away first.

'Would you like to sit down?'

She jerked her head No.

He coughed. 'I would rather for us to be friends.'

Gilly smirked.

'We're not going to have fighting on the playground.' He looked directly at her. 'Or anywhere else around here. I think you need to understand that, Gilly.'

She tilted her head sassily and kept her eyes right on his.

'You're at a new school now. You have a chance to — uh — make a new start. If you want to.'

So Hollywood Gardens had warned him, eh? Well, so what? The people here would have learned soon enough. Gilly would have made sure of that.

She smiled what she knew to be her most menacing smile.

'If there's any way I can help you — if you just feel like talking to somebody . . .'

Not one of those understanding adults. Deliver me! She smiled so hard it stretched the muscles around her eyes. 'I'm OK,' she said. 'I don't need any help.'

'If you don't want help, there's no way I can make you accept it. But, Gilly' — he leaned forward in his chair and spoke very slowly and softly — 'you're not going to be permitted to hurt other people.'

She snuffled loudly. Cute. Very cute.

He leaned back; she thought she heard him sigh. 'Not if I have anything to do with it.'

Gilly wiped her nose on the back of her hand. She saw the principal half reach for his box of tissues and then pull his hand back.

'You may go back to your class now.' She turned to go. 'I hope you'll give yourself — and us — a chance, Gilly.'

She ignored the remark. Nice, she thought, climbing the dark stairs. Only a half day and already the principal was yo-yoing. Give her a week, boy. A week and she'd have the whole cussed place in an uproar. But this afternoon, she'd cool it a little. Let them worry. Then tomorrow or maybe even the next day, *Wham*.

from *The Great Gilly Hopkins* by Katherine Paterson

Reading for Meaning

1 What was Monica's task at recesstime?

2 What was Monica doing instead?

3 How did Gilly manage to gain possession of a basketball?

4 Why did Gilly miss getting the first ball through the basketball hoop?

5 Why did Gilly consider the boy players not worthy of her notice?

6 What did Gilly do to the boy who tried to pull the ball from her hands?

7 What evidence can you find to show that Gilly was skilled with a basketball?.

8 How did Gilly react to the boys chasing her?

9 What happened when the boys finally caught her?

10 What is the meaning of 'The fighting evaporated under her glare'?

11 'She'd actually drawn blood in the fracas.' What had Gilly done?

12 What did the headmaster do about the boys who had been sent to him?

13 'The principal looked away first.' What caused this?

14 Do you think the principal's treatment of Gilly is fair and reasonable? Why or why not?

15 What was Gilly's plan for the future?

16 What did you learn about Gilly's character from your reading of this passage?

The Test

As you read this description you may find that you can identify with Lennie's anxiety about doing tests.

Lennie leant over his desk, pencil in hand, waiting for the Science tests to be passed out. He always got a worried feeling when he was waiting to take a test. Even if he knew everything there was to know about a subject — something that had never happened — he knew he would still be worried.

He erased a mark on his desk and then pencilled it back. He beat out a rhythm from *The Adams Family*, snapping his fingers when he got to the two clicks. He jiggled his leg. He turned to the boy sitting next to him and said, 'Hey, Frankie, is the petiole the stem or is the stipule the stem? I'm mixed up.'

Frankie shrugged.

He turned round. 'Letty Bond, is —'

'The petiole is the stem,' she said in a bored voice, 'the stipules are extra leaves.' She clicked open her ballpoint pen.

Lennie turned back to the front of the room and raised his hand. 'Miss Markham?'

'Yes, Lennie.'

'Can we take our tests in pencil or do we have to have a ballpoint pen?'

'Pencil's fine.'

'But can we use pen if we want to?' He asked this on behalf of Letty Bond who he thought might be growing anxious.

'Either one is fine.'

Lennie's throat was dry. The tests were coming. He put down his pencil, wiped his hands on his shirt and picked up his pencil.

He took the tests from the girl in front of him, selected the top one and passed the rest to Letty Bond.

'Well, here we go,' he said with false liveliness. He glanced at Letty Bond. She had already written her name at the top of the page and was ready to take on the first question.

Lennie turned back to his desk. The test was mimeographed in purple ink, and for a moment Lennie had a vision of another red 23 at the top of his. He let out his breath in one long unhappy sigh. He felt like writing the 23 there and saving Miss Markham the trouble.

Glancing down the page he decided to skip the first part which was fill-in-the-blanks and go on to the second part which was a plant with all the parts to be labelled. He had done that last night for the schoolteachers — twice.

Very carefully he printed the word 'petiole' in the line opposite the stem. Then he looked at the word. It looked wrong. Quickly he turned his pencil and erased the word. He wet his lips. He wanted to turn round and ask Letty Bond if she was sure the petiole was the stem. It seemed to him . . . Nervously he printed 'petiole' back in the same space.

He printed in four more words and then he got up. With his eyes on his paper he went to the teacher's desk. 'Miss Markham?'

'Yes, Lennie.'

'Is that word spelt right?'

'I'm sorry but I can't give you any help after the tests are passed out.'

'Oh.' He stood there for a moment staring down at the word he had written. 'Stupile.' He had never felt more miserable in his life. He gave Miss Markham a weak smile. He said, 'I feel kind of stupile myself today.'

'I do believe though,' Miss Markham went on kindly smiling back at him, 'you should look at what you've written very carefully. There may be something wrong.'

'Thank you, Miss Markham.'

As Lennie hurried back to his desk Miss Markham said, 'Remember, spelling counts, class.'

Lennie erased the word and respelt it. He filled in two more blanks and erased one. His test now had a worked-over look. He had worn through the paper in two places. He thought that anyone who thinks school isn't hard ought to take a look at his paper.

He bent over his desk, wet his pencil-point and filled in another blank. He went on to the multiple-choice section and filled in three of those. He glanced again at the word 'stepile.'

'Time's up, class,' Miss Markham said.

Lennie looked up, startled. He turned to Frankie. 'Are you through?'

Frankie shrugged.

'Are you through, Letty Bond?'

'I've been through since ten thirty,' she said. He glanced at her desk. She was writing a note to someone named Anne. It started: 'Am I bored!'

Lennie spun round and glanced in desperation at his test. Only half of the blanks were filled. Quickly he began filling in the rest, guessing, putting anything down so that Miss Markham would see a full, completed sheet when she got to his test. That was bound to make a better impression.

'Lennie.' It was Miss Markham.

'Yes'm.' He kept writing. He did not have time to look up.

'I have to have your test now.'

'Yes'm.'

'The next class is coming in.'

'One more word.' In desperation Lennie kept writing. Cammie Hagerdorn was standing by his desk, waiting to take Lennie's seat. Lennie looked up.

'Hard, huh?' Cammie said.

'Hard for me.' Lennie sighed. He got up, dropped his test on Miss Markham's desk and went out into the hall. Shoulders sagging, he went slowly to World Studies.

from The TV Kid by Betsy Byars

Reading for Meaning

1 How did Lennie feel when he was waiting to take the test?

2 How do you know that Letty Bond is a good science student?

3 Why was Lennie's liveliness false?

4 Why did Lennie decide to skip the first part and go on to the second part?

5 What is Miss Markham's attitude to Lennie?

6 Why did Lennie's test now have a 'worked-over look'?

7 'Lennie looked up, startled.' Why was Lennie startled?

8 How do you know that Letty Bond found the test easy?

9 Why did Lennie glance 'in desperation' at his test?

10 Why did Lennie try to have all the blanks filled in?

11 'Hard, huh?' Why does Cammie Hagerdorn say this?

12 What do the words 'shoulders sagging' suggest about Lennie's state of mind?

13 What comments would you make about Lennie as a science student?

14 Do you think Lennie is a likeable boy? Give reasons for your viewpoint.

15 Did you find this description true to life? Why or why not?

Hypnotising the School

There never has been, nor will there ever be, a headmaster like the Demon Head-master.

After a moment, the Headmaster appeared. He stalked up the aisle between the chairs, his long gown flapping behind him, seeming even taller than Dinah had remembered. Slowly he climbed the steps up to the stage and turned to look down on the crowded hall below him. There was no need for him to call for silence. Everyone, teachers and children alike, was gazing at him. With a thin smile, he reached up and took off his glasses and his huge green eyes stared out at them.

Dinah felt that he was looking directly at her. She could not move her eyes away from his steady green stare. Then he began to speak.

'Funny,' he said gently, 'that you should all be so tired. So early in the afternoon.'

But that's what he said before, Dinah thought, with a jerk of surprise. *When I was in his office. It's peculiar.*

Her amazement had jolted her out of the dreamy vagueness that his voice was producing in the others. All of a sudden, she felt grimly stubborn. She had had enough peculiar happenings for one day. She tried to turn her attention away from the tall black figure on the stage, so that she could think. But it was very difficult. There seemed to be no escaping those eyes. Then, all at once, like a light, she had a little flicker of understanding.

That's it! She thought triumphantly. *When he takes his glasses off — when I see his eyes — I want to go to sleep. And that's when things get peculiar.*

With an almost gleeful feeling, she shut her own eyes tightly, blacking out the Hall, the rows of yawning children and the compelling green stare. This time she would not get caught.

'You all look very tired,' said the Headmaster's hissing voice.

No I don't, Dinah said rebelliously, inside her head, behind her closed eyes.

'*So* tired,' he went on. 'Your hands and feet are heavy, and your eyelids are like lead.'

No they're not, Dinah thought ferociously. She turned her head sideways and, with great caution, opened one eye. All around her, she could see heads starting to nod. Children were rubbing their eyes. Teachers were giving huge, uncontrollable yawns. Then, gradually, the eyelids closed. Dinah shut her own eyes again and listened.

'You are asleep,' the Headmaster hissed down the Hall.

Ha Ha! No I'm not, Dinah's inside voice said rudely and triumphantly. She was going to do it. She was going to get the better of him.

'When you wake up,' his voice went on silkily, 'you will remember that you saw a film about ants. If anyone asks, you will say, "It was a film about ants. It was very interesting. We saw how they build their nests and look after their eggs and how their Queen lives." If you are asked any more questions, you will say, "I don't remember." Now, repeat that, please. What did you do in Assembly today?'

'It was a film about ants . . .' the children started, their voices wooden, in perfect unison. Dinah joined in, trying to sound as lifeless as the rest of them, but all the time she was gloating, because *she* knew that what she was saying was a lie. Even if she did not understand why she was supposed to be lying.

As the children stopped speaking, there was a pause and, unable to resist the urge, Dinah opened her eyes a fraction to glance at the rows and rows of apparently sleeping children, their faces turned to the front and their hands clasped in their laps. There was something sinister about the sight and, before she could stop herself, she shuddered. Instantly, she closed her eyes tightly and dropped her head forward, imitating theirs, but it was too late. From the front of the Hall she heard heavy footsteps coming down the aisle towards her.

They came closer and closer, leather soles sounding loud on the wooden floorboards, and stopped right beside her chair.

'Dinah Glass, open your eyes,' said the Headmaster's voice softly.

Mechanically, she opened them, letting her gaze settle on a distant point, way past the Headmaster, hoping that he would think she was asleep. She could not see his face, but for a moment she thought that she had succeeded in deceiving him. He stood perfectly still, watching her.

Then she heard him say, 'Your left arm is completely numb. You can feel nothing.'

Oh yes I can, her mind said obstinately — a split second before she realised what he was going to do.

He leaned forward and she felt a sharp pain, darting into her left forearm. Unable to stop herself, she winced, looking down to see him pull out the pin with which he had pricked her.

'As I thought,' he said sharply. 'Pretending. Look at me, Dinah, when I'm speaking to you.'

She went on looking stubbornly at the floor.

'Look at me!' This time his voice was loud and threatening. Frightened in spite of herself, Dinah looked up.

He was staring straight at her, a lock of pale hair falling over his forehead and his green eyes wide and translucent.

'I can see that you are not yet accustomed to our ways,' he said, more quietly. 'I hope you are not going to be a person who won't cooperate with me.'

'It depends what you want,' Dinah said coldly.

'But it's not what *I* want.' He sounded almost amused. 'It's what *you* want.'

'What I want?'

'Yes,' he crooned. 'What you want. You want to go to sleep. Because you're so tired. So very, very tired.'

Too late, she realised that she had let herself get caught off guard. This time, try as she would, she could not close her eyes or turn them away from those great pools of green that seemed to swim closer and closer . . .

'You are so sleepy,' murmured the Headmaster. 'You feel you have to go to sleep . . .'

I'll forget it all, Dinah thought frantically. *I'll forget everything I've discovered. What a waste.*

As her eyelids began to droop, she gathered all her energies together, to try and fix something in her mind.

Remember it, remember it, hypnotism, hypnotism, HYPNOTISM. Grimly, she struggled to concentrate. Remember it, *remember it, hypnotism, hypno-, hyp-. . .*

But the words in her head drifted off into silence and floated away on a great tide of sleep as she slumped slowly forwards in her chair.

This time she did not feel a thing when the Headmaster stuck the pin into her arm.

from *The Demon Headmaster* by Gillian Cross

Reading for Meaning

1 Why was there no need for the Headmaster to call for silence?

2 What effect was the Headmaster's voice having on the students?

3 Why was it difficult for Dinah to turn her attention away from the Headmaster on stage?

4 What did Dinah realise when she saw the Headmaster's eyes with his glasses removed?

5 What was happening to the children and teachers all around Dinah?

6 'You are asleep.' What was Dinah's reaction?

7 What does 'their voices wooden, in perfect unison' reveal about the children?

8 What did Dinah do to make the Headmaster think that she was asleep?

9 How did the Headmaster test to see whether Dinah was asleep or not?

10 Why did Dinah finally look up at the Headmaster?

11 'Too late, she realised that she had let herself get caught off guard.' How had Dinah 'let herself get caught off guard'?

12 How did Dinah try to prevent herself from being hypnotised?

13 How did the Headmaster finally know that Dinah was hypnotised?

14 What comments would you make about Dinah's character?

15 Did you enjoy reading this passage? Why or why not?

POETRY

SCHOOL POEMS

Where Do All the Teachers Go?

Where do all the teachers go
When it's 4 o'clock?
Do they live in houses
And do they wash their socks?

Do they wear pyjamas
And do they watch TV?
And do they pick their noses
The same as you and me?

Do they live with other people?
Have they mums and dads?
And were they ever children?
And were they ever bad?

Did they ever, never spell right?
Did they ever make mistakes?
Were they punished in the corner
If they pinched the chocolate flakes?

Did they ever lose their hymn books?
Did they ever leave their greens?
Did they scribble on the desk tops?
Did they wear old dirty jeans?

I'll follow one back home today
I'll find out what they do
Then I'll put it in a poem
That they can read to you

Peter Dixon

'Excuses, Excuses!'

Late again Blenkinsopp?
What's the excuse this time?
Not my fault sir.
Who's fault is it then?
Grandma's sir.
Grandma's? What did she do?
She died sir.
Died?
She's seriously dead alright sir.
That makes four grandmothers this term Blenkinsopp
And all on PE days.
I know. It's very upsetting sir.
How many grandmothers have you got Blenkinsopp?
Grandmothers sir? None sir.
You said you had four.
All dead sir.
And what about yesterday Blenkinsopp?
What about yesterday sir?
You were absent yesterday.
That was the dentist sir.
The dentist died?
No sir. My teeth sir.
You missed the maths test Blenkinsopp!
I'd been looking forward to it sir.
Right, line up for PE.
Can't sir.
No such word as 'can't' Blenkinsopp.
No kit sir.
Where is it?
Home sir.
What's it doing at home?
Not ironed sir.
Couldn't you iron it?
Can't sir.
Why not?
Bad hand sir.
Who usually does it?
Grandma sir.
Why couldn't she do it?
Dead sir.

Gareth Owen

Questions

1 What is happening at the beginning of the poem?

2 Why is the poem called 'Excuses, Excuses!'?

3 What did you find unusual about Blenkinsopp's excuses?

4 Do you think Blenkinsopp was telling the truth or not? Give reasons for your viewpoint?

5 What does Blenkinsopp say his attitude was to the maths test?

6 Why does Blenkinsopp say he can't line up for PE?

7 How does Blenkinsopp finally outwit the teacher?

8 Do you admire Blenkinsopp? Why or why not?

9 What do you learn about the character of Blenkinsopp's teacher?

10 Did you find the poem funny or serious? Explain your viewpoint.

Sarky Devil

Our teacher's all right, really,
But he can't stop making
These sarcastic remarks.

Nev Stephens, who's got no one to get him up,
Creeps in fifteen minutes late
Practically every morning —
Always with a new excuse.
And old Sarky says,
'Good evening, Stephens,
And what little piece of fiction
Have you got for us today?'

He even sarks the clever kids:
Says things like
'Proper little Brain of Britain, aren't we?'
And only yesterday when Maureen
(Who's brilliant at everything)
Complained of a headache,
He says, 'Perhaps it's the halo
Pinching a bit, Maureen.'

And then there's Bill Nelson
Who's just one of these naturally scruffy kids
Who can't keep anything clean —
Well, his homework book's a disgrace,
And Sarky holds it up
Delicately, by a corner,
At arm's length, and he says,
'Well, Lord Horatio,
Did you have your breakfast off this
Before or *after* the dog had a chew at it?'

Even the one who's getting sarked
Laughs —
Can't do much else, really;
And the rest of the class
Roars, of course,
And feels like one big creep.

It's a good job we understand
Old Sarky.

Eric Finney

Questions

1 What is Sarky's main fault?

2 Why is Nev Stephens late most mornings?

3 Why does Sarky call Nev's excuse a 'little piece of fiction'?

4 What kind of student is Maureen?

5 What is Bill Nelson's problem?

6 How does Sarky react to Bill Nelson's work?

7 What does the student who's 'getting sarked' do?

8 How does the rest of the class react to Sarky's comments?

9 Why do you think the members of the class feel 'like one big creep'?

10 Why has the poem been called 'Sarky Devil'?

11 Which part of the poem did you enjoy most? Why?

I Dreamt I Took Over My Secondary School

I dreamt I took over my secondary school
Sacked the headmaster for breaking the rules,
Kept the teachers outside during break in the cold
And took all their cigarettes: 'You're really too old
To be smoking — haven't you learnt *yet?*' I said.
'Learn to say no; you're too easily led!'
I told them to stop talking and messing about,
'The staff room's a cess-pit. Get it cleaned out!
And, deputy, don't drive that car like a bat out of hell —
Wait in the car-park till the end-of-school bell.'
I called in the matron and checked them for nits,
Tested their eyes and then tested their wits.
Gave the staff an IQ test, kept them in after school;
Made them read out their answers so they'd each feel a fool.
I sent several home to change shirts or their ties
Or put on dull dresses of more suitable size.
I gave lots of homework, which I didn't explain —
They put up their hands and asked questions in vain.
'You should have been listening,' I said with a smile;
'Hand in tomorrow. Now line up single file!'
I ignored their excuses that they had to go out,
'Your work must come first!' I said with a shout.
'Reports will be issued at the end of the term —
If you've not shown improvement, I'll have to be firm:
It may be the thumbscrews, it may be the rack . . .
I'm going to wake up now . . . but I'll be back!'

Trevor Millum

a.m.

Hair neat as knitting,
face clean as glass,
quite the most elegant
kid in the class.

Knees white as lilies,
ears pink as shells,
two glossy school shoes
bright as brass bells.

Jumper steam-ironed,
pristine the blazer,
badge on the smart tie
shines like a laser.

Knife-edged grey pants,
crisp, white shirt clean,
spotless, uncreased like
a new magazine.

p.m.

Missing a shoe-lace,
ditto school tie,
hair like a loo brush,
one blackened eye.

Stains on the jumper
totalling thirty,
ears slightly grubby,
knees just plain dirty.

Shirt smeared with dribble
(licked by a dog),
school badge exchanged for
smelly dead frog.

New blazer vanished,
shirt black as sorrow.
Repeat the performance?
Most likely tomorrow!

Robin Klein

Questions

1 What was the boy's hair like in the morning?

2 How had his hair changed by the afternoon?

3 What words indicate that the boy's knees were clean in the morning?

4 What were the boy's knees like in the afternoon?

5 The boy's ears were 'slightly grubby' in the afternoon. What were they like in the morning?

6 What words indicate that the boy's shoes were very clean in the morning?

7 What simile indicates that the boy's badge was very shiny in the morning?

8 Why doesn't the boy have his school badge in the afternoon?

9 Why are the boy's pants described as 'knife-edged'?

10 What has happened to the boy's shirt by the afternoon?

11 What does this poem show you about the character of the boy?

12 Why has the poet divided her poem into two sections, 'a.m.' and 'p.m.'?

WRITING

DESCRIBING PLACES

Here are descriptions of places by well-known authors. As you read each one, notice how vividly the scene is described. You almost feel that you are present — seeing, hearing and feeling.

BLUNT STREET

Andy Hoddel stood on the pavement in Blunt Street and watched his friends taking turns on a skateboard. The street went plunging downhill into a deep hollow and rose steeply again beyond it. On this side of the street, the pavement ran down under high blank walls; on the opposite side, a row of quaint old cottages tipped downhill with the street. The cottages were clumsy and ugly, squashed together in terraces, and each with a tiny square of front garden. To make up for their sameness and their squat, narrow ugliness they were all painted different colours: sooty blue, grimy green, pink fading to yellow, white turning grey. They all wore television antennae like crazy parasols on their roofs.

from *I Own the Racecourse* by Patricia Wrightson

THE VIEW FROM ABOVE

Far below him lay the sea, a sea bluer than any sky he had ever seen. The land curved in and out along its edge: in and out, up and down, all green and golden, with here and there the red of flowers too far off to be clearly seen. Down by the sea a road ran along the foot of the mountain, and near it lay villages whose bright colours gleamed dazzlingly. There were trees with many changing tints of green, and over it all shone the warming sun — not white-hot and spiteful and scorching, as the sun had shone upon the camp in the summertime, but with a warm golden loveliness.

from *I Am David* by Ann Holm

AFTER THE FIRE

The house was no more than a broken shell. A black jagged piece of wall still held a window-frame: the glass was gone and the window faced down the paddock: it stared emptily at the dark heap of bloated dead cows. There was no furniture in the ruins: there was nothing but the ashes of someone's living. Blackened pots stood on the stove; cracked cups and plates lay among the ashes of what may have been a table. From the top of the chimney there drifted a peaceful curl of smoke: it had been built for fire. The water tank had collapsed: the water had run out and doused the burning grass about it: there was a darker patch, like the shadow of a futile gesture. By the side of the house a few clothes, smoke-darkened, hung on a line that ran from a peg in the chimney to an iron pipe driven upright into the ground.

from *The Sundowners* by Jon Cleary

THE BEACH

The beach was yellow sand, but at the water's edge a rubble of shell and algae took its place. Fiddler crabs bubbled and sputtered in their holes in the sand, and in the shallows little lobsters popped in and out of their tiny homes in the rubble and sand. The sea bottom was rich with crawling and swimming and growing things. The brown algae waved in the gentle currents and the green eel grass swayed and little sea horses clung to its stems. Spotted botete, the poison fish, lay on the bottom in the eel-grass beds, and the bright-coloured swimming crabs scampered over them.

On the beach the hungry dogs and the hungry pigs of the town searched endlessly for any dead fish or sea bird that might have floated in on a rising tide.

from *The Pearl* by John Steinbeck

YOUR TURN TO WRITE

DESCRIBING A PLACE YOU KNOW

What are some of your favourite places? Try to picture in your mind one such place that is special for you. Imagine that you are actually there. What do you see and hear? What are your feelings? Write down all your impressions and sensations.

PICTURES OF PLACES

From magazines and newspapers, collect pictures of all kinds of places. The list that follows will give you some idea of what to look for.

- a snow scene
- a city scene
- a river scene
- a school scene
- at the supermarket

- a farm
- a bike track
- a drought scene
- an airport
- at a sportsground

- a factory
- inside a restaurant
- a holiday resort
- a flood scene
- an ocean scene

Then, working by yourself or with others, write descriptions to go beneath two or three of the best pictures you have chosen.

LANGUAGE

ADJECTIVES

Adjectives are descriptive words. They give colour, shape, size, strength, feeling (or whatever else may be needed) to nouns. Good writers use adjectives to give life to their writing. Look at these examples from *The Demon Headmaster*. The adjectives are in heavy type.

- She could not move her eyes from his **steady green** stare.
- Teachers were giving **huge uncontrollable** yawns.

Cartoonist also use adjectives. See how many adjectives you can find in the following Garfield cartoon.

Missing Adjectives

On the following page you will find a description of one of the meanest characters in fiction. His name is Ebenezer Scrooge. To emphasise Scrooge's meanness, Charles Dickens, the famous novelist, has used many adjectives. Twelve of these adjectives have been removed from the passage and placed in the box. Write out the description of Scrooge and insert the correct adjective in each space. The first letters have been given to help you.

clutching	solitary	wrenching	old
pointed	red	thin	low
hard	frosty	generous	blue

SCROOGE

Oh! but he was a tight-fisted hand at the grindstone. Scrooge! a squeezing, wrenching............, grasping, scraping, clutching........., covetous, old sinner! Hard................ and sharp as flint, from which no steel had ever struck out generous.......... fire; secret, and self-contained, and solitary............ as an oyster. The cold within him froze his old................ features, nipped his pointed............ nose, shrivelled his cheek, stiffened his gait; made his eyes red................, his thin................ lips blue................, and spoke out shrewdly in his grating voice. A frosty............ rime was on his head, and on his eyebrows, and his wiry chin. He carried his own low................ temperature always about with him; he iced his office in the dog-days, and didn't thaw it one degree at Christmas.

from A Christmas Carol by Charles Dickens

Adjectives in Action

Write down each pair of words and complete the adjectives as you do so.

1 dusty road
2 excruciating pain
3 contaminated water
4 appetising meal
5 electrified fence
6 diligent student
7 comfortable lounge
8 chivalrous knight
9 primitive people
10 magnificent view
11 memorable occasion
12 juicy apple

13 mountainous terrain
14 microscopic bacteria
15 handsome actor
16 sparkling wine
17 smooth skin
18 successful attempt
19 stubborn resistance
20 squalid dwelling
21 hidden treasure
22 fragile glass
23 fragrant scent
24 neighbouring town

Adjectives and Their Endings

The following groups of adjectives have the same endings. Insert the correct adjectives in the blank spaces below each box.

detachable	changeable	noticeable	avoidable	advisable

1 Some accidents are *avoidable* .
2 The handle of the saucepan was *detachable* .
3 The weather was *changeable* .
4 If your illness persists it is *advisable* to see a doctor.
5 He had a *noticeable* limp.

painful	spiteful	beautiful	plentiful	truthful

1 It was a *beautiful* scene.
2 His enemy made a *spiteful* remark.
3 Potatoes are *plentiful* this season.
4 He had a *painful* boil.
5 The witness gave a *truthful* account of the accident.

nervous	dangerous	studious	famous	melodious

1 The song was *melodious* .
2 The unexploded bomb was still *dangerous* .
3 She is so *studious* that she will certainly pass her examination.
4 She was a *famous* tennis champion.
5 He was *nervous* about travelling by plane.

Using Better Adjectives

The word *nice* is used in each of the sentences. Replace it with a better adjective from the box.

fragrant	comfortable	refreshing	energetic
absorbing	melodious	fertile	sunny
glamorous	affectionate	picturesque	delicious

1 They enjoyed a *nice* dinner   *delicious*

2 The guests had a *nice* swim.   *refreshing*

3 She purchased a *nice* perfume.   *fragrant*

4 The young man had a *nice* dog.   *affectionate*

5 I am reading a *nice* book.   *absorbing*

6 It was a *nice* day.   *sunny*

7 The room overlooked a *nice* scene.   *picturesque*

8 The chair was very *nice*.   *comfortable*

9 He was playing a *nice* tune.   *melodious*

10 She was wearing *nice* clothes.   *glamorous*

11 We all enjoyed a *nice* game of tennis.   *energetic*

12 The paddock has *nice* soil.   *fertile*

Creating Opposites by Using Prefixes

By adding the prefixes *un*, *in* or *dis*, create adjectives opposite in meaning for each of the following:

1 *un*fortunate

2 *un*necessary

3 accurate

4 *dis*loyal

5 *in*adequate

6 *in*credible

7 honourable *dis*

8 pleasant *un*

9 convenient *in*

10 *dis*courteous

11 *un*conscious

12 *dis*similar

13 popular *un*

14 considerate *in*

15 satisfied *un*

16 *un*selfish

17 *in*visible

18 certain *un*

19 *dis*orderly

20 healthy *un*

21 *un*truthful

22 honest *dis*

23 *dis*respectful

24 dependent *in*

PUNCTUATION

THE APOSTROPHE — AVOIDING CONFUSION

People are often confused about the difference between these words:

- **it's** (it is) **its** (ownership)
- **you're** (you are) **your** (ownership)
- **who's** (who is) **whose** (ownership)
- **they're** (they are) **their** (ownership) **there** (a place)

Show your understanding by inserting the correct words from the brackets in the spaces provided.

1 I wonder ..whose........ book it is.   (whose, who's)

2 ..It's.......... probable that the car has lost ..its............ exhaust pipe.   (it's, its)

3 I will call in to ..their......... house on the way to school.   (they're, their, there)

4 ..You're......... going to be late for ..your.......... exam.   (your, you're)

5 ..They're...... just sitting over ..there.......... .   (they're, their, there)

6 Guess ..who's....... coming to dinner.   (whose, who's)

7 I think ..it's........... her birthday tomorrow.   (it's, its)

8 ..They're....... on ....their....... way to school now.   (their, there, they're)

9 The dog knows ..it's.......... time for ..its........... bath.   (it's, its)

10 ..Who's........ afraid of the big bad wolf?   (whose, who's)

DRAMA

FRACTURED FAIRY TALES

Cinderfella and the Ugly Misters

by Maureen Stewart

CHARACTERS
Cinderfella
Princess Charmpits
Hairy Godfather
Ugly Mister 1
Ugly Mister 2
Ugly Mister 3
Ugly Mister 4
Ugly Mister 5

SCENE ONE

A kitchen. Cinderfella is nailing down lino.

(Enter Ugly Misters.)

Ugly Mister 1 Come on, Cinders, you haven't half finished! Get a move on!
Ugly Mister 2 Yeah.
Ugly Mister 3 Yeah, yeah!
Ugly Mister 4 Yeah, yeah, yeah!
Cinderfella I'm doing my best. Honest I am.
Ugly Mister 2 That's not good enough. Hey, fellas, tonight is the night!
Cinderfella What's on tonight?
Ugly Mister 4 Don't you know anything?
Ugly Mister 1 Tonight's the big game, stupid. Everyone knows that. And we're going.
Ugly Mister 5 Yeah. Later. First we have to go to the pool room, remember?
Ugly Mister 3 That's right! Hey, Cinderfella, crumple my jeans, will ya, so when I come back from pool they're all ready for tonight.
Ugly Mister 2 Mine too. And shine my boots.
Ugly Mister 1 And polish my bike.
Ugly Mister 4 Fix the buttons on that coat of mine, will ya, Cinders?
Ugly Mister 5 And pump up my bike. It's got a flat.
Cinderfella Aw, listen, Uglies, I'm flat out myself! Haven't even got this lino done yet. Give me a break!
Ugly Mister 1 All he ever says is 'Give me a break!' Gets kind of boring after a while.
Ugly Mister 3 You're not kidding. Listen, Cinders, the biggest break you ever got was when you came to live here. So get to it!
Ugly Mister 2 Come on, the pool table is waiting.
Ugly Mister 4 What he really means is Princess Charmpits is waiting.
Cinderfella Who's she?
Ugly Mister 2 Never you mind, Cinders. Just get into that work and finish the lino.
Ugly Mister 3 You mean you haven't heard of Princess Charmpits?
Ugly Mister 2 She's mine, anyway. After the game tonight, I'm going to ask her back here for coffee. Make sure there's some hot, Cinders.
Ugly Mister 1 You know who she is anyway, Cinderfella. Remember that time you were getting the hamburgers and that blonde chick went past with her dog? The one you said hello to.
Ugly Mister 2 What do you mean by saying hello to my girl?
Cinderfella Is she your girl? She doesn't know I say hello, because I always wait till she goes past before I say it.

(Ugly Misters laugh.)

Ugly Mister 5 That's just what we'd expect from you, you freak! Wait till a chick goes past before you say hello!
Cinderfella Who'd say hello to me?
Ugly Mister 2 Not Princess Charmpits, that's for sure.
Cinderfella *(Sighing)* Well, I'd better get this lino finished.
Ugly Mister 2 Don't forget my boots!

Ugly Mister 4   And my buttons!

Ugly Mister 1   And my bike!

Ugly Mister 3   And when you've crumpled my jeans, how about getting us some hamburgers? We should be back from the pool room in an hour or so.

Ugly Mister 5   Mine's without onion.

Ugly Mister 2   Mine's with an egg and sauce.

Ugly Mister 3   Mine's with lotsa lettuce and pepper.

Ugly Mister 4   Mine's without tomato.

Ugly Mister 1   They never have tomato on, you fool.

Ugly Mister 4   Well, that's easy then. Without tomato.

Ugly Mister 1   And mine's with bacon and lettuce!

Cinderfella   Wait a minute! Steady on! Do you think I'm Superman or something?

Ugly Mister 2   No, just stupid. Come on, Uglies, we'll be late for pool.

Ugly Mister 3   Don't forget mine's with lotsa lettuce and pepper, Cinders.

(Ugly Misters exit.)

Cinderfella   *(Looking up from the lino — he throws the hammer on the ground.)*   They make me sick! All they ever do is give me orders. How can I remember all that? Oh well, better start on the boots, I guess.

(He gets up and moves to the door. Enter Hairy Godfather. He is dressed very strangely.)

Hey, who are you? I mean, *what* are you?

Hairy Godfather   I'm your Hairy Godfather.

Cinderfella   Didn't know I had one.

Hairy Godfather   Well you have now. What's your problem?

Cinderfella   My problem? You mean my *problems*. I have hundreds of them. First of all, I have to do a million things for the Ugly Misters. Like shine their boots, crumple their jeans, fix their bikes . . . oh, you wouldn't understand. They make me sick.

Hairy Godfather   Now, don't get so upset about it! They make me sick too. That's why I'm here. I'll help you.

Cinderfella   That's very kind of you, old fella, but how could you possibly help me? Even with your help, I couldn't get all that done. Then there's the hamburgers. And they give me their orders so quickly I can never remember them.

Hairy Godfather   I can help you. Look!

(He does a strange little dance, and sings.)

All ya gotta do is (snap!)
Snap ya fingers,
Snap ya fingers *now!*

Cinderfella   *(Laughing)*   Well, you've got a crazy style about you. But apart from making me laugh, which is pretty hard, how can that help me?

Hairy Godfather   Go into their room. Go on!

Cinderfella   *(Going out the door)*   That's just where I'm going! To start crumpling jeans and . . .   *(He runs back in, with a shiny pair of boots.)*   Look! They're done! And the jeans are all crumpled! Hey, you're a magician!

Hairy Godfather   No, just your Hairy Godfather. Go and look at the bikes.

(Cinderfella runs out again, and then runs back.)

Cinderfella   Hey! You're great! Their tyres are all pumped up, and the bikes are polished. It's terrific! I can't believe it! Why are you doing all this?

Hairy Godfather   You need a break.

Cinderfella   That's what I'm always saying!

Hairy Godfather   And I'm your Hairy Godfather, so I've come to give you one.

Cinderfella   Well, you're just great. I've only got the hamburger orders to get, and I'm finished!

Hairy Godfather   Why can't they get their own hamburgers?

Cinderfella   They never do anything for themselves. Not since I came here. And they're my cousins, sort of far removed. When my folks died I had to come here. So I have to pay them for it by doing all the work.

Hairy Godfather   Yes, I know all about it. I know most things. Where are they going tonight? I know, but you tell me.

Cinderfella   To the big game. I'd like to go, of course, because there is a girl going I like to look at. I see her sometimes walking her dog when I'm out buying things. She's really pretty. I'd like to go, just to look at her.

Hairy Godfather   Well why don't you?

Cinderfella   No hope! For one thing, I've got to rush out and get these hamburgers. For another, I've got no bike. And it's too far to walk. For another, I haven't any gear to wear, not even a coat.

Hairy Godfather   Well, Cinders, first things first.

(He breaks into his song and dance act.)

All ya gotta do is (snap!)
Snap ya fingers,
Snap ya fingers *now!*

(A tray with wrapped hamburgers slides on to the stage.)

Cinderfella   *(Walking over to the tray)*   Wow! Hey, you are magic! How did you do that?

(He unwraps one.)

Hairy Godfather   Don't bother checking them. They're all right. Even the one with lotsa lettuce and pepper.

Cinderfella   You're just the greatest!

Hairy Godfather   *(Picking up a hamburger)*   Here's yours.

Cinderfella   With onions and mustard! My favourite! How did you know?

Hairy Godfather   *(Smiling)*   I'm your Hairy Godfather, remember?

Cinderfella   *(Eating madly)*   Do I ever!

Hairy Godfather   Eat away!

(He hums and dances around the kitchen.)

I have a great plan.
You're going to the game!
And from that moment on,
Life just won't be the same!
Listen, Cinders, I can hear the Uglies. When they go off to the game, I'll be back. See ya.

(He exits, dancing.)

Cinderfella   I must be dreaming!

(Uglies enter.)

Ugly Mister 1   Hey, look, Uglies. Food!

Ugly Mister 2   Well he's finally got with it. Good on ya, Cinders!

(They start eating their hamburgers.)

Ugly Mister 3   These are great. Mmmmmm. Pepper and lettuce!

Ugly Mister 4   And without tomato!

Ugly Mister 2   And a nice, drippy egg and sauce. Hey, Cinders, you're finally earning your keep.

(A couple of the Ugly Misters go out the door. Shouts of surprise are heard.)

Look, my jeans are crumpled!
And my boots are polished!
And my flat is fixed!
And my bike is just gleaming!

(They come back in.)

Cinderfella, you finally made it.

Cinderfella   Can I come to the big game then, fellas?

Ugly Misters   *(Together)*   No!

Ugly Mister 1   You just wouldn't fit in.

Ugly Mister 2   And Princess Charmpits wouldn't like you.

Cinderfella   What makes you think a pretty girl like that would like you, Ugly?

Ugly Mister 2   Well, well. He's getting smart. Just because he can get a bit of work done on time for a change.

Ugly Mister 4   Oh, leave him alone. Come on, Uglies. Let's get ready.

(The Ugly Misters finish their hamburgers and move off to get ready.)

Cinderfella   *(To himself)*   They make me sick. They really do. Even when I do things right they can't be nice. Rotten Uglies.

(Ugly Misters return.)

Ugly Mister 2   *(Combing his hair)*   How do I look?

Ugly Mister 5   Just gorgeous. She'll go for you like a shot, Ugly. Come on, fellas, let's move.

Ugly Mister 3   Yeah. So long, Cinders.

Ugly Mister 1   Better have that coffee hot. We'll be back about ten.

Ugly Mister 2   With Princess Charmpits.

(They exit. Cinderfella watches them sadly.)

Cinderfella   She's too good for him.

(Enter Hairy Godfather.)

Hi! Didn't really expect to see you again, Hairy Godfather. You've been pretty good to me already. Not that it made them any better. They wouldn't let me go to the game.

Hairy Godfather   Who cares? You're going anyway.
Cinderfella   How?
Hairy Godfather   *(Singing and dancing)*
    All ya gotta do is (snap!)
    Snap ya fingers,
    Snap ya fingers *now!*

(A new dragster is pushed on to the stage. Cinderfella catches it.)

Cinderfella   Wow. *Wow!* You mean this is mine?
Hairy Godfather   Only for tonight. And if you aren't back by ten it turns into an
    orange.
Cinderfella   *(Riding it around the stage)*   You're just the greatest! Wow. Imagine me
    with a bike! I can't believe it. Don't worry, I'll be back by ten. I have to be. The
    Uglies will be back by then too, and I'm making coffee. Wow!
Hairy Godfather   There is just one more thing. Here it comes!

(A leather coat is thrown on stage.)

Cinderfella   *(Props up the bike and runs over to the coat)*   Oh boy! How about this?
    A real leather coat. Hey, you can't mean it's for me to wear. . .
Hairy Godfather   I sure do! Put it on.
Cinderfella   *(Putting the coat on)*   Hey, it's a perfect fit. I can't believe it!
Hairy Godfather   That's up to you. Now don't forget, Cinders. Be back by ten or that
    bike becomes the biggest orange you ever saw.
Cinderfella   *(Riding off stage)*   No worries!
Hairy Godfather   They make 'em cute these days . . .

(He goes off, dancing.)

SCENE TWO

The same kitchen, four hours later. Cinderfella rushes in, without his coat and bike.

Cinderfella   Whew! Must be half past ten at the earliest. Lucky I beat them.

(He rushes around putting out mugs for coffee. Enter Ugly Misters.)

Ugly Mister 1   What a game!
Ugly Mister 4   Best this season, that's for sure.
Ugly Mister 3   Good on you, Cinders. Got the coffee ready I see.
Cinderfella   Well, nearly.
Ugly Mister 2   Hey, Cinders. You wouldn't have been there tonight, by any chance,
    would you?
Cinderfella   Why do you say that?
Ugly Mister 5   Oh, ignore him. He's just picking on you because he couldn't get to talk
    to Princess Charmpits. She had her big brother there and didn't even come close to
    us.

Ugly Mister 2   Listen. If she'd seen me she'd have fallen for me like a ton of bricks. Wait till the next game!

Ugly Mister 4   But there was a guy there who looked just like you, Cinders. He really did. Same stupid head and everything.

Ugly Mister 5   How could Cinders get there?

Cinderfella   Maybe I can do things you guys don't know about. Maybe I can get places by magic.

(A loud knocking is heard.)

Ugly Mister 1   Hey, there's someone at the door.

Cinderfella   It must be my Hairy . . . look, I'll go.

(He rushes to the door. Princess Charmpits is there when he opens it.)

Oh! it's you!

(Cinderfella is embarrassed. Princess Charmpits enters.)

Ugly Mister 2   What did I tell you! She's come for coffee.

Ugly Mister 4   How lucky can you be?

Princess Charmpits   *(Holding out Cinderfella's leather coat)*   Hello. This is yours. You were sitting next to us. My brother is waiting for me outside. He knew you lived here.

Cinderfella   *(Taking the coat)*   Gee . . . thanks. Didn't think you even saw me.

Princess Charmpits   I've seen you for a long time. Whenever I take my dog for a walk I see you. You're always carrying lots of things.

Ugly Mister 2   Well, can you beat that! Get her some coffee, will you, Cinders?

Cinderfella   Sure. Do you have milk and sugar?

Princess Charmpits   Yes. But I won't have any, thanks. My brother is waiting. Do you do all the work around here?

Cinderfella   It's a long story.

Ugly Mister 4   And a boring one.

Ugly Mister 2   Don't worry about Cinderfella. He's useless. Where did you get that coat, anyway, Cinders?

Cinderfella   From my Hairy Godfather.

(Ugly Misters laugh.)

Ugly Mister 1   Now I've heard everything.

Princess Charmpits   *(Taking an orange from her bag)*   This yours? I found it on the steps.

(Ugly Misters shake their heads.)

Cinderfella   It's mine. I mean, it was mine. For the night, that is. Hairy Godfather said if I wasn't back by ten the bike would change into an orange. And it did! Crazy stuff!

Ugly Mister 2   You're right off your head, you are. All this talk about Hairy Godfathers.

Princess Charmpits   I think he's just great. At least he's got an imagination, which is more than I can say for you!

Ugly Mister 2   I like that! Cinders having imagination!

Cinderfella   Suddenly I feel like I have heaps of it. Are you sure you won't have coffee, Princess?

Princess Charmpits   No, I must go. But I'll tell you what. Let's both have coffee together tomorrow afternoon. Near the hamburger shop, you know the place. And this time say hello when I can hear you!

Cinderfella   Hey, I'd love that!

Princess Charmpits   I don't suppose you want a job, do you? My brother is looking for someone to help out in the shop . . . anyway, we'll talk about that tomorrow. See you.

(She goes out. The Uglies stare at Cinderfella in amazement. Cinderfella stares at the orange and the coat, and shakes his head in amazement too.)

Ugly Mister 5   I wouldn't believe it if I hadn't seen it with my own eyes. Fancy you getting onto Princess Charmpits like that.

Ugly Mister 2   Yeah!

Ugly Mister 4   Yeah, yeah!

Ugly Mister 3   Yeah, yeah, yeah!

Ugly Mister 1   How did ya do it? I mean, how did ya even get there tonight? And what's the truth about that coat?

Cinderfella   You won't believe me, but . . .

(He sings and dances like the Hairy Godfather.)

All ya gotta do is (snap!)
Snap ya fingers,
Snap ya fingers *now!*

(The Uglies watch as he dances off stage.)

FRACTURING YOUR OWN FAIRY TALES

Now it's your turn to try some on-the-spot creations of your own. Discuss how *Cinderfella and the Ugly Misters* has been humorously 'fractured', then write your own Fractured Fairy Tale. Here are some suggestions.

Fairy Tales for Fracturing

1 Jack and the Beanstalk
2 Goldilocks and the Three Bears
3 Hansel and Gretel
4 Little Red Riding Hood
5 Snow-White and the Seven Dwarfs
6 Beauty and the Beast
7 Rapunzel
8 Aladdin and His Wonderful Lamp
9 Rumpelstiltskin
10 The Three Little Pigs
11 Dick Whittington and His Cat
12 The Sleeping Beauty
13 The Ugly Duckling
14 The Frog Prince

DEAR DIARY . . .

3

DIARIES

The Great Sock Rebellion

Adrian Mole is an English schoolboy who confides his desires, disasters and secret thoughts to his diary. In the diary entries that follow, Adrian writes about his school and his parents.

Thursday June 4th

. . . I went to school. I was feeling rebellious, so I wore red socks. It is strictly forbidden but I don't care any more.

Friday June 5th

Miss Sproxton spotted my red socks in assembly! The old bag reported me to pop-eyed Scruton. He had me in his office and gave me a lecture on the dangers of being a nonconformist. Then he sent me home to change into regulation black socks. My father was in bed when I got home . . . I watched *Play School* with Maxwell until he came downstairs. I told him about the sock saga.

He instantly turned into a raving loonie! He phoned the school and dragged Scruton out of a caretakers' strike-meeting. He kept shouting down the phone; he said, 'My wife's left me, I've been made redundant, I'm in charge of an idiot boy,' – Maxwell, I presume – 'and you're victimising my son because of the colour of his socks!' Scruton said if I came to school in black socks everything would be forgotten but my father said I would wear whatever colour socks I liked. Scruton said he was anxious to maintain standards. My father said that the England World Cup team in 1966 did not wear black socks, nor did Sir Edmund Hillary in 1953. Scruton seemed to go quiet then. My father put the phone down. He said, 'Round one to me.'

This could well get into the papers: 'Black socks row at school'. My mother might read about it and come home.

Saturday June 6th

Oh Joy! Oh Rapture! Pandora is organising a sock protest! She came round to my house today! Yes! She actually stood on our front porch and told me that she admired the stand I was taking! I would have asked her in, but the house is in a squalid state so I didn't. She is going round the school with a petition on Monday morning. She said I was a freedom fighter for the rights of the individual. She wants me to go round to her house tomorrow morning. A committee is being set up, and I am the principal speaker! She wanted to see the red socks but I told her they were in the wash . . .

Monday June 8th

Woke up, dressed, put red socks on before underpants or vest. Father stood at the door and wished me luck. Felt like a hero. Met

Pandora and rest of committee at corner of our road; all of us were wearing red socks. Pandora's were lurex. She has certainly got guts! We sang 'We shall not be moved' all the way to school. I felt a bit scared when we went through the gates but Pandora rallied us with shouts of encouragement.

Pop-eyed Scruton must have been tipped off because he was waiting in the fourth-year cloakroom. He was standing very still with his arms folded, staring with poached-egg eyes. He didn't speak, he just nodded upstairs. All the red socks trooped upstairs. My heart was beating dead loud. He went silently into his office and sat at his desk and started tapping his teeth with a school pen. We just stood there.

He smiled in a horrible way then rang the bell on his desk. His secretary came in, he said, 'Sit down and take a letter, Mrs Claricoates.' The letter was to our parents, it said:

Dear Mr and Mrs .... ,
It is my sad duty to inform you that your son/daughter has deliberately flaunted one of the rules of this school. I take an extremely serious view of this contravention. I am therefore suspending your son/daughter for a period of one week. Young people today often lack sufficient moral guidance in the home, therefore I feel that it is my duty to take a firm stand in my school. If you wish to discuss the matter further with me do not hesitate to ring my secretary for an appointment.
    Yours faithfully,
    R. G. Scruton
    Headmaster

Pandora started to say something about her O levels suffering but Scruton roared at her to shut up! Even Mrs Claricoates jumped. Scruton said that we could wait until the letters had been typed, duplicated and signed and then we had better 'hot foot it out of school'. We waited outside Scruton's office.

Pandora was crying (because she was angry and frustrated, she said). I put my arm round her a bit. Mrs Claricoates gave us our letters. She smiled very kindly, it can't be very easy working for a despot.

We went round to Pandora's house but it was locked, so I said everyone could come round to my house. It was quite tidy for once, apart from the dog hairs. My father raged about the letter. He is supposed to be a Conservative but he is not being very conservative at the moment.

I can't help wishing that I had worn black socks on Friday.

Tuesday June 9th
MOON'S FIRST QUARTER
My father saw Scruton today and told him that if he didn't allow me back to school in whatever colour socks I like he would protest to his MP. Mr Scruton asked my father who his MP was. My father didn't know ...

Monday June 15th
The Red Sock Committee has voted to give way to Scruton for the time being. We wear red socks underneath our black socks. This makes our shoes tight but we don't mind because a principle is involved.

from *The Secret Diary of Adrian Mole Aged 13¾* by Sue Townsend

Reading for Meaning

Thursday June 4th
1 Adrian went to school 'feeling rebellious'. What did this feeling cause him to do?

Friday June 5th
2 How did Mr Scruton react to Adrian's red socks?

3 What did Adrian's father do when Adrian told him about 'the sock saga'?

4 What evidence did Adrian's father use to show that black socks were unimportant?

Saturday June 6th
5 What important news did Adrian have for his diary on Saturday June 6th?

6 What praise did Pandora give Adrian?

7 Explain how this triumphant diary entry ends weakly and humorously.

Monday June 8th
8 What was unusual about the way Adrian dressed?

9 How do we know that the Red Sock Committee was in high spirits on the way to school?

10 How was Mr Scruton staring at the committee?

11 How do we know that Adrian felt some fear as he went upstairs to Mr Scruton's office?

12 In his letter to parents, how did Mr Scruton punish the committee?

13 How did the letter criticise the parents?

14 How did Mr Scruton tell the students to get out of the school?

15 Why was Pandora crying?

16 With what wish does Adrian end his June 8th entry?

Tuesday June 9th
17 How did Mr Scruton win over Adrian's father?

Monday June 15th
18 How did the members of the Red Sock Committee uphold their principle?

Your Opinion
19 What do you think is the most interesting feature of Adrian's diary?

20 What have you learned about Adrian from his diary entries?

The Intruder

Ann Burden, a teenager, believes she is the sole survivor of a nuclear war. The valley where she lives is one place that has not been affected by the war. However, as she notes in her diary, her peaceful solitude is shattered by the approach of a sinister-looking intruder.

May 20th

I am afraid.

Someone is coming.

That is, I think someone is coming, though I am not sure, and I pray that I am wrong. I went into the church and prayed all this morning. I sprinkled water in front of the altar, and put some flowers on it, violets and dogwood.

But there is smoke. For three days there has been smoke, not like the time before. That time, last year, it rose in a great cloud a long way away, and stayed in the sky for two weeks. A forest fire in the dead woods, and then it rained and the smoke stopped. But this time it is a thin column, like a pole, not very high.

And the column has come three times, each time in the late afternoon. At night I cannot see it, and in the morning, it is gone. But each afternoon it comes again, and it is nearer. At first it was behind Claypole Ridge, and I could see only the top of it, the smallest smudge. I thought it was a cloud, except that it was too grey, the wrong colour, and then I thought: there are no clouds anywhere else.

I got the binoculars and saw that it was narrow and straight; it was smoke from a small fire. When we used to go in the truck, Claypole Ridge was fifteen miles, though it looks closer, and the smoke was coming from behind that.

Beyond Claypole Ridge there is Ogdentown, about ten miles further. But there is no one left alive in Ogdentown.

I know, because after the war ended, and all the telephones went dead, my father, my brother Joseph and cousin David went in the truck to find out what was happening, and the first place they went was Ogdentown. They went early in the morning; Joseph and David were really excited, but Father looked serious.

When they came back it was dark. Mother had been worrying — they took so long — so we were glad to see the truck lights finally coming over Burden Hill, six miles away. They looked like beacons. They were the only lights anywhere, except in the house — no other cars had come down all day. We knew it was the truck because one of the lights, the left one, always blinked when it went over a bump. It came up to the house and they got out; the boys weren't excited any more. They looked scared, and my father looked sick. Maybe he was beginning to be sick, but mainly I think he was distressed.

My mother looked up at him as he climbed down.

'What did you find?'

He said, 'Bodies. Just dead bodies. They're all dead.'

'All?'

We went inside the house where the lamps were lit, the two boys following, not saying anything. My father sat down. 'Terrible,' he said, and again, 'terrible, terrible. We drove around, looking. We blew the horn. Then we went to the church and rang the bell. You can hear it five miles away. We waited for two hours, but nobody came. I went into a couple of houses — the Johnsons', the Peters' — they were all in there, all dead. There were dead birds all over the streets'. . .

[Ann's family went in search of help once more, but this time they did not return. Ann is left completely alone.]

May 21st

. . . There are some things I need to explain. One is why I am afraid. Another is why I am writing in this composition book, which I got from Klein's store a mile up the road.

I took the book and a supply of ballpoint pens back in February. By then the last radio station, a very faint one that I could hear only at night, had stopped broadcasting. It had been dead for about three or four months. I say *about*, and that is one reason I got the book: because I discovered I was forgetting when things happened, and sometimes even *whether* things happened or not. Another reason I got it is that I thought writing in it might be like having someone to talk to, and if I read it back later it would be like someone talking to me. But the truth is I haven't written in it much after all, because there isn't much to write about.

Sometimes I would put in what the weather was like, if there was a storm or something unusual. I put in when I planted the garden because I thought that would be useful to know next year. But most of the time I didn't write, because one day was just like the day before, and sometimes I thought — what's the use of writing anyway, when nobody is ever going to read it? Then I would remind myself: some time, years from now, *you're* going to read it. I was pretty sure I was the only person left in the world.

But now I have something to write about. I was wrong. I am not the only person left in the world. I am both excited and afraid. . .

[As the person approaches her valley, Ann prepares to hide and observe.]

May 24th

It is a man, one man alone.

This morning I went as I planned. I put on my good slacks, took the ·22 and hung the binoculars around my neck. I climbed a tree and saw him coming up the road. I could not

really see what he looks like, because he is dressed, entirely covered, in a sort of orange plastic-looking suit. It even covers his head, and there is a glass mask for his eyes — like the wet suits skin divers wear in cold water, only looser and bulkier. Like skin divers, too, he has an air-tank on his back. But I could tell it was a man, even though I could not see his face, by his size and the way he moves.

The reason he is coming so slowly is that he is pulling a wagon, a thing about the size of a big trunk mounted on two bicycle wheels. It is covered with the same orange plastic as his suit. It is heavy, and he was having a hard time pulling it up Burden Hill. He stopped to rest every few minutes. He still has about a mile to go to reach the top.

I have to decide what to do.

Still May 24th
Now it is night.

He is in my house.

Or possibly not in it, but just outside it, in a small plastic tent he put up. I cannot be sure, because it is too dark to see clearly. I am watching from the cave, but the fire he built — outside the house, in the garden — has burned down. He built it with my wood.

He came over the top of Burden Hill this afternoon. I had come up to watch, having eaten some lunch and changed back to my blue jeans. I decided not to show myself. I can always change my mind later.

I wondered what he would do when he reached the top. He must have been pretty sure, but not quite, that he was coming to a place where things were living. As I said, you can see it from the ridge, but not too well — it is a long way. And maybe he had been fooled before; maybe he thought it was a mirage.

There is a flat place where the road first reaches the top of the hill — a stretch of about a hundred yards or so before it starts descending again, into the valley. When you get just past the middle of this you can see it all, the river, the house, the barn, the trees, pasture, everything. It has always been my favourite sight, maybe because when I saw it I was always coming home. Being spring, today it is all a new fresh green.

When he got to that place he stopped. He dropped the shaft of the wagon and just stared for about a minute. Then he ran forward down the road, very clumsy in his plastic suit, waving his arms. He ran to a tree by the roadside and pulled a branch, tearing off the leaves and holding them close to his glass face mask. You could tell he was thinking: Are they real?

I was watching from a place only a little way up the hillside, a path in the woods. I had my gun beside me. I did not know whether he could hear or not with that mask on, but I did not move or make a sound.

All at once he pulled at the mask, at a fastening at the neck of it, as if he were going to take it off. So far I could not see his face at all, but only the glass plate, so I was staring. Then he stopped, and instead ran back to the wagon. He unsnapped the plastic cover at one end and pulled it open. He reached inside and took out a glass thing — a sort of tube with a metal rod in it, like a big thermometer. It had some kind of a dial or gauge on it to read — I couldn't see from where I was, but he held it in front of his mask and turned it slowly, studying it. He walked back down the road to the tree, looking at the rod. He held it down close to the road, then up high in the air. Then back to the wagon again.

He took out another machine, something like the first one but bigger; after that he pulled out a black, round thing: it was an earphone, with a wire dangling from it. He plugged the wire into the machine and put the earphone up beside his mask, next to his ear. I could tell what he was doing: using one machine to check against the other. And I knew what they must be; I had read about them but never seen one: radiation counters, Geiger counters they call them. He walked down the road, a long way this time — half a mile at least, watching one counter, listening to the other.

Then he took off the mask, and shouted.

It startled me so that I jumped back. I started to run — then I stopped. He was not shouting at me. He was cheering — a long 'Haaay' sound, the kind they make at football games. He didn't hear me (luckily); the shout went echoing down the valley, and I stood absolutely still again, though my heart was still thumping — it was so long since I had heard a voice except my own, when I sing sometimes.

Then silence. He put his hands beside his mouth and shouted again, aiming down the hill. This time he called, very loudly:

'Anybody here?'. . .

. . . I am still afraid. And yet it is — what is the word I mean? — *companionable* to know there is someone else in the valley.

from *Z for Zachariah* by Robert O'Brien

Reading for Meaning

May 20th

1 Why do the first few words in the diary create suspense?

2 What evidence does the diarist, Ann Burden, have for the presence of another person?

3 In the paragraph beginning 'Beyond Claypole Ridge . . .' what horrible surprise is presented to the reader?

4 Why did Ann's father, brother and cousin have to go to Ogdentown after the war ended?

5   What did they find in Ogdentown?

6   What word did her father use and repeat to describe the scene and his feeling about the situation in Ogdentown?

7   'I took the book and a supply of ballpoint pens back in February.' Why did Ann decide to keep a diary?

8   In what way was the diary going to be like another person to Ann?

9   Why didn't Ann write much in her diary?

10 What kinds of things did Ann record in her diary?

11 When Ann realised she was not the only person left in the world, what were her feelings?

May 24th

12 What four things did Ann do as the lone man came up the road on the morning of May 24th?

13 How was the man dressed?

14 How did Ann know it *was* a man?

15 Why was the man moving slowly towards Ann?

16 On what note of uncertainty does this diary entry end?

Still May 24th

17 What did Ann decide to do about the lone man?

18 Why did the man react to a tree by running to it, pulling a branch and tearing off the leaves?

19 What precautions were taken by the man before he took off his mask?

20 As he took off his mask what did he do?

21 'I started to run — then I stopped.' Why did she stop?

22 As the passage ends, how does Ann feel about the presence of another person in the valley?

Your Opinion

23 What creates the suspense or the feeling of acute anticipation in this passage?

24 How would you describe the character of Ann Burden?

In the Secret Annexe

When the Germans invaded Amsterdam during the Second World War, Anne Frank, a young Jewish girl, went into hiding with her family and four other people (the Van Daan family and Mr Dussel, a dentist). They remained hidden in a 'Secret Annexe' for two years until they were betrayed and sent to their deaths at a concentration camp in Germany. Only her father survived. During this time Anne kept a diary which was later found and published. Her pet name for the diary was 'Kitty'. Here are some excerpts from Kitty.

Thursday 10th December, 1942

Dear Kitty,

. . . Dussel had opened his dental practice. For the fun of it, I must just tell you about his first patient. Mummy was ironing; and Mrs Van Daan was the first to face the ordeal. She went and sat on a chair in the middle of the room. Dussel began to unpack his case in an awfully important way, asked for some eau-de-Cologne as a disinfectant and vaseline to take the place of wax.

He looked at Mrs Van Daan's mouth and found two teeth which, when touched, just made her crumple up as if she was going to pass out, uttering incoherent cries of pain. After a lengthy examination (in Mrs Van Daan's case, lasting in actual fact not more than two minutes) Dussel began to scrape away at one of the holes. But, no fear — it was out of the question — the patient flung her arms and legs about wildly in all directions until at one point Dussel let go of the scraper — that remained stuck in Mrs Van Daan's tooth.

Then the fat was really in the fire! She cried (as far as it was possible with such an instrument in one's mouth), tried to pull the thing out of her mouth and only succeeded in pushing it farther in. Mr Dussel stood with his hands against his sides calmly watching the little comedy. The rest of the audience lost all control and roared with laughter. It was rotten of us, because I for one am quite sure that I should have screamed even louder. After much turning, kicking, screaming, and calling out, she got the instrument free at last and Mr Dussel went on with his work, as if nothing had happened!

This he did so quickly that Mrs Van Daan didn't have time to start any fresh tricks. But he'd never had so much help in all his life before. Two assistants are pretty useful: Van Daan and I performed our duties well. The whole scene looked like a picture from the Middle Ages entitled 'A Quack at Work'. In the meantime however, the patient hadn't much patience; she had to keep an eye on 'her' soup and 'her' meal. One thing is certain, Mrs Van Daan won't be in such a hurry to allow herself to be treated again!

Yours, ANNE

Wednesday 10th March, 1943

Dear Kitty,

We had a short-circuit last evening, and on top of that the guns kept banging away all the time. I still haven't got over my fear of everything connected with shooting and 'planes . . . The AA guns roar so loudly that you can't hear yourself speak. Mrs Van Daan, the fatalist, was nearly crying, and said in a very timid little voice, 'Oh, it is so unpleasant! Oh, they are shooting so hard,' by which she really means 'I'm so frightened.'

It didn't seem nearly so bad by candlelight as in the dark. I was shivering, just as if I had a temperature, and begged Daddy to light the candle again. He was relentless, the light remained off. Suddenly there was a burst of machine-gun fire, and that is ten times worse than guns. Mummy jumped out of bed and, to Pim's annoyance, lit the candle. When he complained her answer was firm: 'After all, Anne's not exactly a veteran soldier.' And that was the end of it.

Have I already told you about Mrs Van Daan's other fears? I don't think so. If I am to keep you informed of all that happens in the 'Secret Annexe', you must know about this too. One night Mrs Van Daan thought she heard burglars in the attic; she heard loud footsteps and was so frightened that she woke her husband. Just at that moment the burglars disappeared and the only sounds that Mr Van Daan could hear were the heartbeats of the frightened fatalist herself. 'Oh, Putti (Mr Van Daan's nickname), they are sure to have taken the sausages and all our peas and beans. And Peter, I wonder if he is still safely in bed?' 'They certainly won't have stolen Peter. Listen, don't worry and let me go to sleep.' But nothing came of that. Mrs Van Daan was far too nervous to sleep another wink. A few nights after that the whole Van Daan family was woken by ghostly sounds. Peter went up to the attic with a torch — and scamper — scamper! What do you think it was running away? A swarm of enormous rats! When we knew who the thieves were, we let Mouschi sleep in the attic and the uninvited guests didn't come back again; at least not during the night.

Peter went up to the loft a couple of evenings ago to fetch some old newspapers. He had to hold the trapdoor firmly to get down the steps. He put his hand down without looking . . . and went tumbling down the ladder from the sudden shock and pain. Without knowing it he had put his hand on a large rat, and it had bitten him hard. By the time he reached us, as white as a sheet and with his knees knocking, the blood had soaked through his pyjamas. And no wonder; it's not very pleasant to stroke a large rat; and to get bitten into the bargain is really dreadful.

Yours, ANNE

from *The Diary of Anne Frank*

Reading for Meaning

Thursday 10 December, 1942

1 '. . . Mrs Van Daan was the first to face the ordeal.' What was going to happen to Mrs Van Daan?

2 What was Mr Dussel going to use for disinfectant and dental wax?

3 How did Mrs Van Daan behave when her two bad teeth were touched?

4 What did Mrs Van Daan do when Dussel began scraping away at one of the holes in her teeth?

5 What happened after the scraper remained stuck in Mrs Van Daan's tooth?

6 What were Anne's feelings about everyone laughing at Mrs Van Daan?

7 Why didn't Mrs Van Daan start 'fresh tricks'?

Wednesday 10 March, 1943

8 What causes Anne to be afraid?

9 How did Mrs Van Daan show she was frightened?

10 Why did Anne's mother light the candle?

11 What did Mrs Van Daan's burglars in the attic turn out to be?

12 What evidence can you find to show that Mouschi was a cat?

13 Up in the loft Peter 'put his hand down without looking'. What happened next?

Your Opinion

14 What do you think is the most interesting feature of this diary?

15 What have you learned about Anne's character from her diary entries?

POETRY

POEMS OF PERSONAL EXPERIENCE

Friday Morning Last Two
Lessons is Games Day

We straggle in twos
Down Endbutt Lane to the playing fields,
In a gap-toothed murmuring line
Filling the pavement.
Mr Pearson strides out in front
The ball tucked firmly under one arm,
His head bent.

We avoid lampposts
And young mothers pushing prams,
Sometimes walk gammy-legged in gutters
Or scuffle through damp leaves.
The morning is filled
With laughter-tongued and pottering mongrels;
Old men tending bare borders
Slowly unbend
And lean upon their brooms to watch us pass.
Their wives in flowered pinnies
Peer through the lace curtains
Of unused front rooms.

At the pitch
We change in the old pavilion
That smells of dust and feet
And has knot holes in the boarding.
Someone
From another class
Has left
One
Blue and white sock behind.

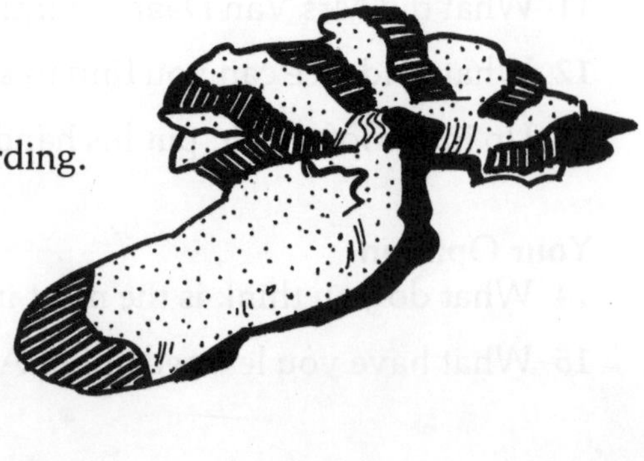

The lads shout about other games
And goals and saves and shots
Or row about who'll wear red or blue.
Pearson blows exasperation
Briskly through his whistle,
'Come on, lads, let's be having you.'

With eighteen a side
We tear after the ball shouting,
Longing to give it a good clean belt,
Perform some piece of perfection —
Beat three sprawling backs in a mazy dribble.
Race full pelt onto a plate-laid-on pass
And crack it full of hate and zest
Past the diving goalie to bulge the net.
But there is no net
And we have to leg it after the ball
To the allotments by the lane
Before we can take centre
To start the game again.

Afterwards,
Still wearing football socks,
Studded boots slung on my shoulder,
I say 'Tarrah' to Trev
At Station Road and drift home
Playing the game again.
Smoke climbs steep from neat red chimneys;
Babies drool and doze
And laugh at the empty sky.
There is the savour of cabbage and gravy
About the Estate and the flowers do not hear
The great crowd roaring me on.

Gareth Owen

Questions

1 What activity is occurring in the first verse?

2 How do you think someone would look walking 'gammy-legged in gutters'?

3 What is the sound-word in the line 'Or scuffle through damp leaves'?

4 How do old men react to the passing of the school students?

5 What do their wives do?

6 Where is the setting of the third verse?

7 What would you smell in the old pavilion?

8 What would you see?

9 In blowing his whistle, what feeling is being expressed by Pearson?

10 'We tear after the ball'. Note the power of the action word 'tear'. Find five other action words in the same verse which you think are just as powerful.

11 '. . . to bulge the net'. What has happened?

12 'Playing the game again'. What is meant by this?

13 What picture of the Estate does the poet present to the reader towards the end of the poem?

14 'The great crowd roaring me on'. What is the boy thinking about?

The Apple-Raid

Darkness came early, though not yet cold;
Stars were strung on the telegraph wires;
Street lamps spilled pools of liquid gold;
The breeze was spiced with garden fires.

That smell of burnt leaves, the early dark,
Can still excite me but not as it did
So long ago when we met in the park —
Myself, John Peters and David Kidd.

We moved out of town to the district where
The lucky and wealthy had their homes
With garages, gardens, and apples to spare
Ripely clustered in the trees' green domes.

We chose the place we meant to plunder
And climbed the wall and dropped down to
The secret dark. Apples crunched under
Our feet as we moved through the grass and dew.

The clusters on the lower boughs of the tree
Were easy to reach. We stored the fruit
In pockets and jerseys until all three
Boys were heavy with their tasty loot.

Safe on the other side of the wall
We moved back to town and munched as we went.
I wonder if David remembers at all
That little adventure, the apples' fresh scent.

Strange to think that he's fifty years old,
That tough little boy with scabs on his knees;
Stranger to think that John Peters lies cold
In an orchard in France beneath apple trees.

Vernon Scannell

Questions

1 What sights does the poet describe in the first verse?

2 To what does the poet compare the light produced by the street lamps?

3 What fragrance did the breeze bring?

4 How are we told in the second verse that the poem is to be about an experience of childhood?

5 Find the words in the poem which mean that apples ready to be picked were present in great numbers in the leafy apple trees?

6 What sound does the poet describe in the fourth verse?

7 Where did the boys store their stolen apples?

8 Why does the poet describe the boys as 'heavy'?

9 'We . . . munched as we went'. Why is 'munched' a better word than 'ate'?

10 How has the poet indicated the passing of time in the first two lines of the last verse?

11 What is the meaning of the last two lines of the poem?

12 What do you think inspired the poet to write this poem?

My Uncle Mick

My Uncle Mick the portrait artist painted Nature's Creatures.
Began with the Venus Fly-trap but he soon got onto Leeches
Because he found inspiring beauty in their hideous features.

His portrait of the Lamprey, whose face is a living grave,
Knocked men cold with horror, made women quake and rave.
'When you have seen what's what,' he said, 'That's how you *should* behave.'

He painted a lifesize portrait of a laughing Alligator
With a man's feet sticking out, and titled 'THE CREATOR
DOING REPAIRS AND MAINTENANCE INSIDE HIS EXCAVATOR.'

'The bigger the fright,' said Uncle Mick, 'The more it can inspire us.'
He filled his ceiling with the portrait of a vicious virus.
Out of his walls came sharks with jaws like doorways to devour us.

But alas his fate was waiting when he painted a tiger's roar.
We found his paints and brushes scattered round upon the floor.
Had the tiger got him? Uncle Mick was seen no more.

We gaze at the tiger's portrait now. Was that my Uncle's fate?
His painting was too lifelike and his rescuers were too late.
Those eyes glare dumbly back at us and our hair stands up straight.

Ted Hughes

Questions

1 What kind of portraits did Uncle Mick choose to paint?

2 What is awful about the Lamprey's face? (A lamprey is an eel-like creature.)

3 How did men and women react to Uncle Mick's portrait of the Lamprey?

4 What was on the ceiling of Uncle Mick's room?

5 What were on the walls?

6 Why is 'a tiger's roar' an unusual subject for a painting?

7 What mystery surrounded the disappearance of Uncle Mick?

8 How do we know that Uncle Mick's painting was frightening to look at?

9 What makes this an unusual but interesting poem?

10 Imagine that you have a relative who has an unusual occupation, and then try
writing a poem about this person.

The Female Highwayman

Priscilla on one summer's day
Dressed herself up in men's array;
With a brace of pistols by her side
All for to meet her true love she did ride.

And when she saw her true love there
She boldly bade him for to stand.
'Stand and deliver, kind sir,' she said,
'For if you don't I'll shoot you dead.'

And when she'd robbed him of all his store,
Said she, 'Kind sir, there's one thing more;
The diamond ring I've seen you wear,
Deliver that and your life I'll spare.'

'That ring,' said he, 'my true love gave;
My life I'll lose but that I'll save.'
Then, being tender-hearted like a dove,
She rode away from the man she love.

Anon they walked upon the green,
And he spied his watch pinned to her clothes,
Which made her blush, which made her blush
Like a full, blooming rose.

' 'Twas me who robbed you on the plain,
So here's your watch and your gold again.
I did it only for to see
If you would really faithful be.
And now I'm sure that this is true,
I also give my heart to you.'

Anon

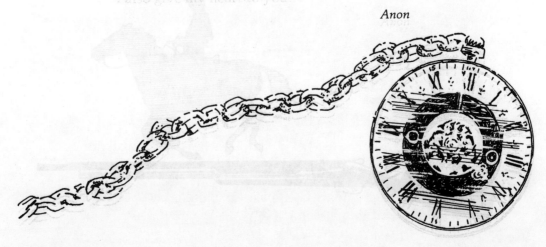

The Last Song of Billy the Kid

I'll tell you the story of Billy the Kid.
I'll tell of the things that this young outlaw did
Way out in the West when the country was young.
When the gun was the law and the law was a gun.

Now the Mexican maidens play guitars and sing
Songs about Billy, the boy bandit-king
But with drinkin' and gamblin' he come to his end,
Shot down by Pat Garrett who once was his friend.

Pat Garrett rode up to the window that night,
The desert was still and the moonlight was bright,
Pat listened outside while the Kid told his tale
Of shooting the guard in the Las Cruces jail.

'I rode down the border and robbed in Juaréz,
I drank to the ladies the happiest of days,
My picture is posted from Texas to Maine
And women and ridin' and robbin's my game.'

All the while Billy bragged Pat waited outside.
Bill said to his friends, 'I ain't satisfied.
Twenty-one men I have put bullets through,
The sheriff, Pat Garrett, must make twenty-two.'

Then Pat Garrett fired and his thumb-buster cracked.
Billy fell dead, he was blowed through the back.
Pat rode away, left the Kid lying dead,
And this is the last song of Billy the Kid.

Anon

WRITING

KEEPING A DIARY OR JOURNAL

Monday March 2nd
Today in English, we talked all about how to keep a diary, and the sorts of things to write in it. Paul Kelly, our teacher, says we have to have a special book for it, and he would be rapt if some people could keep it up for the whole year. He said to try and write about the most important thing that happens during the day, and if nothing happens, then just talk about things that have happened in the past that are interesting memories, or about the things you want to get off your chest. He reckons it's better to get down quickly what's going on in your brain and how you feel about it, instead of worrying about writing perfectly.

I'm going to start and talk about . . .

from *Breaking Up* by Frank Willmott

Keeping a diary or journal usually involves writing down the daily events of your life. Some of these events will be important, while others will be the routine details of your day-to-day existence. You might include descriptions of the people you meet, the films you see, or perhaps a quotation from an interesting book you are reading. A diary or journal gives you an opportunity to write down the thoughts, ideas and feelings you have about *any* matter of importance to *you*.

Many people find that keeping a diary or journal often becomes like confiding in a close friend. So the diary is addressed as 'Dear Diary', or in the case of Anne Frank with a pet name, 'Dear Kitty'.

The following diary extract is from the book *So Much To Tell You . . .* by John Marsden. It is about the life of a lonely girl in a boarding school who feels she is shunned by her fellow students, even though some of them, especially Cathy, make an effort to be friends with her. The diarist confides a certain kind of pain and suffering to the secrecy of her diary.

LONELINESS

March 7
I am the Phantom, the Ghost Who Walks, in the Dorm, in class, all around the School. People don't notice that I exist any more. I like it that way. Sometimes they look at me with sympathy, or say or do something kind, like offering me a bite of a Mars Bar. At those times they use the sort of voice people have when they're talking to little

children, or pet puppies. Other times they get angry at me and yell. Other times they're cruel and make jokes about me. Mostly it's Sophie, but I don't want to make her sound like she's evil or anything. She just likes people who are loud and funny and noisy. I know it must be awful for them, having me in their Dorm. But I did not steal her money. What would I want with money?

Today Cathy got fed up with me, for no particular reason that I know of. She came into the Dorm in a bad mood, swearing at everyone and complaining about everything. Then she found some of my undies on her bed, where I'd put them while I was sorting my laundry. She got mad and threw them at me and said: 'And don't think we're going to keep feeling sorry for you all year.' I was scared and very very sick inside me but I didn't run away like I normally do.

Now we're in Prep again and she has sent me a note:

I'm sorry about yelling at you. I was in a foul after Science, 'cos Hardcastle virtually accused me of cheating. It wasn't anything you did. I'm sorry — I think you're nice and I want to be friends. *Cathy*

It's about 20 minutes since she sent it to me. I cannot look at her. I cannot move. I have spent the whole time with my head down, looking at this page. Now I have just started writing again. I want to die or hide or run away. I am scared to look at her. I can handle, have handled, most things in my life, but not this.

from *So Much To Tell You . . .* by John Marsden

Questions

1 How does the girl dramatise her loneliness in the opening sentence of her diary entry?

2 How is she critical of the people who are sympathetic or kind to her?

3 What other reactions to her do people have?

4 On March 7th who 'got fed up' with her and why?

5 What happened when Cathy 'got mad'?

6 How did Cathy try to make up for her outburst?

7 The girl in this extract probably liked keeping her diary. What suggests this?

8 What do you learn about the personal nature of a diary from this extract?

The following extract is from *The Diary of a Teenage Health Freak* by Aidan Macfarlane and Ann McPherson. The teenage health freak is Peter Payne, aged 14. The entry concerns a fight between Peter and his sister Susie (Sally is his older sister). It is written with a good deal of robust humour.

THE BIG BUST UP

Friday 22nd February

Pouring with rain — got soaked going to school. Both Mum and my maths teacher asked me if I had got out of bed the wrong side. Felt exhausted and had a headache all day. . .

Then came the BIG bust up. Real Clint Eastwood style on a domestic scale. I spilt some tea by mistake. Susie said it was on purpose because it was her turn to clear and wash up, and that I had to wipe it up. Didn't see why I should as it was HER turn. She made a face and stomped to the kitchen with a pile of dishes. So I spilt her tea, and when she came back told her now she had something of her own to clear up. She tried to hit me. I caught and twisted her arm. She fell and hit the table and the milk bottle fell and smashed on the floor. At this point Mum reappeared looking as black as thunder. Told her it was all Susie's fault and Susie, lying as usual, said it was all mine. Mum threw a washing-up cloth at Susie and a brush at me, telling us to get on with clearing it up. Then she walked out in a real bate.

Immediately Susie slopped milk all over my new trainers, whispering, 'I hate you', so told her she was a real pain and no wonder Kate didn't like her any more. As I said it, I was aware, with terrible certainty and delighted fear, that it would provoke violence. She hit me on the arm with her milk-sodden tea towel, so I screamed and collapsed (unhurt) on the floor clutching my arm, accidently cutting myself on the broken glass on the floor. At that instant both Mum and Dad appeared — Mum at one door speechless with rage, and Dad at the other, fresh from beastie bashing, equally speechless. Mum recovered first, yelling, 'BOTH TO BED — NOW.' Dad blurted out, 'Do what your mother says.' I cried, 'But I'm bleeding,' and Susie said, 'But it was all his fault, why do you always pick on ME?' 'BED,' Mum screamed, so, deliberately dripping blood all up the stairs, stamped up to my room, slamming the door. Lay listening to Susie sobbing. Maybe 'feeling fed up' is infectious.

What seemed hours later, Sally came up to fetch us for supper. In Susie's room the sobbing immediately began again, followed by a shout of, 'No — leave me alone, everybody hates me.' In my worst whiney voice I recited as loud as I could:

'Nobody likes me, everybody hates me,
Think I'll eat some worms.
Big fat juicy ones,
Slip slap slimy ones,
Watch them squiggle and squirm.
Bite their heads off,
Suck their guts out,
Throw their skins away.
Everybody wonders why I live on three fat worms a day.'

Sally shouted at me to shut up. When I stopped I heard her say, much to my surprise, 'No, they don't hate you. We all love you very much, including Pete.' Lies, lies, lies.

Supper was a dead silent affair. Had neither the energy nor the nerve to reject my beans and kidneys — even though I didn't feel hungry. Dad made one or two of his feeble jokes which disappeared into the atmosphere without a ripple. Came straight up after supper to write this. Sometimes writing about things seems to make them better.

from *The Diary of a Teenage Health Freak* by Aidan Macfarlane and Ann McPherson

Questions

1 Why was the morning and the day of Friday 22nd February a miserable one for Peter?

2 How did 'the BIG bust up' between Peter and his sister Susie start over something trivial?

3 How did their mother handle the argument?

4 What happened after Peter provoked violence?

5 How does Peter indicate in his diary entry the loudness of the screaming and yelling?

6 How would you describe the poem that Peter used in his diary?

7 Why did Peter go straight up after supper to write in his diary?

8 What kind of mood was Peter in when he wrote this diary entry?

9 Do you consider that any part of the entry is so personal that Peter probably wouldn't want anyone else to read it?

10 What do you learn about Peter's character from this diary entry?

WRITING A PAGE FROM THE DIARY OF . . .

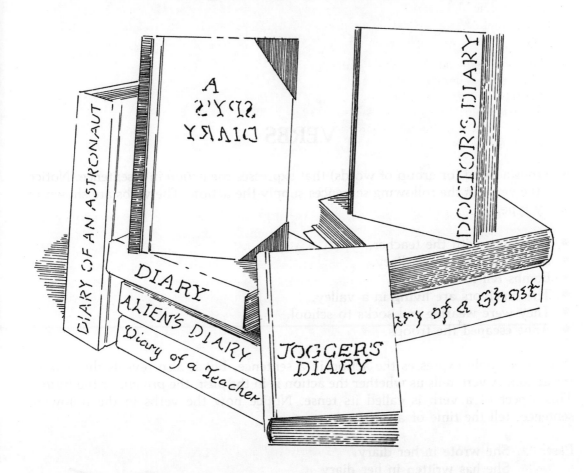

Imagine that you are one of the diarists listed below. Write a detailed diary entry for one day or several days in that person's life. Make your entry or entries as personal as you can. Try confiding your secrets to your diary as to a friend. Make sure that you give the date of each entry.

Diarists
- a doctor
- a jogger
- the Queen of England
- an explorer
- a school teacher
- a space alien
- a ghost
- Garfield (or another cartoon character)
- a police officer
- an astronaut

- a zoo animal
- a newspaper reporter
- Superman or Superwoman
- the president of the USA
- a school bus driver
- a spy
- a national park ranger
- an Olympic athlete
- a magician
- a lifesaver

LANGUAGE

VERBS

A verb is a word (or group of words) that expresses the *action* in a sentence. Notice how the verbs in the following sentences supply the action. The verbs are shown in heavy type.

- He **argues** with the teacher.
- She **is writing** in her diary.
- Bombs **fell** from the sky.
- The survivors **are living** in a valley.
- They **were wearing** red socks to school.
- Anne **escaped** the troops.

A verb not only expresses the action in a sentence, but it also reveals the *time* of the action. A verb tells us whether the action is in the *past*, the *present* or the *future*. This aspect of a verb is called its **tense**. Notice how the verbs in the following sentences tell the time of an action.

Past: She **wrote** in her diary.
           She **has written** in her diary.
           She **was writing** in her diary.

Present: She **writes** in her diary.
           She **is writing** in her diary.

Future: She **will write** in her diary.
           She **shall write** in her diary.

I am writing

Verbs create the action in all kinds of writing. In the following exercises you are asked to examine the use of verbs in comic strips, a recipe and a diary entry.

Verbs in Comic Strips

© Diogenes Design Ltd

1 In the first and last frames of the Footrot Flats comic strip above, what verbs are in the present tense?

2 In the second and third frames, what verbs are in the past tense?

© United Media Syndicate

1 What verbs can you find in the Garfield comic strip above?

2 How has the cartoonist used verbs to create humour?

Verbs in a Recipe

A RECIPE FOR A PUDDING

4 cups S.R. flour	1 teaspoon nutmeg	Cooking time: 3 hours.
½ cup sugar	500 g/1 lb currants	
1 dessertspoon dripping		

Dissolve the dripping in a pint of hot water. Mix the flour, nutmeg, currants and sugar all together then add the hot water and dripping, add enough more water as to make a sloppy mix, but not runny. When all mixed put into a cloth — like Christmas pudding

— and <u>boil</u> for 3 hours. <u>Place</u> a saucer in the bottom of the pot to <u>stop</u> the pudding from <u>burning</u> on the bottom. <u>Make</u> sure the water is <u>boiling</u> before you <u>place</u> the pudding in. <u>Serve</u> with custard.

from *Outback Cooking in the Camp Oven* by Jack and Reg Absolom

1 How many verbs can you find in the recipe?

2 Do most of the verbs in the recipe deal with the past, the present or the future?

Verbs in Adrian Mole's Diary

Thursday January 1st
These are my New Year's resolutions:

1. I will help the blind across the road.
2. I will hang my trousers up.
3. I will put the sleeves back on my records.
4. I will not start smoking.
5. I will stop squeezing my spots.
6. I will be kind to the dog.
7. I will help the poor and ignorant.
8. After hearing the disgusting noises from downstairs
   last night, I have also vowed never to drink alcohol.

1 Do most of the verbs in Adrian's New Year's resolutions deal with the past, the present or the future?

2 What does the word 'will' tell you about a verb?

3 Which one of the resolutions deals with a different time from the others?

4 Which of the resolutions do you like most? Why?

Verb Forms

Here is an exercise that will test your knowledge of how verbs change their form according to the time (tense) they reveal. In each of the following sentences put the correct form of the verb in the space provided. The first one has been done as an example.

1 Has the film ....begun..... yet?   (begin)

2 We ..drove........ to the valley yesterday.   (drive)

3 He was ..bitten......... by the dog.   (bit)

4 She was tired after she had ..swum........... one kilometre. (swim)

5 You will break......... the cup if you drop it. (broke)

6 Yesterday we .spoke......... to the dentist. (speak)

7 Tomorrow we will ..know......... whether we have won. (knew)

8 He has .drawn........ a picture on the wall. (draw)

9 They have .grown......... their own vegetables for years. (grew)

10 This time last year we were .decideing... to go to college. (decide)

11 I .had gone..... to the gym yesterday. (go)

12 The sail was ..torn.......... by the wind. (tore)

13 Last week the dog .ate........... all its dinner. (eat)

14 After it was pulled out of the pool, the cat ..shake..... the water from its fur. (shake)

Verbs That Command

Verbs that command or direct you to take action are listed in the box below. Select the appropriate verb from the box to complete each of the expressions that follow. The first one has been done as an example. Sometimes the first letters are given to help you.

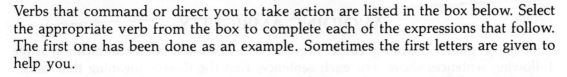

listen	observe	hoist	guard
reduce	conserve	persist	ascend
apologise	create	calculate	repair
elect	punish	apply	resuscitate

1 ......listen..... to the radio

2 ...apologise.. for your rudeness

3 p..unish...... an offender

4 ..apply...... for a job

5 e.lect........... a mayor

6 ..calculate your answer to the sum

7 c.reate....... a poem

8 r.esuscitate.... the drowning victim

9 p..rsist.......... in your efforts

10 reduce....... your weight

11 ..hoist........ the flag

12 o.bserve...... an eclipse of the moon

13 repair..... a breakage

14 ascend......... a mountain

15 .conserve..... the environment

16 guard.......... the treasure

Verbs and Their Meanings

Match each of the verbs in the left-hand column with its correct meaning in the right-hand column.

Verbs	Meanings
accumulate	finish
exceed	stretch out
intrude	blow up with air or gas
erode	gather together
anticipate	go beyond
conceal	make an uninvited entry
ignore	influence by argument
refund	foresee, look forward to
extend	eat away
complete	take no notice
persuade	hide
inflate	pay back — especially money

GETTING IT RIGHT
AVOIDING AMBIGUITY

Ambiguity (double meaning) causes considerable confusion in communication as the following sentences show. For each sentence, find the double meaning that causes the confusion, then rewrite the sentence so that it conveys the correct meaning. You may be able to do this by rearranging the sentence, but sometimes you will need to change the wording. The first one has been done as an example.

1 They kept a tiger in a cage that could roar.
  In a cage they kept a tiger that could roar.

2 For sale: lovely old cottage that will not last very long.

3 There is a pot for cooking stew that is said to be 100 years old.

4 Wanted: sensible young woman to wash, iron and milk two cows.

5 The rescue team found the man who got lost in the bush with the help of the Boy Scouts.

6 She asked if she could try on the dress in the window.

7 Advertisement: You can run more than one kilometre on one slice of bread.

8 Student wants washing and cleaning three days a week.

9 Headline: MAN CRITICAL AFTER BEING RUN OVER BY TRUCK

10 Boat for sale, one owner, green in colour.

DRAMA

DIARY DRAMA IN REAL LIFE

Some diaries have been published after the death of the diarist. One famous example is the diary of Captain Scott. This English explorer was beaten in a race to the South Pole in 1911 by the Norwegians. On his return journey from the Pole, Scott and his companions perished from lack of food and the dreadful cold. Captain Scott's diary was found beside his body by the rescue team.

Arrange your class into five or six groups. Each group is then to work as a team of scriptwriters whose task it is to turn the following entries from Scott's diary into a drama script. When this has been done, assign a part to each group member and perform your script for the class. You will find suggestions for scriptwriting after the diary entries.

Scott of the Antarctic's Final Hours

Friday 16 March or Saturday 17

Lost track of dates, but think the last correct. Tragedy all along the line. At lunch, the day before yesterday, poor Titus Oates said he couldn't go on; he proposed we should leave him in his sleeping-bag. That we could not do, and we induced him to come on, on the afternoon march. In spite of its awful nature for him he struggled on and we made a few miles. At night he was worse and we knew the end had come.

Should this be found I want these facts recorded. Oates's last thoughts were of his mother, but immediately before he took pride in thinking that his regiment would be pleased with the bold way in which he met his death. We can testify to his bravery. He has borne intense suffering for weeks without complaint, and to the very last was able and willing to discuss outside subjects. He did not — would not — give up hope till the very end. He was a brave soul. This was the end. He slept through the night before last, hoping not to wake; but he woke in the morning — yesterday. It was blowing a blizzard. He said, 'I am just going outside and may be some time.' He went out into the blizzard and we have not seen him since.

I take this opportunity of saying that we have stuck to our sick companions to the last. In the case of Edgar Evans, when absolutely out of food and he lay insensible, the safety of the remainder seemed to demand his abandonment, but Providence mercifully removed him at this critical moment. He died a natural death, and we did not leave him till 2 hours after his death. We knew that poor Oates was walking to his death, but though we tried to dissuade him, we knew it was the act of a brave man and an English gentleman. We all hope to meet the end with a similar spirit, and assuredly the end is not far.

At the Pole (from left to right: Oates, Bowers, Scott, Wilson, Evans)

I can only write at lunch and then only occasionally. The cold is intense, –40° at midday. My companions are unendingly cheerful, but we are all on the verge of serious frost-bites, and though we constantly talk of fetching through I don't think any one of us believes it in his heart.

We are cold on the march now, and at all times except meals. Yesterday we had to lay up for a blizzard and today we move dreadfully slowly. We are at No 14 pony camp, only two pony marches from One Ton Depôt. We leave here our theodolite, a camera, and Oates's sleeping-bags. Diaries, etc, and geological specimens carried at Wilson's special request, will be found with us or on our sledge.

Thursday 29th March
Since the 21st we have had a continuous gale from wsw and sw. We had fuel to make two cups of tea apiece and bare food for 2 days on the 20th. Every day we have been ready to start for our depôt 11 *miles* away, but outside the door of the tent it remains a scene of whirling drift. I do not think we can hope for any better things now. We shall stick it out to the end, but we are getting weaker, of course, and the end cannot be far.

It seems a pity, but I do not think I can write more.

R. Scott

Last entry:
For God's sake look after our people.

from *Scott's Last Expedition* (the personal journals of Captain R. F. Scott)

SUGGESTIONS FOR SCRIPTING SCOTT'S DIARY

First of all, list your characters.

CHARACTERS

Captain Scott	Edgar Evans
Dr Wilson	Lieutenant Bowers
Titus Oates	Narrator

Next, outline the story of the diary entries. Work out what you think the characters would have said and done. Use these guidelines to help you.

Friday 16 March or Saturday 17
How do Scott, Wilson and Bowers react to Oates's suggestion to leave him behind?
What do they do when he goes out into the snow?
Do they try to stop him?
Be sure to bring out the sadness and tragedy of the scene.

Thursday 29 March
What are some of the things Scott, Wilson and Bowers talk about during their last hours?
— Evans and Oates?
— their life in England?
— their families?
— the cold?
— their lack of food?
— how they will face death?
— the chances of being rescued?

Having outlined the story, you are ready to write your script. Here is an example of how your script could be set out.

THE LAST HOURS

Narrator   . . . .
Scott   . . . .
Wilson (*sadly*)   . . . .
Bowers (*wearily*)   . . . .
Oates (*determined*)   . . . .
Evans   . . . .

Once your script is written, your group then acts it out for the rest of the class. Discuss the differences between each group's interpretation of the diary entries.

THE PULSE OF THE CITY

4

NOVELS

Death in the Park

Streetgang warfare sometimes goes further than anyone wants, as Ponyboy and Johnny discover.

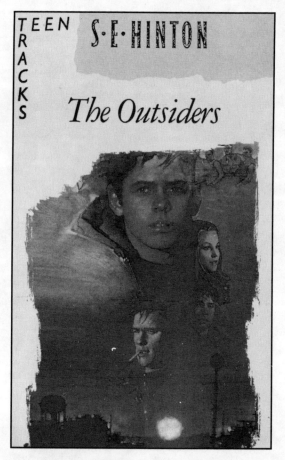

The park was about two blocks square, with a fountain in the middle and a small swimming pool for the little kids. The pool was empty now in the fall but the fountain was going merrily. Tall elm trees made the park shadowy and dark, and it would have been a good hangout, but we preferred our vacant lot, and the Shepard outfit liked the alleys down by the tracks, so the park was left to lovers and little kids.

Nobody was around at two-thirty in the morning, and it was a good place to relax and cool off. I couldn't have gotten much cooler without turning into a popsicle. Johnny snapped up his jeans jacket and flipped up the collar.

'Ain't you about to freeze to death, Pony?'

'You ain't a'woofin',' I said, rubbing my bare arms between drags on my cigarette. I started to say something about the film of ice developing on the outer edges of the fountain when a sudden blast from a car horn made us both jump. The blue Mustang was circling the park slowly.

Johnny swore under his breath, and I muttered, 'What do they want? This is our territory. What are Socs doing this far east?'

Johnny shook his head. 'I don't know. But I bet they're looking for us. We picked up their girls.'

'Oh, glory,' I said with a groan, 'this is all I need to top off a perfect night.' I took one last drag on my weed and ground the stub under my heel. 'Want to run for it?'

'It's too late now,' Johnny said. 'Here they come.'

Five Socs were coming straight at us, and from the way they were staggering I figured they were reeling pickled. That scared me. A cool deadly bluff could sometimes shake them off, but not if they outnumbered you five to two and were drunk. Johnny's hand went to his back pocket and I remembered his switchblade. I wished for that broken bottle. I'd sure show them I could use it if I had to. Johnny was scared to death. I mean it. He was as white as a ghost and his eyes were wild-looking, like the eyes of an animal in a trap. We backed against the fountain and the Socs surrounded us. They smelled so heavily of whisky and English Leather that I almost choked. I wished desperately that Darry and Soda would come along hunting for me. The four of us could handle them easily. But no one was around, and I knew Johnny and I were going to have to fight it out alone. Johnny had a blank, tough look on his face—you'd have had to know him to see the panic in his eyes. I stared at the Socs coolly. Maybe they could scare us to death,

but we'd never let them have the satisfaction of knowing it.

It was Randy and Bob and three other Socs, and they recognised us. I knew Johnny recognised them; he was watching the moonlight glint off Bob's rings with huge eyes.

'Hey, whatta ya know?' Bob said a little unsteadily, 'here's the little greasers that picked up our girls. Hey, greasers.'

'You're outa your territory,' Johnny warned in a low voice. 'You'd better watch it.'

Randy swore at us and they stepped in closer. Bob was eyeing Johnny. 'Nup, pal, yer the ones who'd better watch it. Next time you want a broad, pick up yer own kind—dirt.'

I was getting mad. I was hating them enough to lose my head.

'You know what a greaser is?' Bob asked. 'White trash with long hair.'

I felt the blood draining from my face. I've been cussed out and sworn at, but nothing ever hit me like that did. Johnnycake made a kind of gasp and his eyes were smouldering.

'You know what a Soc is?' I said, my voice shaking with rage. 'White trash with Mustangs and madras.' And then, because I couldn't think of anything bad enough to call them, I spit at them.

Bob shook his head, smiling slowly. 'You could use a bath, greaser. And a good working over. And we've got all night to do it. Give the kid a bath, David.'

I ducked and tried to run for it, but the Soc caught my arm and twisted it behind my back, and shoved my face into the fountain.

I fought, but the hand at the back of my neck was strong and I had to hold my breath. I'm dying, I thought, and wondered what was happening to Johnny. I couldn't hold my breath any longer, I fought again desperately but only sucked in water. I'm drowning, I thought, they've gone too far . . . A red haze filled my mind and I slowly relaxed.

The next thing I knew I was lying on the pavement beside the fountain, coughing water and gasping. I lay there weakly, breathing in air and spitting out water. The wind blasted through my soaked shirt and dripping hair. My teeth chattered unceasingly and I couldn't stop them. I finally pushed myself up and leaned back against the fountain, the water running down my face. Then I saw Johnny.

He was sitting next to me, one elbow on his knee, and staring straight ahead. He was a strange greenish-white, and his eyes were huger than I'd ever seen them.

'I killed him,' he said slowly. 'I killed that boy.'

Bob, the handsome Soc, was lying there in the moonlight, doubled up and still. A dark pool was growing from him, spreading slowly over the blue-white cement. I looked at Johnny's hand. He was clutching his switchblade, and it was dark to the hilt. My stomach gave a violent jump and my blood turned icy.

'Johnny,' I managed to say, fighting the dizziness, 'I think I'm gonna be sick.'

'Go ahead,' he said in the same steady voice. 'I won't look at you.'

I turned my head and was quietly sick for a minute. Then I leaned back and closed my eyes so I wouldn't see Bob lying there.

This can't be happening. This can't be happening. This can't be . . .

'You really killed him, huh, Johnny?'

'Yeah.' His voice quavered slightly. 'I had to. They were drowning you, Pony. They might have killed you. And they had a blade . . . they were gonna beat me up . . .'

'Like . . .'—I swallowed—'like they did before?'

Johnny was quiet for a minute. 'Yeah,' he said, 'like they did before.'

Johnny told me what happened: They ran when I stabbed him. They all ran . . .'

from *The Outsiders* by S. E. Hinton

Reading for Meaning

1 What two features could be seen in the middle of the park?

2 Why was the park left to lovers and little kids?

3 Why had Johnny and Ponyboy gone to the park?

4 What evidence is there to indicate just how cold it was?

5 What was the first indication that other people were around?

6 In which general direction was the Soc's territory from the park?

7 Why were the Socs out of their territory?

8 '. . . from the way they were staggering I figured they were reeling pickled.' What do you think 'reeling pickled' means?

9 How could Ponyboy see that Johnny was 'scared to death'?

10 What expressions did Johnny and Ponyboy have on their faces as they faced the Socs?

11 What emotions did Ponyboy experience after Bob began talking?

12 Why did Ponyboy spit at the Socs?

13 What happened when Ponyboy could not hold his breath any longer?

14 'Then I saw Johnny.' The short sentence suggests something is terribly wrong. What is there about Johnny's appearance that confirms this?

15 Suggest two reasons why Ponyboy is sick.

16 What two reasons does Johnny give for having to kill Bob?

17 What is your attitude towards Johnny at the end of this extract?

18 What are your feelings about what has happened?

The Space Cyclone

Clara is *so* miserable she has to get away from everyone — even if that means a terror ride!

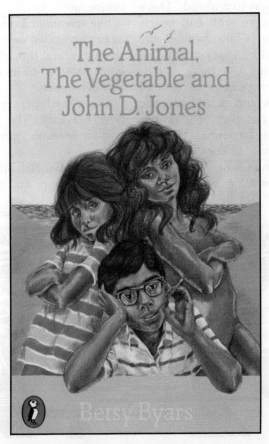

Clara looked up. Her eyes focused on the huge dome of the Space Cyclone, the one place nobody would follow her. 'I'm going on that one,' she said.

'Are you out of your mind? The Space Cyclone?'

'Yes.'

'You know you'll get sick. Just once I would like to drive home from an amusement park with you when you didn't smell like puke. Dad, don't let her go!' Deanie turned back to her father, dodging people until she had his attention.

'Clara,' her father called mildly, 'don't go if it's going to make you sick.'

Clara kept walking. 'You're going to be miserable!' Deanie sang out behind her. Deanie's voice sounded so much like her mother's that Clara almost turned around to see if by some miracle her mother had actually arrrived to take her home.

The Space Cyclone was just ahead. There was a sign warning people with bad hearts not to go on the ride. Clara handed the attendant her book and he tore out the last ticket. Clara got into line.

There were three teenage boys in front of her, a family of five behind. Clara was the only person who was not part of a group, but she was relieved to be alone. The line moved back and forth, snaking forward slowly. All too soon Clara was there. 'Remove your sunglasses,' a woman in a space outfit told her, 'and remain seated until the end of the ride.'

Clara nodded.

The car slid forward and slowly began to climb. It was so dark Clara couldn't see anything. Space music began. Computerised chords whined, rose and fell eerily. A cold came in the air.

Suddenly, without warning, the car lunged over the top and, twisting and turning, began to spiral down through the darkness. Clara heard herself scream. Stars exploded in her face. Meteorites flew at her. Space vehicles attacked. Her stomach turned as the car plunged down into a black hole and up again.

The car began another slow climb. Clara leaned back. She breathed deeply. She had never heard her body so loudly before. Blood pumped. Her ears popped. Her stomach throbbed. She was like an orchestra tuning up.

She screamed as the car went over the top again, screamed as it plunged — this time so steeply Clara thought the car had actually come loose from its tracks and was hurtling through space.

She closed her eyes, clapped her hands over her ears. The music was mixed with human screams now, both building to a climax.

The car twisted, spiralled, dipped one last, sickening loop, and then straightened. It slid

out into the light and stopped with a sure, mechanical click.

Clara bobbed forward in her seat. She opened her eyes. She felt as strange as an explorer seeing things for the first time. This is called light and these are people and you have just been on something called a ride.

The loudspeaker said, 'Please step out of your car and walk through the door marked Re-entry.

Clara tried to get to her feet, failed, and sat back in the space capsule. 'Wasn't that awful?' a woman asked cheerfully as she passed.

'Yes,' Clara answered. She got slowly to her feet and leaned over the car like a wilted flower.

'I'm going again as soon as I can get in line.' The woman leaned closer. 'Are you all right, honey? You look funny.'

Clara smiled weakly. 'I always look this way,' she said. Stumbling slightly, she got out of the capsule and headed for Re-entry.

from *The Animal, The Vegetable and John D. Jones* by Betsy Byars

Reading for Meaning

1 Why does Clara choose to ride the Space Cyclone?

2 How does Clara's sister, Deanie, react when she finds out that Clara intends riding the Space Cyclone?

3 What argument does Deanie use to try to stop Clara?

4 What sort of person do you think Deanie is, judging from this extract? What evidence is there for your viewpoint?

5 What warning does the public receive about the Space Cyclone?

6 How does Clara differ from others in the queue?

7 Why do you think Clara has to remove her sunglasses?

8 As the car begins to climb what special effects set the mood for the ride?

9 What causes Clara to scream?

10 'She was like an orchestra tuning up.' Explain what was happening to Clara.

11 What frightens Clara even more in the Space Cyclone's second plunge?

12 What external sounds, other than the space music, does Clara hear during her ride?

13 'She felt as strange as an explorer seeing things for the first time.' Why do you think Clara experiences this strange sensation?

14 'Wasn't that awful?' Why do these words seem humorous, coming from this particular woman?

15 How do we know that the Space Cyclone ride has had a physical effect on Clara?

16 What did you learn about Clara's character from this incident?

Cat and the Parkway

Taking a cat on holidays can present a few problems, as Davey discovers. Note that the American word 'parkway' means a highway which runs through a park or other landscaped area.

It's like this, Cat
Emily Neville

I get up early the next morning and help Mom button up around the house and get the car loaded before Pop gets home in the afternoon. He hoped to get off early, and I've been pacing around snapping my fingers for a couple of hours when he finally arrives about six o'clock. It's a hot day again.

I don't say anything about Cat. I just dive in the back seat and put him behind a suitcase and hope he'll behave. Pop doesn't seem to notice him. Anyway, he doesn't say anything.

It's mighty hot, and traffic is thick, with everyone pouring out of the city. But at least we're moving along, until we get out on the Hutchinson River Parkway, where some dope has to run out of gas.

All three lanes of traffic are stopped. We sit in the sun. Pop looks around, hunting for something to get sore about, and sees the back windows are closed. He roars, 'Crying out loud, can't we get some air, at least? Open those windows!'

I open them and try to keep my hand over Cat, but if you try to hold him really, it makes him restless. For the moment he's sitting quiet, looking disgusted.

We sit for about ten minutes, and Pop turns off the motor. You can practically hear us sweating in the silence. Engines turn on ahead of us, and there seems to be some sign of hope. I stick my head out the window to see if things are moving. Something furry tickles my ear, and it takes me a second to register.

Then I grab, but too late. There is Cat, out on the parkway between lanes of cars, trying to figure which way to run.

'Pop!' I yell. 'Hold it! Cat's got out!'

You know what my Pop does? He laughs.

'Hold it, my eyeball!' he says. 'I've been holding it for half an hour. I'd get murdered if I tried to stop now. Besides, I don't want to chase that cat every day of my vacation.'

I don't even stop to think. I just open the car door and jump. The car's only barely moving. I can see Cat on the grass at the edge of the parkway. The cars in the next lane blast their horns, but I slip through and grab Cat.

I hear Mom scream, 'Davey!'

Our car is twenty feet ahead, now, in the centre lane, and there's no way Pop can turn off. The cars are picking up speed. I holler to Mom as loud as I can, 'I'll go back and stay with Kate! Don't worry!'

I hear Pop shout about something, but I can't hear what. Pretty soon the car is out of sight. I look down at Cat and say, 'There goes our vacation.' I wonder if I'll be able to catch a bus out to Connecticut later. Meanwhile, there's the little problem of getting back into the city. I'm standing alongside the parkway, with rail-road tracks and the Pelham golf course on the other side of me, and a good long walk to the subway.

A cat isn't handy to walk with. He keeps trying to get down. If you squeeze him to hang on, he just tries harder. You have to keep juggling him, like, gently. I sweat along back, with the sun in my eyes, and people in cars on the parkway pointing me out to their children as a local curiosity.

One place the bulrushes and marsh grass beside the road grow up higher than your head. What a place for a kids' hideout, I think. Almost the next step, I hear kids' voices, whispering and shushing each other.

Their voices follow along beside me, but inside the curtain of rushes, where I can't see them. I hear one say, 'Lookit the sissy with the pussy!' Another answers, 'Let's dump 'em in the river!'

I try to walk faster, but I figure if I run they'll chase me for sure. I walk along, juggling Cat, trying to pretend I don't notice them. I see a drawbridge up ahead, and I sure hope there's a cop or watchman on it.

The kids break out of the rushes behind me, and there's no use pretending any more. I flash a look over my shoulder. They all yell, 'Ya-n-h-h-h!' like a bunch of wild Indians, but they're about fifty feet back.

I grab Cat hard about the only place you can grab a cat, around one upper forearm, and I really run. The kids let out another war whoop. It's uphill to the bridge. Cat gets his free forepaw into action, raking my chest and arm, with his claws out. Then he hisses and bites, and I nearly drop him. I'm panting so hard I can't hardly breathe anyway.

A cop saunters out on my approach to the bridge, his billy dangling from his wrist. Whew — am I glad! I flop on the grass and ease up on Cat and start soothing him down. The kids fade off into the tall grass as soon as they see the cop. A stone arches up towards me, but it falls short. That's the last I see of them.

As I cross the bridge, the cop squints at me. 'What you doing, kid? Not supposed to be walking here.'

'I'll be right off. I'm going home,' I tell him, and he saunters away, twirling his stick.

It's dark by the time I get to the subway,

and most of another hour before I'm back in Manhattan and reach Kate's. I can hear the television going, which is unusual, and I walk in. No one is watching television. Mom and Pop are sitting at the table with Kate.

Mom lets loose the tears she has apparently been holding onto for two hours, and Pop starts bellowing: 'You fool! You might have got killed jumping out on that parkway!'

Cat drops to the floor with a thud. I kiss Mom and go to the sink for a long glass of water and drink it all and wipe my mouth. Over my shoulder, I answer Pop:'Yeah, but if Cat gets killed on the parkway, that's just a big joke, isn't it? You laugh your head off!'

Pop takes off his glasses and scratches his head with them, like he always does when he's thinking. He looks me in the eye and says, 'I'm sorry. I shouldn't have laughed.'

Then, of all things, he picks up Cat himself. 'Come on. You're one of the family. Let's get on this vacation.'

At last we're off.

From *It's Like This, Cat* by Emily Neville

Reading for Meaning

1 What two tasks does Davey have to help with on the morning of their vacation?

2 Why does Davey put Cat behind a suitcase?

3 'Pop looks around, hunting for something to get sore about . . .' Give three reasons why Pop might be feeling frustrated at this time?

4 Why isn't Davey able to hold Cat in the back seat?

5 What is the first sign that the traffic is starting to move again?

6 Why does Davey stick his head out the window?

7 Why is Pop unwilling to stop the car while they catch Cat?

8 What problem confronts Davey after his parents' car is out of sight?

9 Where is Davey when he first becomes aware of the gang of kids following him?

10 Why doesn't he run?

11 How does Cat react when Davey starts running?

12 What do the kids do when they see the policeman?

13 Why does Davey's mother cry?

14 'You fool!' Pop bellows. What feelings do you think are really being expressed here?

15 What is it about the day's events that has upset Davey more than anything else?

16 How does his father make amends?

17 What does this extract show you about the character of Davey?

18 Identify one quality in Pop's character that you like. Where do you see this quality in the extract?

POETRY

CITY LIFE

The Building Site

In a haze of brick dust
And red sun
All day the men slog,
Lumbering about
The churned ridges of clay
In clod-hopping boots,
Humping brick hods
On the brawn of red shoulders
Up piped and rattling scaffolding
And uneven boards
To where their mates
With deft flicks from trowels
Make house walls grow
Brick by red brick.
All day too
The great trucks bang and clatter
Back and forth
And the churning mixer
Slops out gobs of concrete
In wholesome pats
On the dusty earth.

At twelve they break up,
Swarming from scaffolding
To drink brown tea
From huge mugs
That they grip in the beef of their fists.
After they kick a ball about
Or lie and bronzie in the sun
Till it's turn-to time again.

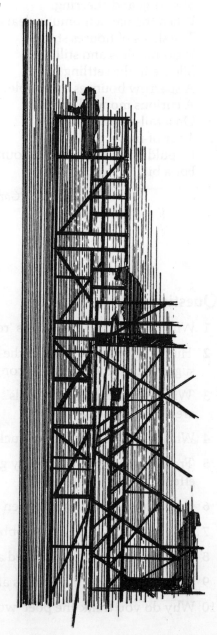

The afternoon shift wears on;
They whistle more
Shout out and laugh
And sing the songs that blare
From two transistors.
At six
They knock off
And pack into a lorry
With their clobber.
Down the rutted track they bound
Shouting and cheering.
When the pandemonium clears
The shells of houses stand
Workmanless and still.
Silence in the settling haze.
A sparrow bounces on rubble,
A curious mongrel snuffles
On a tail-wagging
Tour of inspection.
I wouldn't mind being a labourer
For a bit.

Gareth Owen

Questions

1 Why do you think the sun is 'red' instead of golden?

2 'Humping brick hods / On the brawn of red shoulders'. Which word here suggests that the men are strong?

3 'With deft flicks from trowels'. Which word particularly suggests that the men are skilful workers?

4 What sounds do the great trucks make?

5 'From huge mugs / That they grip in the beef of their fists'. Why is 'beef' an effective word to use here?

6 How can you tell that the men are happier during the afternoon shift?

7 Why are 'knock off' and 'clobber' appropriate words to use in this poem?

8 Why are the houses described as 'shells of houses'?

9 What is the 'haze' that settles after the workmen leave?

10 Why do you think the poet 'wouldn't mind being a labourer / For a bit'?

The Dump

Across the tip we played,
Where summers ran screaming
On schooldays-end legs
And cogwheels gnawed the cinder path
With hungry teeth of rust. It was there that
Gantries looped their smashed and awry arms
And toppled into pools of ebony oil,
Where cables hissed and slithered in the wind.

All those hot summer days of childhood
The tip smelt of oil and rust and grass.
Great boilers boomed like stranded whales,
Their skin, a dry, red, crispy shingle,
That burst into a flame of copper moths
Beneath the bricks we threw.

Then we left them to their dying;
Watched the birds nest in their clutches,
Those cast-off old machines that grabbed the sky.
The fire weed and the ragwort made their way
Through spokes and ducts and sumps
And flashed green rags of banners in the sun.

My playground was a tip,
My countryside a waste of brick and dust,
Where grass and rain gnawed, picked and bit
As the slowly changing landscape fell to rust.

Mike Harding

Questions

1 Where did the poet play during his summer school holidays?

2 'Where summers ran screaming / On schoooldays-end legs'. How do you think legs run at the end of a schoolday? What is the poet saying about the way summers seemed to go?

3 A 'gantry' is a crane. How do we know the gantries here are wrecked?

4 'Where cables hissed and slithered in the wind'. What animal do you think the cables are being compared to? Give reasons for your answer.

5 Why is the description of the 'great boilers' as 'stranded whales' a good one?

6 Why is the 'skin' of these boilers red?

7 What used to happen when the children threw bricks at the boilers?

8 Why does the poet describe the boilers as 'dying'?

9 Why are the machines described as 'cast-off'?

10 What signs of life are there in the tip?

11 Which words suggest that the grass and rain only affect the landscape slowly?

12 How does the poet seem to feel about growing up with the tip as a playground?

In Favour of Pushing Your Car Over a Cliff and Buying a Bike

I am a mighty Garage,
On the corner of the Square,
And it is all my pleasure,
To provide a quick repair,
Or I can do your service,
In the blinking of an eye,
I wouldn't say it's thorough,
But it'll get you by.

If you break down, we might tow you in,
I suppose that's what we're for,
Despite the astronomic bill,
It's still a bloody chore,
We'll glare beneath your bonnet,
And we'll reel it off so pat,
Did you know that needs replacing?
And that? And that? And that?

Or we might buy your little car,
For half of what it's worth,
After we've convinced you,
It's got every fault on earth,
But pass me by and presto!
In the window it'll be,
As Clean! One Owner! Spotless!
And the price tag that you see,

Will bear no fond resemblance,
To the price in our demands,
When we said how much we'd give you
Just to take it off your hands.
The price will strangely rocket,
And the things we said were wrong,
Without help from the mechanics
Are conveniently gone!

But when the next poor muggins
He comes looking for a car,
And asks a few odd questions,
They won't get him very far,
We don't say the sub-frame's rotten,
Or the whining from the rear,
Is out of the back axle,
And not ringing in his ear.

For I'm such a busy garage,
And my memory is short,
I don't want people trusting me,
Or troubles of that sort,
We don't want you dissenters,
Butting into our sales pitch,
We just sit here, on the corner,
Growing big. And fat. And rich.

Pam Ayres

Road Up

What's wrong with the road?
Why all this hush?—
They've given an anaesthetic
In the lunch-hour rush.

They've shaved off the tarmac
With a pneumatic drill,
And bandaged the traffic
To a dead standstill.

Surgeons in shirt-sleeves
Bend over the patient,
Intent on a major
Operation.

Don't dare sneeze!
Don't dare shout!
The road is having
Its appendix out.

Norman Nicholson

Old Johnny Armstrong

Old Johnny Armstrong's eighty or more
  And he humps like a question-mark
Over two gnarled sticks as he shuffles and picks
  His slow way to Benwell Park.

He's lived in Benwell his whole life long
  And remembers how street-lights came,
*And how once on a time they laid a tram-line,
  Then years later dug up the same!

Now he's got to take a lift to his flat,
  Up where the tall winds blow
Round a Council Block that rears like a rock
  From seas of swirled traffic below.

Old Johnny Armstrong lives out his life
  In his cell on the seventeenth floor,
And it's seldom a neighbour will do him a favour
  Or anyone knock at his door.

With his poor hands knotted with rheumatism
  And his poor back doubled in pain,
Why, day after day, should he pick his slow way
  To Benwell Park yet again? —

*O the wind in park trees is the self-same wind
  That first blew on a village child
When life freshly unfurled in a green, lost world
  And his straight limbs ran wild.*

                              Raymond Wilson

Questions

1 Why is Johnny Armstrong 'like a question mark'?

2 What information in the second verse gives us an idea of just how old Johnny is?

3 How do we know that Johnny lives high up in a council flat?

4 What is the traffic below Johnny's flat compared to?

5 Why is Johnny's flat described as a 'cell'?

6 What information do we have that tells us Johnny is lonely?

7 How do we know that it is difficult for Johnny to go to the park each day?

8 What question seems to puzzle the poet?

9 Why *does* Johnny go to the park each day?

10 Who is the 'village child' referred to in the last verse?

11 What does Johnny remember when he is at the park?

12 What feelings for Johnny does the poem arouse in you?

Street Boy

Just you look at me, man,
Stompin' down the street
My crombie stuffed with biceps
My boots is filled with feet.

Just you hark to me, man,
When they call us out
My head is full of silence
My mouth is full of shout.

Just you watch me move, man,
Steady like a clock
My heart is spaced on blue beat
My soul is stoned on rock.

Just you read my name, man,
Writ for all to see
The walls is red with stories
The streets is filled with me.

Gareth Owen

Susannah Potts

Susannah Potts—
if you've annoyed her,
the only thing
is to avoid her!

Just by glaring
Susannah can cause
Dobermann pinschers
to quake at the paws.

Three Rose Crescent?
A postal bungle—
by rights she should live
in a tropical jungle!

Her scowl is such
that Goths and Vandals
would faint with shock
within their sandals.

Susannah Potts
next to Darth Vader
makes him look like
a shy First Grader.

Susannah Potts!
I'd give my right arm
to have just half
your sinister charm!

Robin Klein

WRITING

CHOOSING THE RIGHT WORDS

Good writers are not content to choose a word that is 'near enough' to the one they want. They aim for their writing to:

- be full of action
- have a strong impact
- create a particular mood or atmosphere

They achieve these effects by working to find the right words, even though often this means doing several draft versions of a piece of writing.

ACTION WORDS

Below is a paragraph from the novel *Avalanche*. Notice the action words in heavy type.

AVALANCHE

And then it happened. In the middle of the night. Just below the top of the Kühelihorn a great mass of snow **broke loose** with a crash like an explosion. Slowly it began to shift, it seemed to hesitate, but only for a little. A few seconds later the avalanche **hurtled** down, its path growing wider and wider, the force of the air **driven** before it **blasting** the village even before the **thundering** mass **leapt** upon the snow-covered houses and sheds like a wild beast.

from *Avalanche* by A. Rutgers van der Loeff

Now read carefully this scene from *The Turbulent Term of Tyke Tyler*. Write down as many action words as you can.

FATTY

Danny brought a mouse out of his pocket. Fatty, his big black and white piebald.

Danny placed the mouse in the middle of Linda Stoatway's yellow hair, waving in front of him.

Linda Stoatway let out a scream and shot forward, trying to pull out the mouse and her hair as well. She fell over a third-year girl in front of her who toppled on to the boy in front. It's a small hall and there isn't much room. Like ninepins a whole line of children fell forward in it. The one in the front row crashed into Champers at the piano. There was a horrible loud chord — or dischord — and in the confusion, Fatty could be seen heading for the side where the Staff stand. Mrs Somers seemed to be his target. She screeched a high shrill shriek, and climbed the two lowest rungs of the wall bars. Mr Merchant, our teacher, spotted Fatty and did a flying tackle, landing at Mrs Somers's feet. But Fatty had already moved on, travelling at tremendous speed towards the platform, pursued by several children who all thought they were good mouse-catchers. Very nippily, Chief Sir ran down the steps, picked up Fatty, and mounted the platform again. He looked round the hall. Children crept back to their places. He stood there, not saying a word, until it seemed that something would burst in that hall. No one moved. He stroked Fatty, who looked quite happy sitting there in his hand.

Then he said in a voice like a laser beam:

'I should like the owner of this little fellow to come to my room at playtime.'

from The Turbulent Term of Tyke Tyler by Gene Kemp

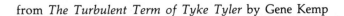

WORDS THAT HAVE IMPACT

Often writers choose one word rather than another because it has more impact on the reader. For example, 'a ferocious wind' will normally be a better descriptive phrase than 'a strong wind' because the word 'ferocious' has more impact than the word 'strong'. In the following passage twelve-year-old Paul Anderson is carting water from the Gidgee Bore to relieve the water shortage on his drought-stricken property. Read the passage carefully, then work through the questions that follow.

THE JOURNEY HOME

Peter's whinny and his sharp velvety sneeze in the night brought back the present again. He was standing by the trolley, snorting the tickle of dust out of his nostrils and stamping impatiently. The passing storm and the cool sweep of the new breeze had roused him, and he was anxious to set off for home.

'Coming,' Paul shouted, picking his way round the broken edges of the quarry. 'No need to stamp and fuss.' He reached the trolley and rubbed Peter's nose. 'Hullo, boy. Lonely, eh?' He pushed the pony's ears in under his armpit. 'Well, we'll be on the track in a second.' Paul took the bucket and climbed on to the trolley. 'Must have a drink first.' He dipped the bucket far down into the drum for water. 'Have to. Got a throat like a pepper-pot.'

There was only a foot of dirty water left in the bottom of the drum, but he managed to ladle some of it out and lifted the whole bucket clumsily to his lips. The water swilled and spilt down his chin and ran in a stream from his elbows. He panted and blew as he drank.

'Ah-h!' he said at last, setting down the bucket in front of Peter's nose. 'Hydatids or no hydatids, I needed something wet to put out the fire on my tongue.' He listened in silence for a moment to the sound of Peter's drinking. Then he put aside the bucket and harnessed the horse back in the trolley again.

Now, for the first time on that terrible homeward journey, Paul rode on the trolley and guided Peter with the reins. They skirted the eerie arc round the bottom of the hill until they intercepted the vague scrabble of the track; then they struck out for home.

from *The Water Trolley* by Colin Thiele

Observing the Impact of Words

1 Note the expression 'snorting the tickle of dust' in the first paragraph. The writer could easily have used another expression as an alternative. He could have written 'snorting the fine dust' or 'snorting the few grains of dust', but 'tickle' is better. It is fresh and it helps us immediately connect the dust to Peter's sneeze. Paul's horse sneezes a 'sharp velvety sneeze'. Why are the words 'sharp' and 'velvety' good words to have used?

2 Why is 'picking his way' a good description for the way Paul walks? Write out your own alternative expression. Which is better? Why?

3 'Well, we'll be on the track in a second.' Why is 'track' a better word than 'road'?

4 Why is the sentence 'Have to' better in this extract than 'I really have to' would have been?

5 The word 'pepper-pot' seems to fit perfectly to describe Paul's throat in the sentence 'Got a throat like a pepper-pot'. Why is it an appropriate word? Create an alternative. Which is better? Why?

6 The word 'clumsily' is used to describe the way Paul lifts the bucket to his lips. What does this word suggest about Paul's physical condition?

7 'The water . . . ran in a stream from his elbows.' How does the word 'stream' cause us to picture in a certain way the amount of water being spilt?

8 'I needed something wet to put out the fire on my tongue.' Why is 'fire' a word with impact?

9 'They skirted the eerie arc round the bottom of the hill . . .' What does the word 'eerie' tell us about Paul's feelings as he rode past that spot?

10 '. . . the vague scrabble of the track . . .' How does the description 'vague scrabble' help us to picture the condition of the track?

WORDS THAT CREATE A MOOD OR ATMOSPHERE

In the following extract Dylan Thomas uses descriptive words to create an atmosphere, a feeling for this particular incident and day. You will note that many of the words are completely unexpected, and unusual, but they are very effective.

FEELING GOOD — ALMOST

And on one occasion, in this long dissolving year, I remember that I boarded a London bus from a district I have forgotten, and where I certainly could have been up to little good, to an appointment that I did not want to keep.

It was a shooting green spring morning . . . The sun shrilled, the buses gambolled, policemen and daffodils bowed in the breeze that tasted of buttermilk. Delicate carousal plashed and babbled from the public-houses which were not yet open. I felt like a young god. I removed my collar-studs and opened my shirt. I tossed back my hair. There was an aviary in my heart, but without any owls or eagles. My cheeks were cherried warm, I smelt, I thought, of sea-pinks. To the sound of madrigals sung by slim sopranos in waterfalled valleys where I was the only tenor, I leapt on to a bus. The bus was full. Carefree, open-collared, my eyes alight, my veins full of the spring as a dancer's shoes should be full of champagne, I stood, in love and at ease and always young, on the packed lower deck. And a man of exactly my own age—or perhaps he was a little older—got up and offered me his seat. He said, in a respectful voice, as though to an old justice of the peace, 'Please, won't you take my seat?' and then he added—'Sir.'

from *Quite Early One Morning* by Dylan Thomas

GOING AFTER THE RIGHT WORDS

Write your own descriptive paragraphs on three of the following topics. Letting the writing samples on the previous pages inspire you, strive to make the first a description full of action, the second a description using words with lots of impact, and the third a description that creates a mood or atmosphere. Write draft copies and a final version of each paragraph as *you* go for the right words!

- The last push to the mountain summit
- Accident outside the newsagent
- Fully-clothed in the swimming pool
- The storm
- Waiting in the queue for an injection
- Encounter with a snake
- The spending spree

- Death of a pet
- Time machine
- Rock concert
- The Grand Final
- Custard pie shootout!
- When I really get hungry . . .
- Heatwave!

LANGUAGE

ADVERBS

As their name implies, adverbs add meaning to the action expressed in a verb. Often they tell:

1 *How* something has been done
   e.g. He swam **slowly** across the river.

2 *When* something has been done
   e.g. She came **often** to visit her mother.

3 *Where* something has been done
   e.g. Place the book **there**!

It is important to note that adverbs may also add to the meaning of adjectives, and other adverbs:

- The ocean was very calm.
- He spoke **particularly** calmly to the policeman.

Quite often adverbs end in 'ly' and this may make them easier to identify.

Forming Adverbs

Complete each sentence below by forming an adverb from the word in brackets.

1 The blue Mustang was ..slowly........ circling the park.   (slow)

2 The pool was empty now but the fountain was splashing merrily....... .   (merry)

3 I wished desperately..... that Darry and Soda would come along hunting for me.   (desperate)

4 The four of us could handle them easily............ .   (easy)

5 Bob spoke a little unsteadily........ .   (unsteady)

6 I stared at the Socs cooly............ .   (cool)

7 I lay there ..weakly........ breathing in air and spitting out water.   (weakness)

8 My teeth chattered ...unceasingly... .   (unceasing)

9 I turned my head and was ..quietly........ sick for a minute.   (quiet)

10 His voice quavered ...slightly....... .   (slight)

Selecting Adverbs

Choose the appropriate adverb from the box to complete each of the sentences below. In each case the first letter has been given.

gently	apparently	along	barely	nearly
later	practically	early	hardly	finally

1 I got up e..early........... the next morning.

2 I'd been pacing around a couple of hours when he f..inally.......... arrived.

3 At least we're moving a..long........... , until some dope runs out of gas.

4 You can p..ractically..... hear us sweating in the silence.

5 The car's only b..arely........... moving.

6 I wonder if I'll be able to catch a bus out to Connecticut l..ater........... .

7 You just have to keep g..ently.......... juggling the cat.

8 Then he hisses and bites, and I n..early.......... drop him.

9 I'm panting so hard I can h..ardly.......... breathe anyway.

10 Mom lets loose the tears she has a..pparently...... been holding onto for two hours.

Adverbs with Similar Meanings

Identify the two adverbs with similar meanings from each group below.

Example: awkwardly happily fearfully clumsily
(Answer: awkwardly, clumsily)

1 alertly anxiously nervously gently
2 courteously politely carefully wearily
3 tearfully boldly confidently shyly
4 strongly precisely approximately exactly
5 gladly steadily happily forcefully
6 timidly jokingly jovially angrily
7 calmly definitely quickly peacefully
8 fully purposely warmly deliberately
9 silently passionately quietly generally
10 suddenly clearly brutally cruelly

Replacing the Word Groups

Rewrite the sentences below, replacing each word group in italic type with an appropriate adverb. The first letter of each one has been provided for you.

Example: *In a quiet way*, the mouse explored the room.   (s................)
Silently, the mouse explored the room.

1 The mountain climber pulled himself *in a tired manner* onto the rock shelf. (w.............)
2 Please behave *with good manners* when you meet the guests.   (p.............)
3 The questions were all answered *with no mistakes*. (c.............)
4 *Every day* the old man walked to the park. (d.............)
5 *Every now and then* huge seas prevent the fishermen going out. (o.............)
6 The car was driven *with no caution* along the highway.   (r.............)
7 We were asked to begin work *right away*. (i.............)
8 Have you answered the question *without lying*? (t.............)
9 The books were stacked *in a tidy way* on the shelf. (n.............)
10 *In a short time* the food was ready. (s.............)

Adverb Opposites

Write down the adverb from the left-hand column and match it with its opposite from the right-hand column.

timidly	silently
swiftly	lovingly
strongly	wisely
despairingly	outside
hatefully	weakly
foolishly	boldly
loosely	dangerously
safely	slowly
noisily	tightly
inside	hopefully

GETTING IT RIGHT

USING ADJECTIVES OR ADVERBS

Choose either the adverb or the adjective from the brackets to complete each sentence correctly.

1 The work was .... (final/finally) completed.

2 She played .... (good/well).

3 He acted .... (foolishly/foolish) when the visitors arrived.

4 The .... (proudly/proud) father showed everyone the photos of his new daughter.

5 The owner was .... (falsely/false) accused by the police.

6 The dog barked .... (angry/angrily) at the intruder.

7 Secret agents made a .... (savage/savagely) attack on the palace.

8 The fete was .... (large/largely) successful because of Sarah's efforts.

9 The sky was .... (sudden/suddenly) full of birds.

10 We worked .... (busy/busily) in the garden.

DRAMA

JOKE ACT-OUTS

The following act-out situations are based on jokes. Choose one of the jokes, then follow the directions and try to bring out the humour through acting.

Canoe Number 99

Characters: canoe-hire owner, daughter

The owner of a canoe-hire business is watching over people who have hired canoes. He walks down to the edge of the water, looks at his watch, then raises his binoculars and looks out on the water. He checks his watch again, then raises a loud hailer and calls out: 'Canoe number 99, your time is up. Please come in now. Canoe number 99, your time is up. Please come in now.'

His little daughter runs down to join him. 'But, Daddy,' she says, 'you only have *seventy* hire canoes!' The owner lifts up his binoculars again and stares out to sea. Then raising the megaphone again, he calls out: 'Canoe number 66, are you in trouble?'

DIRECTIONS

This one should be quite easy. Either mime the use of binoculars and a megaphone, or else make use of on-hand substitute props, such as a rolled up sheet of paper for the megaphone.

My Brother the Taxi Driver

Characters: car driver, passenger

A driver and passenger are driving along a busy city street when the light ahead turns red. The passenger says: 'Look out, the light's turned red!'

'Ah, no worries, mate,' the driver answers. 'My brother the taxi driver always goes through red lights! It's quite safe,' and pressing his foot to the floor he drives straight through.

Up ahead another set of lights appears. The same thing happens. The light is red and the passenger says: 'Look out, it's gone red!'

'No worries,' says the driver. 'My brother the taxi driver always goes straight through red lights. He reckons it's safe.' And he pushes his foot down and charges through.

Another set of lights appears and this time the passenger says: 'Ah, we'll be right this time. The light's just turned green.' Straight away the driver slams on his brakes and screeches to a halt. Angrily, the passenger says: 'What did you do that for? It's green, we can go through.'

'Not on your life, mate,' the driver says. 'My brother the taxi driver is working this area, and he always goes straight through red lights!'

DIRECTIONS

There is plenty of opportunity here for the passenger to show his anxiety (even panic) as they drive through red lights. Props can include two chairs side by side, and there can be a props manager who holds up cardboard RED LIGHT and GREEN LIGHT signs at the appropriate times.

The Tramp

Characters: man, tramp

A man is seated on the front verandah of his house reading the paper. A tramp comes through the front gate and up the path towards him. He clears his throat and asks: 'Hey, mister, any work I can do to earn some money?'

The man studies him for a minute and then says: 'Sure. Go around the back. You'll find a can of green paint and a brush in the shed. I want you to paint the porch. I'll pay you ten bucks.'

The tramp exits, and the man continues to read his paper. A minute passes and then the tramp comes back, green paint on his fingers. The man looks up from his paper: 'You finished already?'

'Yeah,' replies the tramp.

'I was sure it would take you an hour,' says the man.

'That's not the only mistake you made,' says the tramp. 'It wasn't a Porch; it was a Mercedes!'

DIRECTIONS

This act-out will require the house owner to look comfortably well-off. The scene begins with him studying the paper. The passing of time when the tramp is painting can be suggested by the turning over of a few pages in slow motion. When the tramp returns, the house owner should check his watch before registering his surprise at the time.

The Pig with the Wooden Leg

Characters: farmer, visitor, pig

A farmer is showing a visitor around his farm. Suddenly the visitor notices a pig with a wooden leg walking by. 'Hey, how come that pig over there has a wooden leg?' he asks.

'Ah, that's quite a story,' the farmer answers. 'That's an amazing pig. Let me tell you about him. One night we were asleep in the house when a fire broke out. By the time we had woken up, the house was ablaze and there didn't seem to be any way we could get out. Then, suddenly, that pig appeared from nowhere, crashing through the burning walls. He dragged the missus and me to safety and saved our lives!'

'Wow,' said the visitor, 'that's some story. But why has he got a wooden leg?'

'Just a minute,' said the farmer, 'I'm not finished yet. A week or so later I was ploughing down in the south paddock when I hit a tree root and the tractor tipped over, pinning me underneath. I thought I was a goner for sure. But suddenly, out of nowhere, that pig comes. He digs around with his snout, digging a big hole underneath the tractor, and once again drags me out, just before the tractor goes up in flames. Yeah, that's quite a pig!'

'That's amazing,' said the visitor, 'but you still haven't told me why he's got a wooden leg?' 'Well,' answered the farmer, 'if you've got a pig that good, you're not gonna eat him all at once, are you?'

DIRECTIONS

Plenty of room here for dramatic gestures and animated action. Let yourself go! Probably the farmer would talk with a slow drawl.

ADVERTISING

5

THE ROLE OF ADVERTISING

Anyone who has ever wanted to sell something can understand why advertisements first came into being. The person who wants to sell *has* to find a way of letting others know. This is the major role that advertising plays in our world. Advertisements *inform* people about the products that are for sale (e.g. books, boats, food) and the services that are available (e.g. from banks, real estate agents, government departments).

But advertisements usually go further. As well as providing information about products and services, they try to *persuade* people to buy. They encourage a response. You will notice the importance of this in most of the advertisements in this chapter.

There are a number of different advertising media. These include:

- newspapers and magazines
- television
- cinema
- radio
- handbills, promotional leaflets, 'junk mail'
- billboards
- signs on buildings, buses, taxis etc.
- phone calls

Each medium is different so, naturally, advertisements differ. You can put a photo or illustration with a newspaper advertisement, but not with a radio commercial. Radio calls for a different approach, a different type of advertisement. By looking at examples of advertisements from the main media, we will be able to discover what some of these distinctive features are, and how advertisers make use of them.

NEWSPAPER AND MAGAZINE ADVERTISEMENTS
WHAT GRABS YOUR ATTENTION?

Newspaper and magazine advertisements usually consist of a photo or illustration, a headline and the body-copy (words written about the product or service). Usually the picture or the headline has to grab the reader's attention, otherwise he or she is unlikely to read the body-copy which contains information about the product and often urges a response.

Consider the magazine ad opposite. After studying the headline and the photo, read through the body-copy. Then answer the questions that follow.

You'll find Celuform at home just about anywhere in Australia.

Unfortunately most dream homes are anything but a dream to maintain.
Now there is a remarkable building board that is simply a dream to live with.
Celuform. It never needs painting and is low maintenance.
It's lightweight, flexible, insulated and easy to install. Celuform is tough
and resists scratches and dents. And most importantly,
Celuform makes your home look magnificent.
Also available: Celuform Lattice, never needs painting.

DURAFORM BUILDING PROFILES
(A Unit of James Hardie Building Products Pty Limited Inc in NSW)

P.O. BOX 211 SEVEN HILLS N.S.W. 2147.

I WOULD LIKE TO KNOW MORE ABOUT CELUFORM:

NAME

ADDRESS

P/C

Thinking about the Celuform Ad

1 What would make this ad stand out from others in a magazine?

2 Why does this feature of the ad attract attention?

3 What emotions does it arouse in you? What emotions do you think the advertiser *wants* to arouse in readers? Why?

4 What product is the ad promoting?

5 Explain how the headline ('You'll find Celuform . . .') relates to the photo. What point do the headline and photo make about the product?

6 Why might this 'dream home' be difficult to maintain?

7 How does the first line of the body-copy, about dream homes, relate to the photo? What makes this particular home seem like a 'dream home'?

8 Identify five attractive features of Celuform from the ad.

9 What does the body-copy identify as the most important feature of Celuform?

10 How does this ad encourage readers to take action?

The Toyota ad opposite has a different kind of appeal. Study the ad carefully before answering the questions below.

Opening the Lid on Toyota Oil

1 What has the advertiser done in this ad to attract the attention of readers?

2 What word in the headline connects the photo and the headline?

3 By using a picture of Herman Munster to promote their oil, the advertisers have attempted to appeal to our sense of humour. How successful do you think this is?

4 What audience is the ad aimed at? Would it appeal to a Nissan owner?

5 The ad warns against using 'the wrong oil'. What reason is given?

6 What special features of Toyota Motor Oil make it superior according to the ad?

7 What response from readers does the ad call for?

8 The Toyota slogan used in the ad is: 'Keep the feeling!' What 'feeling' is suggested by the writing style used for the slogan?

9 How would you rate the effectiveness of this ad?

Now examine the Repco Cycles ad on pages 146–7. In particular, look carefully at the photo. Its message is not immediately obvious.

Using any other oil in your Toyota would be monstrous.

The wrong oil can do horrible things to your engine.
So Toyota has introduced a high performance
Motor Oil made especially to suit Toyota engines.
In fact, Toyota Motor Oil is blended in
Australia to meet the specifications of the
Toyota Motor Corporation.
So for your next oil change,
see your Toyota dealer about
using the oil with your engine's
name on it.

Keep the feeling!
TOYOTA
Genuine parts · Quality service

Whether it's the gruelling Tour de France, or a gentle ride through the park, Repco Cycles has a bicycle for you – with all the technology and reliability that has carried the Repco Cycling Team to victory around the world.

Repco Cycles also has the colours and designs you're looking for, in a complete range of cycles. There are tiny tot trainers, flying BMXs, classic tourers, racing lightweights and versatile all-terrain bikes.

All with the Repco Cycles 15 year warranty. So to race on, or ride on, you can choose a

Repco. Number One on two wheels.

epco cycle that's right for you.

    See your Authorised Repco Cycle Dealer.
e'll help you select the cycle you need to give
ou maximum performance and comfort.
ecause he's a professional, he will ensure
ou make the right choice.

NUMBER ONE ON TWO WHEELS

Cycling through the Repco Ad

1 What grabs your attention in this ad?

2 From your examination of the photo, which cyclist is riding a Repco bike? What evidence is there?

3 Which cyclist is leading the race? What evidence does the photo provide?

4 The background of the photo is blurred. Does this matter? What effect do you think it has?

5 What strikes you most in the headline?

6 The ad's body-copy outlines a number of valuable features of Repco cycles. Identify four of these features.

7 Advertisers usually like to include their product's name more than once in an ad. How many times does the name 'Repco Cycles' appear in this ad? What benefit can the advertiser get from repetition?

8 In one sentence for each, summarise the ad's message about the **quality** and **availability** of Repco cycles.

WHAT AUDIENCE IS THE AD AIMED AT?

Advertisements are usually prepared for a specific group of people, the target audience. The advertising agency tries to build an accurate profile of the target audience and develops the ad so that it will appeal to this group. Advertisers know that certain words, types of pictures and subjects are more likely to appeal to some groups than others. They often seek to create an appealing atmosphere for the target group.

For example, if an ad for baby food is directed at a target audience of young mothers, the advertiser is likely to use pictures of smiling chubby babies, fun times, happy families, and so on. The words used in the ad might emphasise the idea that good, responsible parents provide only the best baby food for their youngsters. Of course, completely different words and pictures would be chosen for a clothing ad aimed at a target audience of teenagers.

Study the two advertisements that follow and answer the questions.

EVERY ARTIST NEEDS HIS CANVAS.

Christian Hosoi

CONVERSE Chuck Taylor ALL STARS

© 1988 Converse Inc.

This is the Hairy-nosed Wombat.

Take a long, last look,

There are now just 50 Northern Hairy-nosed Wombats. We are only beginning to understand why.

The total disappearance of any of our wildlife, like the Northern Hairy-nosed Wombat, would be a tragedy. Now and forever. Please help us before it is too late.

or fill in this coupon.

YES I WANT TO HELP SAVE OUR ENDANGERED PLANTS AND ANIMALS

☐ $25.00 Annual Member, including receipt of quarterly Newsletters.

☐ $50.00 Wildlife Supporter, including receipt of quarterly Newsletters and Conservation Programme Brochure.

☐ $100.00 Wildlife Guardian, including Project Reports, quarterly Newsletters and Conservation Programme Brochure.
AND/OR

☐ I would like to donate $_____ to help conserve our wildlife.

For further information on how you can help, phone or write to:

WORLD WILDLIFE FUND AUSTRALIA,
Level 17, St. Martins Tower,
31 Market Street, Sydney. NSW 2000.
G.P.O. Box 528, Sydney, NSW 2001.
Telephone: (02) 261 5572
Or toll free (008) 251 573.
▷ FOR ALL GIFTS YOU WILL RECEIVE A DISTINCTIVE PANDA LAPEL BADGE.

WWF

PLEASE FIND ENCLOSED CHEQUE MADE PAYABLE TO WORLD WILDLIFE FUND AUSTRALIA. AMOUNT $_____

OR CHARGE MY BANKCARD/MASTERCARD/VISA WITH $_____

CREDIT CARD No.:_____   EXPIRY DATE: /   /

NAME:_____   SIGNATURE:_____

ADDRESS:_____   POSTCODE:_____

GIFTS TO WWF AUSTRALIA ARE TAX DEDUCTIBLE.

Comparing the Ads

1 What group would be the target audience for the *Every Artist* ad (page 149)?

2 What group would you see as the target audience for the *Wombat* ad (opposite)?

3 Which ad do you see as being targeted at the larger group? Give a reason for your answer.

4 How has the advertiser used the picture in the *Every Artist* ad to appeal to the target group?

5 What emotions does the *Every Artist* ad seek to arouse?

6 In the *Wombat* ad, what effect do you think the advertiser wants to have on readers by using the line 'Take a long, last look'?

7 What emotions does the *Wombat* ad seek to arouse?

8 The *Every Artist* ad has the endorsement of a skateboard champion, Chuck Taylor. How might this increase its appeal to 'skateheads'?

9 Which ad appeals most to you? Do you fit its intended audience? What is it about the ad that appeals to you?

10 Below is a list of descriptive words and phrases. For each ad, choose three which best describe the target audience.
   — nature-loving
   — young
   — conservation-minded
   — energetic
   — game-for-anything
   — concerned for others

TELEVISION COMMERCIALS

Television ads or commercials make use of the viewer's vision and hearing in presenting a product. Because so many people watch television at specific times, these ads can often reach a wider audience than any other type of ad. Little stories which have plenty of action are often used to present the product. At other times the product is demonstrated. Product slogans, jingles and logos are frequently included. Sometimes printed words are superimposed on the screen, and no one speaks. At other times a voice-over (the commentator talking about the product while the visual runs) is used. One of the great attractions of television commercials is that they offer so many rich possibilities to the advertiser.

FUJI IMAGE PLAZA COMMERCIAL

Three stages of the Fuji Image Plaza commercial are presented on the following pages to help you appreciate how a television commercial is made. First, the **scene drafts** which guide the production of the commercial have been laid out scene by scene with the words underneath. Then the **final script** is provided. This includes the video script (for the camera) and the audio script (for the voice-over and sound effects). Finally, two **photos** from the finished commercial are reproduced.

Scene Drafts

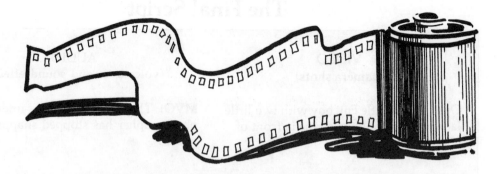

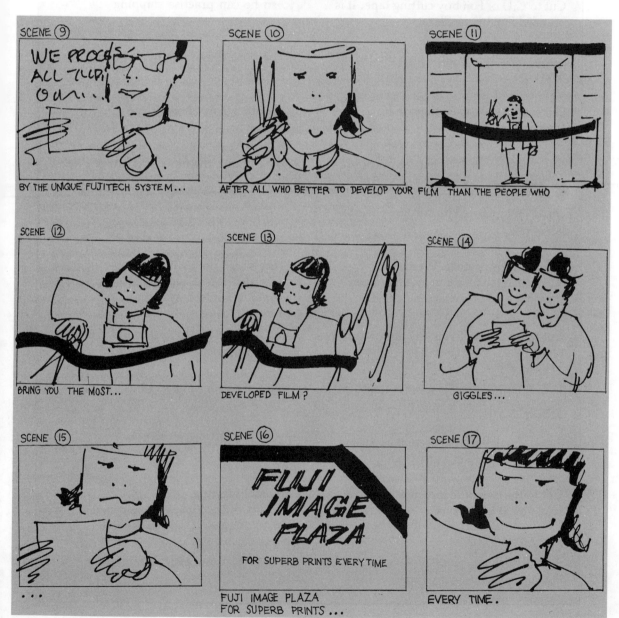

The Final Script

VIDEO (camera shots)	AUDIO (voice-over and sound effects)
Open on the little Fuji boy with two little Japanese girls holding a tape in front of him.	MVO: The world's most undeveloped photographer has stopped snapping for a while . . .
Cut to C.U of Fuji boy cutting tape. It is branded Fuji Image Plaza.	. . . so he can practise snipping . . .
Cut to wide shot as little girls pick up a new tape.	. . . because tomorrow he's opening . . .
Cut to mid shot as he snips the replacement tape.	. . . another Fuji Image Plaza . . .
Cut to wide shot. The Fuji boy is now outside a new Fuji Image Plaza. An opening tape is stretched across the entrance supported by chrome pedestals either end.	And he knows the more Fuji Image Plazas there are . . .
Cut to inside of store. We see an Australian lab assistant and manager standing by a processing machine.	. . . the more places he'll be able to have his film developed with quality assured by the unique Fujitech system.
Cut to mid shot of Fuji boy about to snip tape.	After all, who better to develop your film than the people who bring you . . .
C.U of Fuji boy as his scissors fail to cut the tape. We flash freeze this shot . . .	. . . the most developed film?
. . . and pull back to reveal it as a photograph held in a girl's hand.	SFX: Girls giggling.
Cut to the two little Japanese girls laughing at the picture.	Girls still giggling.
Cut to end super: Fuji Image Plaza For superb prints every time.	MVO: Fuji Image Plaza For superb prints every time.

Photos

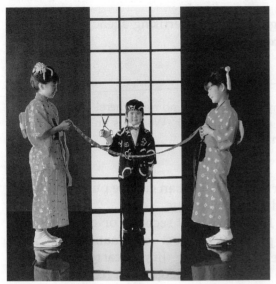 

Understanding Fuji Image Plazas

Refer to the scene drafts, the final script and the photos to answer these questions.

1 Explain what is happening in the opening scenes of the commercial.

2 What message does the commercial give about Fuji Image Plazas?

3 These terms are used in the final script: 'C.U', 'cut', 'super', 'SFX', 'MVO'. What do you think these terms mean?

4 What two meanings are there in the phrase 'the most developed film'?

5 From the scene drafts, which scenes show us that only experts process Fuji film?

6 What system is used to process Fuji film?

7 From the photos, why is the 'Fuji boy' a desirable actor to have 'selling' the messages about Fuji film and Fuji Image Plazas?

8 At the end of the final script the message is given in *two* ways at the same time. What are these?

9 Did you like this commercial? What did you like about it?

10 Do you think this commercial would be *effective* in promoting Fuji film? What reasons do you have for your answer?

RADIO COMMERCIALS

In a humorous radio script, Stan Freberg goes to an advertising agency to get some commercials done, with himself as the product.

> **Ad executive** Yes?
> **Stan** Ah, Stan Freberg.
> **Ad executive** Ah, come right in! Ah, Stan, my boy. Wait. Stand right there! Don't move! I can see it now. The camera dollies in closer and closer. We focus on one eye and superimpose Stan the Man Freberg! What a picture!
> **Stan** But, Mr Gambit. Will that be good on radio?

Radio commercials cannot make use of our vision. They can engage our imagination only through sound. This makes radio advertising unique.

Usually a radio commercial is brief — 15 seconds, 30 seconds or one minute in length. The advertiser sometimes simply provides product information, but more often this is accompanied by a catchy tune called a jingle. Jingles carry the name of the product and are designed to be easy to learn so that people can remember them. At other times the product is presented by means of a mini-drama, often with sound effects to help us imagine the scene, and frequently with some humour so that we identify happy feelings with the product.

Examine the radio commercial script opposite.

Checking on Westpac

1 What is the opening sound effect and what scene does it cause us to imagine?

2 What emotion would you expect Ed to show in his voice when he says 'Hey, what a great car'?

3 What is the connection between the cat's meow and Ed's comment that follows?

4 The first voice-over introduces important information about a Westpac service. What service is referred to? What warning is also given?

5 Which comment gives us the first hint that something is wrong with the car?

6 Why doesn't the car have wheels?

7 The last voice-over explains why the situation would not happen with a Westpac loan. Why wouldn't it happen?

8 What is the purpose of the jingle in the last line?

9 What overall effect does this ad have on you?

10 How is Westpac presented by the ad?

Radio — Car Loans 'Wheels'

Duration	30 Seconds.
Sound effects	(Roller doors open).
Stan	There you go . . . . feast your eyes on that.
Ed	Hey, what a great car.
Stan	Wait till you hear the engine.
Sound effects	(Ignition starts and cat shrieks — meow!).
Ed	It really purrs, doesn't it?
Voice over	If you're buying a new car, don't get in over your head. See Westpac first about a car loan you can afford.
Ed	Great car, pity about the wheels.
Stan	I know.
Ed	When are you going to get some?
Stan	As soon as I can afford them . . . .
Voice over	Westpac Car Loans. We'll get you driving without driving your finances into the ground.
Sung	You can bank on Westpac.

You can bank on Westpac.

DESIGN YOUR OWN ADVERTISEMENTS

1 Imagine that you are working for an advertising agency. You have been asked to write the headline and body-copy to go with a newspaper advertisement about a sensational new loaf of bread. Create an appealing name for the bread. Direct your ad towards those people who take sandwiches to work for lunch. Convince them that they should really try this wonderful new product. When you have designed the ad, lay it out on a sheet of cardboard or paper of A4 size or larger. Make a class display of all the ads and decide which ones are most effective.

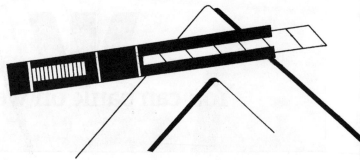

2 Once again, imagine that you work for an advertising agency. However, this time work with two other people in your class. You have been asked to write the headline and body-copy to go with a new car polish called Tortoise Tuff, a very durable, long-lasting wax polish. The ad will be placed in a car magazine. You are to design it as a promotional ad in which people are invited to send you a coupon and you will send them a sample of Tortoise Tuff. Lay out the ad as professionally as you can, then evaluate each finished product as a class.

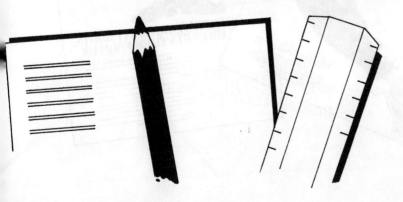

INDIVIDUAL AND CLASS PROJECTS

The first two tasks require you to find newspaper and magazine ads. It will help if each student brings two or three different newspapers or magazines along so that a class pool is developed.

1 Consider the ads from *three* magazines or newspapers.
   a Which ad do you rate as the *best* ad among all the ones you see? What are the reasons for its outstanding achievement?
   b Which ad do you rate as the *worst* ad? Why do you believe it to be so poor in quality?
   c Which ad is the most *appealing* to you personally, so that you really would like to have the product? What would be the target audience for the ad? What makes it so appealing to you?

2 Contrast an ad that you consider to be successful with one you consider to be unsuccessful.
   a How does the artwork or photo differ?
   b How do the headlines differ?
   c How does the body-copy differ in length, appropriateness of language, and layout?

3 Take a class poll to decide what you see as the best and worst ads currently running on both radio and TV. Discuss these ads and develop a list of distinguishing features.

4 Hold a class discussion on the topic: 'Can the ad you love to hate still be a successful ad?'

5 After forming groups of three students:
  a Choose a product. Make up a name for your particular product.
  b Decide who your target audience will be.
  c Design a newspaper/magazine ad for your product. Find a photo or picture, or do your own artwork. Decide on a headline that catches attention and write your copy. Lay out the finished ad on a large sheet of paper or cardboard.
  d View all the ads produced in your class and discuss their merits.

6 Develop a script for a radio commercial which aims to sell the product you worked on in project 5. Record your commercial on cassette. Make use of sound effects, background music or jingles. Listen to all the radio commercials developed by class groups. Which one stands out as the most successful? Why?

TEENAGERS
IN TROUBLE

6

NOVELS

Run off the Road

A frightening duel between a carload of 'punks' and the Glory bus results in a terrible accident.

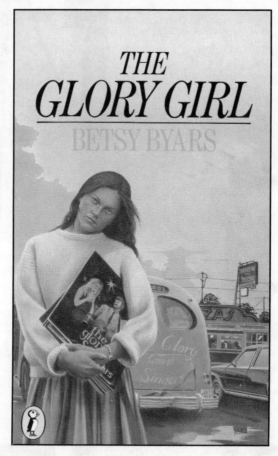

'Dad, I think they're going to try something.'

'What, Anna?' Mrs Glory asked.

'I don't know — force us off the road or something. They're too close.'

Mr Glory's eyes darted to the rearview mirror to check the headlights of the car behind. Then he stepped on the gas. Mrs Glory clasped her hands over her heart as the bus began to shimmy. Danger was everywhere now — in the sluggish window wipers, the boys behind them, the trembling bus. 'Please, John,' she moaned.

'Please what? Please let those punks run us off the road?'

'We don't know that's what they're going to do. Maybe they're in a hurry. Maybe they want to pass.'

'They can pass if they want to,' Mr Glory snapped. 'They have room.'

'John, they don't. Slow down and move over a little. Please!'

With his lips clamped on his cigarette, Mr Glory glanced down at the speedometer. He eased up on the gas pedal. Forty-five . . . forty . . . thirty-five . . . thirty . . .

Anna glanced from the speedometer to the back of the bus where the lights of the other car lit up the window.

'If they wanted to pass,' Mr Glory said beneath his breath, 'they'd pass. Pass, you punks!'

'What's happening?' Joshua asked, rising from his sleeping position. 'What's going on?'

'Nothing,' Anna said, 'just some boys trying to be funny.'

'What are they doing?'

'Nothing, just —'

Joshua scrambled down the aisle and looked out of the back window. 'It's a Triumph,' he called. He knew cars. His voice rose. 'And it's getting ready to bump into us!'

At that moment the Glorys felt the jarring thud as the Triumph struck the back of the bus.

The jolt flung the Glorys forward and then backward in their seats. Angel's eyes snapped open. Matthew awoke as he hit the seat in front of him. The sound of Mrs Glory's sharp scream hung in the air long after they had recovered.

'John, pull over,' Mrs Glory said then in a soft pleading voice, her hands again over her heart. 'Stop. Let them pass.'

Mr Glory did not answer. His eyes darted from the rearview mirror to the road ahead.

'What's happening now?' Anna called back to Joshua. He was at the window again, his forehead against the cold glass.

'Nothing,' he reported. 'The Triumph's still there and it's not slowing down. They're blowing the horn!' His last words were lost in the long, arrogant blast of the Triumph's horn.

'John, *please*.'

At the wheel of the Glory bus, Mr Glory started to tremble. This was something he had never been able to control. All his life the combination of helplessness and fear had caused his bones to rattle. As a boy his nickname had been 'Shaky'.

'John!' Mrs Glory cried sharply. She moved to the edge of her seat. She felt she had lost her husband's attention. He seemed to be in a trance. 'John!'

'He's coming at us again!' Joshua called.

The Glory family tensed. Anna braced herself against the back of her father's seat. Her knuckles were white.

'Hold on,' Mrs Glory cried.

The jolt came then, hard. Anna's head was flung against her father's seat. She heard her mother scream, heard Joshua yell as he was thrown backwards into the aisle. She straightened. In the pale light from the dashboard her eyes were wide with her own fear.

She wet her dry lips. 'Maybe we *should* pull over, Dad.'

Anna put her hand on her father's shoulder as she spoke, and she felt him trembling. It was as frightening as feeling stone tremble. 'Dad?' She had never thought of her father as anything but hard and unyielding. She said again, 'Dad?'

Mr Glory did not answer. His shoulder jerked as he reached down to shift gears, again as he clutched the steering wheel. And beneath was the terrible shivering, as if his very bones had turned to ice. Anna was more alarmed by this than she was by the boys behind them.

'Dad, are you all right?'

As she leaned forward, waiting for his answer, Joshua screamed, 'He's coming at us again!'

Instantly Mr Glory steered the bus to the right in a desperate attempt to avoid the jolt. Anna was thrown sideways. Behind them, tyres screeched.

'That stopped them,' Joshua yelled in triumph.
'They missed!'

'For *now*,' Matthew added. Both boys were at the back of the bus now, peering with white faces at the car behind them.

'I don't believe this,' Matthew added. 'Why doesn't he leave us alone.'

Joshua said, 'I told you we needed a CB. We could call the police!' Joshua was holding on to the seat with both hands now, swaying as wildly as if he were riding a bucking horse.

'He's coming again!'
'Dad, he's coming!'

Mr Glory strained forward. His shoulders flexed as he steered to the right again. This time he went too far. Anna felt the front wheel slip off the crumbling black top and on to the soft earth. Mr Glory yanked the wheel to the left.

The bus wavered on the edge of the road, swerving back and forth. The headlights shone first on the trees to the left, then on the stone bank on the right. The Triumph passed, sending a spray of water up on to the window.

At that moment the window wipers stopped. Mr Glory peered blindly over the steering wheel. The world was lost in a sheet of water. He hit the brakes. For what seemed an eternity, the bus wavered.

Anna, with her hand on her father's shoulder, knew the exact moment when her father lost control of the bus. He was pulling the steering wheel to the left with all his strength, and the bus turned to the right.

Anna gasped as the bus went off the road. A flash of lightning lit up the world and Anna saw trees looming ahead.

For a moment the top-heavy bus swayed in the soft earth. Mr Glory clung to the useless steering wheel, braced for the crash.

Before Anna buried her head in her arms, the window wipers swept across the window for one last time, and Anna saw the trees directly ahead. She held on for dear life.

The head-on crash Anna expected did not happen. At the last moment the bus groundlooped. Skidding in the soft, slick earth it hit the trees sideways.

There was the awful sound of metal scraping against wood and a pause. Then, with a terrible slowness, like a prehistoric animal dying, the Glory bus turned over on to its side. It rested against trees which bent beneath the weight.

The shock jarred Anna from her seat. She plunged across the bus and landed against the opposite window, her shoulder jammed into the cold glass. Drums overturned and crashed against the side of the bus. People screamed.

Then Anna was aware only of the sound of the bus motor, still running, of tyres spinning uselessly in the air. The noises gave her a strange, almost safe feeling, as if the bus were trying to straighten itself and drive on as before.

Anna raised her head. The headlights from the Triumph were shining on the bus now, and in that light Anna could see her mother beside her. Beyond, Angel was trying to sit up, and her father, somehow still suspended in the driver's seat, was struggling to free himself.

In the back of the bus one of the twins called, 'Help!' The other, upside down, called a weaker, 'Me, too.'

Leaning forward Anna heard the screech of tyres as the Triumph drove away. The sound of the engine disappeared in the distance. The light was gone with it, and the Glorys were left with only the dim glow from the dashboard.

'Kids?' Mrs Glory called. Her weak voice was almost lost in the sound of the racing bus engine. The engine was running stronger now than it had ever done on the road.

'I'm all right,' Anna answered. 'I'm right beside you.'

'Angel?'

'I'm all right.'

from *The Glory Girl* by Betsy Byars

Reading for Meaning

1   Why do the opening lines of the passage make you want to go on reading?

2   Why did the bus begin to 'shimmy'?

3   What caused Mrs Glory to moan 'Please, John'?

4   How did Mr Glory react to his wife's 'Please, John'?

5   What disturbing news was relayed by Joshua from the back of the bus?

6   With what kind of sound did the Triumph strike the back of the bus?

7   What effect did the jolt from the car have on the Glorys?

8   Why had Mr Glory's nickname, as a boy, been 'Shaky'?

9   'She felt she had lost her husband's attention.' Why did Mrs Glory feel this?

10 Why was it frightening for Anna when she felt her father's shoulder trembling?

11 ' "That stopped them," Joshua yelled in triumph.' What manoeuvre caused Joshua's excitement?

12 What comparison tells how wildly Joshua was swaying in the bus?

13 What caused Mr Glory to lose sight of everything outside the bus?

14 Explain how Anna knew the exact moment when her father lost control of the bus.

15 'Mr Glory clung to the useless steering wheel, braced for the crash.' Why do you think 'braced' is a more expressive word to use than, say, 'prepared'?

16 What comparison does the writer use to emphasise the terrible slowness with which the bus turned over?

17 One purpose of this piece of writing is to communicate the fear felt by the family. In your opinion, how has the writer managed to do this?

Trouble in the Subway

Sam doesn't usually find himself in trouble with the authorities, but his luck runs out on the day he has to produce his subway pass for the ruthlessly efficient Officer Cruz.

A few days later, rushing from the rain, a cheerful swarm of Burr Academy students invaded the subway station. Sprinting to catch the train roaring in, they barely stopped long enough to hold up their subway passes for the wooden-faced woman in the change booth.

If she had actually taken the time to examine the legitimacy of each pass, and the bearer thereof, there would have been a long bottleneck — thereby inconveniencing and greatly exasperating those adult citizens waiting behind the gaggle of youngsters to buy tokens.

But Transit Officer Felipe Cruz, standing to the side of the booth, was under orders to make spot checks of the swift students — in order to catch stray thieves in the act and also to deter those planning to defraud the Transit Authority at some future crowded moment.

At the top of the stairs, Sam had set his knapsack down — noting angrily that the books were soaking wet because he had forgotten to close it — and searched through his pockets for the subway pass. Finally, he found it in his shoe, where he had put it that morning in case he might get mugged at this subway stop which was still new to him. Picking up his knapsack, bottom side up, Sam watched, in acute disgust, as his books slithered down the stairs. By the time he had collected them all, the other Burr students were long gone, and Officer Cruz had ample leisure to examine this straggler.

'Your pass?' he said to Sam.

Sam took it from between his teeth and handed it to Officer Cruz, who took it gingerly. 'How do I know what else you got in you mouth?' he said sourly as he looked at the pass. 'Your name is Benjamin Bloom?'

'Oh, God!' Sam hit himself on the head. 'I forgot! Listen, Benjy Bloom is a friend of mine, and he borrowed my subway pass and he lost it and so when he found his, he gave it to me.'

'This pass' — Officer Cruz looked at it again — 'expired last June. So, you are using a pass which is not yours — these passes are *not* transferable — and you are using a pass which is no longer valid. You have broken *two* regulations. You are a double delinquent.'

'Aw look' — Sam was shaking his head in despair — 'I didn't even think about needing a new pass. I just started at this new school. Wait, I remember, I was supposed to see about getting a new pass but I had so many other things to get settled so I wouldn't get into trouble, and I didn't want to get in trouble right off in this new school, so I just forgot about the pass, you know, I mean I wasn't trying to get away with anything, I just *forgot*, damn it!'

Officer Cruz bristled. 'Don't you swear at me! You're such a smart-ass, you can come down with me to headquarters and I'll book you as a juvenile offender.'

'I wasn't swearing at *you*!' Sam wailed even more desperately. 'I was swearing at *me*, at all the goddamn trouble I get into for no *reason*.'

Cruz let himself smile a little. 'You think about it, you'll find the reason.' The officer took from his back pocket a long black notebook, thick with official-looking forms. Peeling off one of them, he began to fill it out.

Sam bit his lip, shook his head, and asked, 'What's *that* for?'

'A summons,' Officer Cruz said matter-of-factly. 'You will have to appear in court, nine in the morning, two weeks from today, to answer the charge of subway trespass — which means you weren't entitled to use this pass which wasn't usable in the first place. The judge will decide the penalty. Unless' — Officer Cruz smiled broadly — 'you can talk him out of it, which is as likely as me being the starting pitcher for the Yankees today.' Cruz was much amused at the analogy. 'Yes, sir, maybe I will pitch a no-hit game today.'

Sam, looking at, but not seeing, the ground, was shaking his head again. 'Terrific. I'm going to have to ask for time off from school to appear in court as a *criminal*. That'll really set me up at Burr. You might as well,' Sam said bitterly, 'put the cuffs on.'

'You're going to learn something,' Cruz said coolly. 'You're going to learn something they should have taught you in that school of yours. You're going to learn to watch what you're doing — at all times. Okay, I need your name and address. And no funny business. Give me identification. Real identification.'

Sam slowly pulled a battered wallet out of his knapsack and handed him the Burr identification card — with his picture on it.

Cruz compared the desolate boy in front of him with the truculent boy in the picture, wrote down the name, got his home address from Sam, handed him a summons, and kept a copy of it for the fat black notebook.

'Can I go now?' Sam said heavily.

'Why not?' Officer Cruz shrugged. 'Unless you're going to play some other dumb trick.'

Sam put his hand in his pants pocket, and then desperately, in his other pants pocket, and then in all his jacket pockets, and then dove into his knapsack. 'Oh God,' he said, 'I don't have any money.'

'Don't look at me,' said Officer Cruz. 'I'm not the Welfare. How far you got to go?'

'Seventy-two blocks. I live on Twelfth Street and Fifth Avenue.'

'Jog,' said Officer Cruz. 'It won't take no time.'

from *Does This School Have Capital Punishment?* by Nat Hentoff

Reading for Meaning

1 Why were the Burr Academy students 'rushing'?

2 Why is 'invaded' a better word to use than 'entered'?

3 What did they barely stop long enough to do?

4 Why didn't the woman in the change booth take the time to examine each student's pass?

5 Why did Transit Officer Felipe Cruz 'make spot checks of the swift students'?

6 What made Sam angry at the top of the stairs?

7 Where did Sam finally find his subway pass?

8 Why had he hidden his subway pass?

9 Explain how an accident to Sam's books led to his encounter with Officer Cruz.

10 Why did Officer Cruz take Sam's pass 'gingerly'?

11 How did Sam manage to break two regulations?

12 'Officer Cruz bristled.' What made him do this?

13 What official-looking form did the transport officer begin to fill out?

14 What did this form require Sam to do?

15 In what way was Cruz critical of Sam's school?

16 How did Sam in the flesh differ from the Sam in the identification picture that Cruz was looking at?

17 What final problem does Sam have?

18 What was Cruz's unsympathetic solution to Sam's problem?

19 Does Sam deserve our sympathy in this passage? Give reasons for your viewpoint.

20 Do you think this passage would appeal to high school students? Why or why not?

The River Ran Deep

When two boys swim a swift river which has treacherous currents, the tragedy of drowning becomes reality.

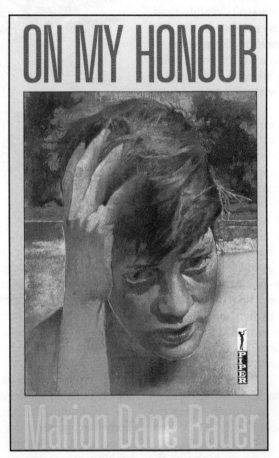

'Come on,' Tony prodded. 'You said out to the sandbar. Are you giving up?'

'You sure you'll make it?' Joel eyed his friend's still faintly heaving chest meaningfully. 'You look pretty tired to me.'

Tony gave him a shove, almost caught him off balance. 'Swim,' he commanded, and Joel plunged into the water and resumed swimming. Tony started beside him but immediately dropped behind. Joel could hear him, blowing and puffing like a whale.

It's not so bad, Joel said to himself, beginning to get his rhythm and discovering the angle that made it possible to keep gaining

against the current. Maybe Tony was right and the river swimming would be a good way to practise . . . now that his father had decided he was old enough to be allowed a bit of freedom.

He started the side stroke. He could watch where he was going better that way, keep tabs on how far he still had to go. He couldn't see Tony coming behind, but he didn't need to see him. He could tell he was there, because he sounded like an old paddle-steamer.

Only a few more metres. Joel caught a toehold in the bottom for a second to look ahead. The water foamed and eddied around the sandbar as if it were in more of a hurry there than other places. He put his head down and began the crawl, angling upriver against the current.

He was gasping for breath each time he turned his head. He wasn't really tired, though. A little nervous, maybe. In the pool the side was always nearby, something to grab on to. Still, he was a pretty good swimmer, and he was doing all right. He *might* be good enough for the swimming team by the autumn.

He should have thought of practising in the river himself. It had been a good idea. Tony was full of good ideas. When they both reached the sandbar, he would apologise, tell Tony he was sorry for what he'd said about his dad. He'd tell him he was sorry about saying Tony would be afraid to swim, too.

'Made it,' he called out, when his hand scraped bottom with his approach to the sandbar. He stood up. 'And I beat you, too!'

There was no answer. Joel turned to check.

Behind him stretched the river, smooth and glistening, reddish-brown, but there was no sign of Tony. There was nothing to indicate that Joel wasn't alone, hadn't come into the water alone to start with. Except, of course, he hadn't.

He started to walk back, pushing through the water impatiently, as though it were a crowd holding him back. 'Tony,' he yelled. 'Where are you?'

A faint echo of his own voice, high like the indistinct mewing of a cat, bounced back at him from the bluffs, but there was no other reply. Joel kept walking forwards, pushing against the wall of water.

Maybe Tony had turned back; maybe he was hiding in the bushes somewhere along the bank, watching him, waiting for him to come unglued.

'All right, Tony Zabrinsky. I know your tricks. Come out, wherever you are.'

There was no answer, not even a giggle from the bushes or some rustling.

'Doggone you, Tony, if you mess with my clothes . . .' But he could see his clothes, the pile of them, lying where he had left them,

his red T-shirt clearly marking the spot.

'Tony!' He began to move forward in lunges, gasping for breath, half choking. Tony had to be hiding. He had to be just off to the side somewhere . . . laughing. There was no other possibility.

It was when Joel stepped into the nothingness of the deep water, the bottom of the river suddenly gone from beneath his feet as if he had hit a black hole in space, that he knew. As he choked and fought his way to the surface, he understood everything.

Tony couldn't swim — not really — and Tony had gone under.

Joel trod water for another few seconds, looking across the deceptively smooth surface of the river. There was nothing there, no faint difference in the appearance of the water, nothing to give a hint of danger. How wide across was the hole? Where did Tony go under? Would he still be where he went down, or would the current have carried him away by now? How long could a person be under water and still live?

The questions came at Joel in a barrage, leaving no space for answers, if there were any.

There wasn't time to wait for them anyway. He made a lunging dive, pulling himself forwards and under with both arms, his eyes open and smarting in the murky water. He

Tony was dead ... dead! And he, Joel, was going to die, too. He couldn't breathe. His lungs were a sharp pain. The air came bursting from his chest like an explosion, and the water rushed in to take its place. The form that had ridden above him brushed against his arm, his side. It was rough, hard, no human body. It was a log. Joel grabbed hold, and his head broke through the light-dazzled surface just as the rest of his body gave in to limpness.

He lay for a few minutes, coughing, spitting water, being moved without any assistance on his part from the eddying whirlpool to the slower, straighter current close to the river bank. When the river bottom came up to meet his feet, he stood.

The sky was an inverted china bowl above his head. A single bird sang from a nearby tree.

Shut up, Joel wanted to shout. *You just shut up*. But he didn't. He didn't say anything. Instead, he bent over double and vomited a stream of water. Strange that river water in small amounts looked clean.

Joel could see everything with a sharp, terrible clarity: the river water he vomited, the bare roots of a tree thrust above the water, the steady flow of the river towards ... where did it go? Towards the Illinois River. And the Illinois River emptied into the Mississippi.

Didn't it? They had studied rivers in school, but he couldn't remember.

He looked around. Still nothing disturbed the smooth surface of the water, and nothing skulked along the bank, no hidden form. He might have been the only human being alive in the entire world.

Joel turned towards home and began to run blindly up the middle of the road. He could feel the river just behind him, a presence, a lurking monster waiting to pounce. A monster that swallowed boys. Joel increased his speed, his heart hammering against his ribs, his bare feet slapping against the dark pavement.

couldn't see more than a few centimetres in front of his face, so he reached in every direction with his hands as he swam, feeling for an arm, a leg, a bit of hair. Anything! He found nothing until he touched something slimy and rotting on the bottom and sprang to the surface.

He ducked under the water again, reaching on every side, looking and feeling until the river sang in his ears, and he burst through to the light, pulling raggedly for air.

The current would have pulled Tony downstream. He let the river carry him a few metres farther on and tried again.

Nothing.

When Joel dived for the fourth time, letting the current carry him farther from the shore, he found himself caught in the grip of that hurrying water. It sucked at him, grinding him against the silty river bottom. As he struggled to rise, grasping at the water with both hands as if he could pull himself up by it, his hand touched something solid.

Was it Tony, floating just above him? He thrashed towards the object, only to have the current draw it from his reach. Then he was swirling, spinning, being pulled towards the bottom again while a dark, boy-shaped object pivoted above him, face down in the muddy water.

from *On My Honour* by Marion Dane Bauer

Reading for Meaning

1 Why did Joel think that his friend Tony looked tired?

2 Joel heard Tony swimming in the water behind him. What did Tony sound like?

3 What did Joel discover as he began to get into his rhythm for swimming?

4 'He couldn't see Tony coming behind him, but he didn't need to see him.' Why didn't Joel need to see Tony?

5 How does the writer describe the way the water flowed around the sandbar?

6 Joel felt a little nervous as he swam towards the sandbar. Why?

7 When Joel turned to check for Tony, all he saw was the river. How did the river look to him?

8 Give the comparison that is used by the writer to show us how the water hindered Joel as he pushed through it to look for Tony.

9 What did the echo of his own voice sound like to Joel as it bounced back at him from the bluffs?

10 What did Joel hope Tony was doing?

11 What two signs of distress did Joel experience as he shouted 'Tony!' and began to move forward in lunges?

12 At what moment did Joel understand everything?

13 What feeling did Joel have about the surface of the river?

14 How did Joel compensate for not being able to see more than a few centimetres under the water?

15 What caused Joel to spring back to the surface?

16 What happened to Joel as he made his fourth dive?

17 What two things told Joel that the form he had seen above him was not a human body?

18 How did the sky look to Joel when he stood up from the water?

19 When Joel looked around and saw that nothing disturbed the surface of the water, what thought came to him?

20 How does the writer make the tragedy of drowning a very real one for the reader?

POETRY

THE TEENAGE YEARS

The Loner

He leans against the playground wall,
Smacks his hands against the bricks
And other boredom-beating tricks,
Traces patterns with his feet,
Scuffs to make the tarmac squeak,
Back against the wall he stays —
And never plays.

The playground's quick with life,
The beat is strong.
Though sharp as a knife
Strife doesn't last long.
There is shouting, laughter, song,
And a place at the wall
For who won't belong.

We pass him running, skipping, walking,
In slow huddled groups, low talking.
Each in our familiar clique
We pass him by and never speak,
His loneness is his shell and shield
And neither he nor we will yield.

He wasn't there at the wall today,
Someone said he'd moved away
To another school and place
And on the wall where he used to lean
Someone had chalked
'watch this space'.

Julie Holder

Questions

1 Why is the title 'The Loner' a good one for this poem?

2 What line in the first verse explains why the boy keeps moving around?

3 How is the playground described at the beginning of the second verse?

4 What comparison does the poet use to describe strife in the playground?

5 How does the second verse end on a depressing note?

6 How do the other students behave towards the boy?

7 What is the meaning of 'And neither he nor we will yield'?

8 Someone had chalked 'watch this space'. What cruelty is there in this message?

9 How true to school life do you think this poem is?

10 What are your feelings towards the boy described in the poem?

Big Fears

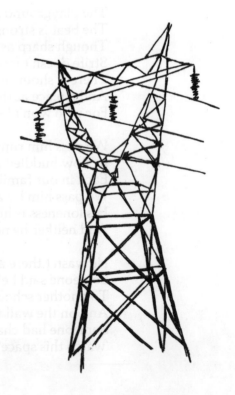

Twenty-five feet above Sian's house
hangs a thick wire cable
that droops and sags between two
electricity pylons.
A notice says it carries 40,000 volts
from one metallic scarecrow to the next,

then on to the next and the next
right across the countryside to the city.
The cable sways above Sian's council house
making her radio crackle and sometimes
making her television go on the blink.

If it's a very windy night
Sian gets frightened because she
thinks the cable might snap,
fall onto the roof and electrocute
everyone as they sleep.

This is Sian's Big Fear.

Outside Matthew's bedroom there
is a tall tree. Taller than the house.
In summer it is heavy with huge leaves.
In winter it stands lonely as a morning moon.

On a windy night, Matthew worries
that the tree might be blown down
and crash through his bedroom window.
It would certainly kill him and his cat
if it wasn't in its own cardboard box.

This is Matthew's Big Fear.

Outside Karen's bedroom there's nothing
but a pleasant view, meadows, hedges, sheep
and some distant gentle hills.
There's nothing sinister, nothing to worry about.

But in the dark Karen thinks
the darting shapes on the ceiling
are really the shadows of ghost's
great cold hands and that the night noises
made by the water pipes are the
screeches and groans of attic skeletons.

John Rice

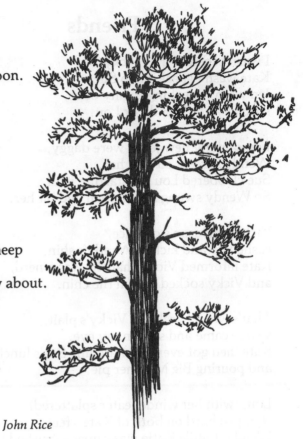

Questions

1 What imaginative comparison does the poet use to describe the electricity pylons?

2 What makes Sian constantly aware of the electricity cable above her house?

3 What is Sian's Big Fear?

4 What comparison is used by the poet to present us with a picture of the tree in winter?

5 When does Matthew worry about the tree?

6 What is Matthew's Big Fear?

7 What feeling does the view from Karen's window arouse in you?

8 What do the darting shapes on the ceiling suggest to Karen's mind?

9 How does Karen's imagination react to the night noises made by the water pipes?

10 Do you think Karen's fears are worse than those of Sian and Matthew? Why?

11 Do you think 'Big Fears' is a good title for this poem? Why or why not?

Friends

I wasn't speaking to Vicky,
Kate wasn't speaking to Sue,
Jen wasn't speaking to any of us,
specially not Wendy or Lou.

Lou said my new jeans were daggy,
Wendy agreed, so I hit her.
Sue clobbered Lou for starting it all,
So Wendy swung round then and bit her.

Vicky, in Susan's defence,
rushed up and kicked Wendy's shin.
Kate informed Vicky that she was a nerd,
and Vicky socked her on the chin.

That's when I grabbed Vicky's plait,
so Sue came and spat in my eye.
Kate then got even by snatching Sue's lunch
and pouring Big M in her pie.

Lou, (with her windcheater splattered)
stamped hard on both of Kate's feet.
Wendy, (while Katie was nursing crushed toes)
cried, 'Do that again, Lou! It's neat!'

I quickly took care of Lou,
leaving Kate to obliterate Wendy,
but Debby Paszkowski poked *her* in the nose
and said that my jeans just weren't trendy!

Both Vicky and I, united,
stuffed Debbie P. into the bin,
but that's when her minder, Lynne Moody,
came barging across to join in.

Lynne, who's a squad swimming champion,
has muscles as strong as an ox.
Without saying pardon, or may I, or please,
she tied us both up with our socks!

Kate, seeking powerful allies,
begged Jennifer for assistance.
(But Jen wasn't speaking to any of us
and was reading, aloof, at a distance.)

Wendy (that traitor and chicken)
edged up to Lynne Moody and hissed,
'Kate reckons you are a feller in drag!'
Lynne Moody bunched up a large fist.

Kate, stuck in L. M.'s half-nelson,
turned blue and started to holler,
so Lou very thoughtfully snuck up on Lynne
and shoved a dog mess down her collar.

Lynne Moody was not very pleased.
Her glare at poor Lou wasn't jolly.
She emptied Lou's schoolbag and jumped on the lot,
then ripped up Lou's copy of Dolly.

Kate was recovering from shock,
so I yelled out to Jenny for aid.
(But she wasn't speaking to any of us,
and continued to read in the shade.)

Sue, sucking up to Lynne Moody,
hooked a claw in the hem of Lou's skirt,
and with manners distinctly unladylike,
rubbed Lou's angry face in the dirt.

So Wendy and I, umbrage taking,
stuck bubble gum into Sue's hair,
and in case she had not got the message,
decorated her nose with a pear.

Lou saw the pear (which was hers)
and turned on us two in a rage.
She said at the zoo she had seen both our dads,
befurred, eating nuts in a cage.

Lynne then insulted us *all*,
with her big mouth as large as a bus.
Gorillas were too bright and brainy, she scoffed,
to father such morons as us!

She said that included Paszkowski —
cry-baby, prize wimp and sook.
So the lot of us ganged up and went for L.M!
(Save Jenny, engrossed in her book.)

Karate and elbows and fury,
fingernails, knuckles and feet!
Our fight made the Battle of Waterloo
look like a Sunday School Treat.

Jen shut her book then, and blinked
at the wild hubbub raging about.
'Small birds in their nests should agree,'
  she observed.
So we all stopped — and sorted *her* out!

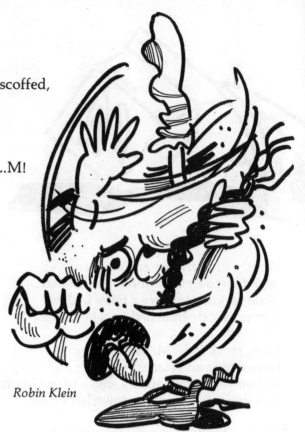

Robin Klein

Questions

1 Do you think the title 'Friends' is suitable? Why or why not?

2 How did Lou start the fight?

3 Why did Vicky sock Kate on the chin?

4 How did the girls suffer in the fifth verse?

5 What comparison tells us about the strength of Lynne's muscles?

6 How did Wendy manage to enrage Lynne?

7 When 'Lou very thoughtfully snuck up on Lynne' what shock did she give Lynne?

8 Why didn't Jenny come to anyone's aid?

9 How did 'Wendy and I' cooperate to change Sue's appearance?

10 What does the poet reveal about the size of the fight between L.M. and the rest of the girls?

11 What surprise occurs in the last verse?

12 Why did you like or dislike this poem?

The Road to Glamour

Protein-rich shampoo —
A split end? Oh, no!
Calamity dire,
disaster and woe!

Who's that at the door?
You can go away!
My beauty routine
takes most of the day.

Tweezer my eyebrows;
I wish they would arch.
They're as straight as two lines
of ants on the march.

Don't bang on the door;
you cannot come in.
I've got a crisis —
a *spot* on my chin!

What's making my nose
shine like a hammer?
Lined with bad words is
the road to glamour!

Sharp-eyed are my fans.
Don't kick down that door!
I'll be here for *hours* —
I've found a blocked pore!

This new astringent
stings like a shocker!
(Life's tough when you're made
Captain of Soccer.)

Robin Klein

WRITING

STORY BEGINNINGS

Have you ever stared at the blank piece of paper in front of you and wondered how to begin your story? If so, perhaps it's because you realise that the opening sentences of any piece of creative writing are crucial to its success. The opening is where you grab the reader's attention, stir his or her imagination and create a sense of anticipation. The opening should invite the reader to read on and find out what happens next as your story unfolds.

One way of learning how to create interesting and absorbing beginnings is to observe carefully the methods used by other writers. Here are the opening sentences from ten popular novels. Read them carefully. The questions that follow are designed to help you appreciate the successful approach adopted by each writer.

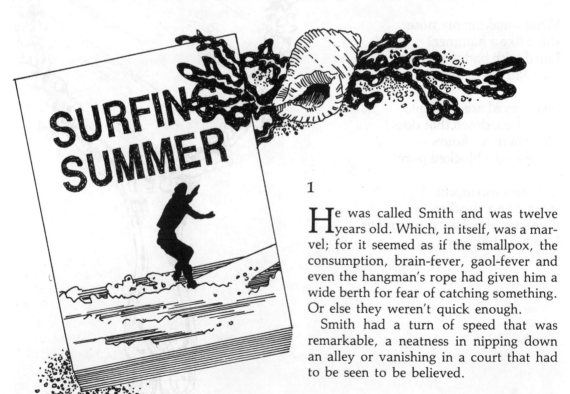

1

He was called Smith and was twelve years old. Which, in itself, was a marvel; for it seemed as if the smallpox, the consumption, brain-fever, gaol-fever and even the hangman's rope had given him a wide berth for fear of catching something. Or else they weren't quick enough.

Smith had a turn of speed that was remarkable, a neatness in nipping down an alley or vanishing in a court that had to be seen to be believed.

from *Smith* by Leon Garfield

2

I hate my father. I hate school. I hate being fat. I hate the principal because he wanted to fire Ms Finney, my English teacher.

from *The Cat Ate My Gymsuit*
by Paula Danziger

3

Chris Cunnigan was making a grilled cheese sandwich. You could tell a lot about him just by watching him work. His shirt cuffs were turned back twice, indicating neatness. There was a sureness in the way he flipped the sandwich that demonstrated unusual cooking skill for a sixteen-year-old boy. Just inside the collar of his shirt was the glitter of a chain, the kind used for a cross or religious medal. He was tall for his age, attractive, and clearly took pains with his appearance. And he was restless.

from *Centre Line* by Joyce Sweeney

4

Ba-room, ba-room, ba-room, baripity, baripity, baripity, baripity — Good. His dad had the pick-up going. He could get up now. Jess slid out of bed and into his overalls. He didn't worry about a shirt because once he began running he would be hot as popping grease even if the morning air was chill, or shoes because the bottoms of his feet were by now as tough as his worn-out sneakers.

from *Bridge to Terabithia*
by Katherine Paterson

5

I will never forgive my mother for calling me Erica with a surname like Yurken.

When an emergency teacher was taking our grade (we got a lot of emergency teachers at our school because the ordinary ones were often away with nervous problems), the emergency teacher would say something like, 'Girl in the end row with the dark hair, what's your name?' But before I could answer, kids would screech out 'Erk!' Or 'Yuk!' Or 'Gherkin!'

from *Hating Alison Ashley* by Robin Klein

6

The run from Lunar Station to Mars is a piece of cake. The passengers take the rocket buses up to the inter-planetary spacer, the *Johannes Kepler*, and settle down for ninety-two days of fun and food, sociability and relaxation. All one hundred and forty-seven of the passengers were enjoying themselves, in just this way, on the thirtieth day out from Earth.

That was when the meteorite hit the spaceship head on. Almost dead centre.

from *Spaceship Medic* by Harry Harrison

7

The Pushcart War started on the afternoon of March 15, 1976, when a truck ran down a pushcart belonging to a flower peddler. Daffodils were scattered all over the street. The pushcart was flattened, and the owner of the pushcart was pitched headfirst into a pickle barrel.

from *The Pushcart War* by Jean Merrill

EARTH QUAKE

MY SISTER IS A WITCH

Jogging is a Health Hazard

8

'There ain't no such thing as ghosts.' Wilf Piggins shifted his bulk against the parapet of the bridge and waited for someone to contradict him. Nobody did. 'And anybody who reckons he's seen one is mad.'

That's me. Kit Huntley leant over the parapet in the twilight and watched the dim reflection of her hair swing in the water. I've seen a ghost. But Wilf will never know.

from *The Edge of the World* by John Gordon

9

Winter came early to the city that year. Josiah Davidson, emerging from the subway, his arms loaded with schoolbooks, shivered against the dank November rain which blew icily against his face and sent a trickle down the back of his neck. He did not see three boys in black jackets who moved out of a sheltering doorway and stalked him.

from *The Young Unicorns* by Madeleine L'Engle

10

Infinitely far off lay dark clouds. The old aeroplane which emerged might have flown through them; might have been formed of them. It butted its way forward, hurled down by air pockets, wafted upwards by thermals, buffeted by turbulence. Nerveless hands gripped the controls, sightless eyes stared through the windows. The roar of piston engines was unvarying, like a savage beast whose jaws have been locked open for ever. The course did not waver: the target and the time of arrival were fixed.

from *The Fourth Plane at the Flypast* by Dennis Hamley

Questions

1 At the beginning of *Smith* we are introduced to an exceptional boy, and our curiosity is immediately aroused. What are the two ways in which Smith is quite exceptional?

2 Why do you think the strong emotion expressed in the opening sentences of *The Cat Ate My Gymsuit* makes a gripping beginning to a story?

3 At the beginning of *Centre Line* a person is described in great detail. At what point in the description does the reader feel that he or she would like to know more?

4 What hint of mystery in the opening lines of *Bridge to Terabithia* causes a reader to want to read on?

5 Another person's misfortune often fascinates the rest of us. Explain how the novel *Hating Alison Ashley* begins in a fascinating way.

6 After reading the opening lines of *Spaceship Medic*, there is no doubt that you would feel compelled to read on. Why is this?

7 Drama and humour are a good combination for a lively and interesting beginning. Why is the beginning of *The Pushcart War* both dramatic and humorous?

8 What irresistible hint of the uncanny is present in the beginning of *The Edge of the World?*

9 The hunt is on in *The Young Unicorns*. Having read the beginning, why do you feel the urge to read more of the novel?

10 The supernatural comes to life in the opening lines of *The Fourth Plane at the Fly Past*. What is the fact you would seek to discover by reading on?

WRITING YOUR OWN BEGINNINGS

Choose two of the titles listed below, and give some thought to the story that might be developed from each title. Then write the opening sentences to go with each of your titles.

- The Great Animal Rescue
- The Haunted Picture Show
- Cycling to Freedom
- The Big Surprise
- My Sister is a Witch
- Danger Down Below
- Earthquake!
- The School That Went Mad
- Surfing Summer
- Jogging is a Health Hazard

WRITING YOUR OWN STORY

A dramatic or lively photo and the first words of a story will probably give you just the stimulus you need to keep on writing. Choose one of the following photos. Notice that it comes complete with the opening words of the story you will write. Continue the story in your own way. As you write, keep referring to your photo for further stimulus. Your story should be about two pages in length.

Out of the blue the idea came to me. It was marvellous. It was wonderful. And it was a certain money-maker. Let me share it with you . . .

Given the time and the energy, anyone can do anything as I discovered when . . .

LANGUAGE

THE SENTENCE

A sentence has two parts called the **subject** and the **predicate**. The subject is the part of the sentence which tells us *who* or *what* performs the action. The main word in the subject is usually a noun or a pronoun. The predicate, which always contains a verb, is the part of the sentence that tells us what is said about the subject.

When you look at the examples below, you will notice that the subject of a sentence can be a single word or a group of words. The same is also true of the predicate.

Subject	Predicate
Joshua	scrambled down the aisle
Mr Glory's eyes	darted to the rearview mirror
The jolt	flung the Glorys forward

Finding the Subject and Predicate

Write down the subject and predicate of each of the following sentences. One good way of identifying the subject is to put the question *who* or *what?* in front of the verb.

1 Anna's head was flung against her father's seat.

2 Mr Glory did not answer.

3 The Glory family tensed.

4 She heard her mother scream.

5 His shoulder jerked as he reached down to shift gears.

6 Her knuckles were white.

7 His last words were lost in the long, arrogant blast of the Triumph's horn.

8 The world was lost in a sheet of water.

9 The sound of the engine disappeared in the distance.

10 The shock jarred Anna from her seat.

11 He hit the brakes.

12 Anna raised her head.

HOW TO RESTRUCTURE SENTENCES

Beginning Sentences with New Subjects

In many sentences the subject *does* the action. However, a sentence may be restructured to show the action being *done to* a new subject, without changing the original meaning of the sentence. By using this technique, you can add interest and variety to your sentences.

Example: **The car** struck the Glory bus.
          The Glory bus was struck by the car.

Here, the Glory bus (the new subject) is having the action done to it by the car.

Restructure the following sentences to show the action being *done to* a new subject. Notice that in each case the new subject has been provided for you.

1 Anna heard the screech of tyres.
  The screech of tyres . was heard by Anna

2 Blood covered his face.
  His face . was covered with blood

3 Joel swam the flooded river.
  The flooded river . was swum by Joel

4 Students invaded the subway station.
  The subway station . was invaded by the students

5 The officer caught the criminal.
  The criminal . was caught by the officer

6 Sam broke two regulations.
  Two regulations were broken by Sam

7 My friend borrowed my subway pass.
  My subway pass . was borrowed by my friend.

8 A flash of lightning lit up the world.
  The world .. was lit up by the flash of lightning

Beginning Sentences with '-ing' Words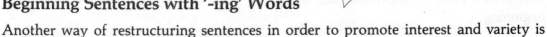

Another way of restructuring sentences in order to promote interest and variety is to use '-ing' words.

Example: Joel **turned** towards home and began to run blindly up the road.
Turning towards home, Joel began to run blindly up the road.

Notice how the '-ing' form of the action word 'turned' is used to begin the sentence.

In each of the following sentences an action word is shown in heavy type. Given the '-ing' form of the action word, your task is to complete each of the new sentences.

1 He let the river carry him a few metres on and tried again.
Letting *the river carry him, he then went a few meteres on tried again.*

2 Cruz **took** the kid by the arm and threatened him.
Taking *the kid by the arm, Cruz threatned him.*

3 She **thought** the bus was out of danger so she looked out of the back window.
Thinking *the bus was out of danger, she looked out of the back window.*

4 Tony **gave** Joel a shove and plunged into the water himself.
Giving *Joel a shove, Tony plunged into the water himself.*

5 He **put** his head down and began to swim.
Putting *his head down, he began to swim.*

6 Mr Glory **trembled** as he drove his bus faster.
Trembling *Mr Glory drove his bus faster.*

7 Anna **leant** forward and heard the screech of tyres as the Triumph drove away.
Leaning *forward, Anna heard the screech of tyres as the Triumph drove away.*

8 Joshua **buried** his head in his arms and thought his last moment had come.
Burying *his head in his arms, Joshua thought his last moment had come.*

Different Beginnings for Sentences

You can begin sentences in different ways, without altering their meaning, by changing the order of the main thoughts expressed.

Example: Anna opened her eyes **when** a bright light startled her.
When a bright light startled her, Anna opened her eyes.

Notice how there is a change in the main order of the thoughts expressed when the sentence is begun with 'when'. However, the meaning of the sentence is unchanged.

Restructure each of the following sentences using the given word as your new beginning.

1 The student was shaking **as** he rubbed at his mouth with his sleeve.
As *he rubbed at his mouth with his sleeve the student was shaking*

2 Mrs Glory started to scream **when** the bus veered off the road.
When *the bus veered off the road, Mrs Glory started to scream*

3 He began to move forward in lunges **because** he was gasping for breath.
Because *he was gasping for breath, he began to move forward in lunges*

4 Sam jumped aside **with** a yell.
With *a yell, Sam jumped*

5 The students were hurrying **because** the train was roaring in.
Because *the train was roaring in, the students were hurrying*

6 He continued to search **while** there was any breath left in his lungs.
While *there was any breath left in his lungs, he continued to search*

7 Her eyes were wide with her own fear **in** the pale light from the dashboard.
In *the pale light from the dashboard, her eyes were wide with her own fear*

8 He saw Tony swimming beside him **whenever** he turned his head.
Whenever *he turned his head, he saw tony swimming beside him*

9 The transit officer waited **while** Sam searched in his knapsack.
While *Sam searched in his knapsack the transit officer waited*

10 Her father pressed his foot hard on the accelerator **in order that** the bus might outmanoeuvre the car.
In order that *the bus might outmanoeuvre the car her father pressed his foot hard on the accelerator*

GETTING IT RIGHT
AGREEMENT OF SUBJECT AND VERB

The action word, or verb, in a sentence should agree with the subject of that sentence.

Example: **The boy is** talking in the corridor.

Here, the subject 'the boy' is one person and is therefore singular, and so the singular form of the verb 'is' must be used.

Example: **The boys are** talking in the corridor.

Here, the subject 'the boys' consists of more than one person and is therefore plural, and so the plural form of the verb 'are' must be used.

The following exercise will help you to make sure that the subjects and verbs in your sentences are in agreement. In each of the following sentences, choose the verb from the brackets that agrees with the subject of the sentence.

1 The ticket officer (were/was) examining all the passes.

2 Her eyes (are/is) wide with her own fear.

3 The bus (have/has) gone over the cliff.

4 The swimmers (see/sees) the deep water ahead.

5 Sam slowly (pull/pulls) a battered wallet out of his knapsack.

6 As the bus (goes/go) off the road, Anna gasps.

7 Then he (were/was) being pulled towards the bottom again.

8 Anna's face (strike/strikes) the metal edge of the seat.

9 The students (finds/find) their passes in their shoes.

10 The front of the bus (were/was) slowly sinking into the rain-swollen waters.

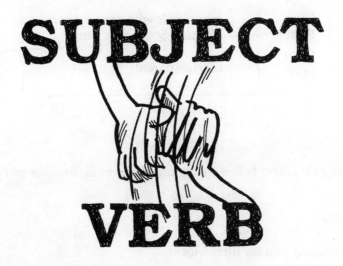

DRAMA

Facing Sarah Sockwell

by Bill Condon

```
┌─────────────────────────────────────────────┐
│              CHARACTERS                      │
│                                             │
│   Maria    ⎫                                │
│   Kelly    ⎬  schoolgirls                   │
│                                             │
│   Gina     ⎫  schoolgirls who are members   │
│   Robbie   ⎬  of Sarah Sockwell's gang      │
│                                             │
│   Mrs O    ⎫                                │
│   Mr O     ⎬  Maria's parents               │
└─────────────────────────────────────────────┘
```

SCENE ONE

A girl walks briskly on stage. When she is halfway across, another girl enters and runs after her.

Maria   Kelly, Kelly!
Kelly   What?
Maria   I've been chasing you for three blocks.
Kelly   I know that.
Maria   Why didn't you stop?
Kelly   I have to do my homework.
Maria   You've never been in a hurry to do your homework in your life, Kelly Martin. The truth is you don't want to help me do you?
Kelly   I don't know what you're talking about, Maria.
Maria   Yes you do. Sarah Sockwell's going to kill me!
Kelly   No she won't. She's never killed anyone yet — she'll just give you a black eye.
Maria   See! You know all about it.
Kelly   The whole school knows. You're really going to cop it.
Maria   Not if you back me up. We'll just go to the library and get out a heap of karate books and study them — and then when Sarah comes for me . . .

Kelly   Maria. Stop. I like you and that, but if you think I am going to fight Sarah Sockwell for you, you're wrong!

Maria   You're joking, right, Kel? Tell me you're joking.

Kelly   No, I mean it, Maria — you started this.

Maria   But you're my best friend.

Kelly   Listen, Maria, my father works an extra job just to pay for my teeth. If I got into a fight and hurt my teeth he'd have a nervous breakdown. You understand don't you?

Maria   I'd help *you*.

Kelly   No you wouldn't — because I wouldn't get in this mess in the first place.

Maria   Remember the time Sally Rogers was going to bash you 'cause you put a blue-tongue lizard in her bag?

Kelly   Yes, I remember — you didn't lift a finger to help me.

Maria   I did so! I rang Sally and told her your father was in the Mafia and she'd be in big trouble if she laid a finger on you.

Kelly   You did that?

Maria   Yes!

Kelly   Wait until I tell my father — his lawyers have been dying to find out who started that rumour!

(Kelly Exits. Maria addresses the audience.)

Maria   This is turning out to be the worst day of my life! Sarah Sockwell's going to kill me because I let her copy during the English exam — that's right, I let her copy — but I gave her all the wrong answers! The teacher just marked the papers and I came third in the class. And guess who came last? Sarah Sockwell! Right this minute I bet she's looking for me. She's gunna tear me apart!

(Sarah's gang enters — Gina and Robbie.)

Gina   Sarah sent us over to give you a message.

Robbie   Yeah — stock up on bandages.

Maria   Look, look, how about I give her some money?

Gina   How much have you got?

Maria   Ten dollars — she can have it all.

Robbie   Hand it over.

(Maria gives them the money.)

Maria   Now she won't hurt me, right?

Gina   Wrong.

Robbie   For this ten bucks, *we* won't hurt you — what Sarah does is her business.

Maria   That's not fair.

Gina   Tough. Sarah's got another message for you too — she'll meet you here at 12 o'clock.

Robbie   High noon! And if you're not here —

Gina   She'll come looking for you.

Robbie   Yeah!

Maria   What am I going to do?!

Gina   You can always go running to mummy for help.

Robbie   Good one, Gina . . . .

(They both laugh.)

Maria   Oh, sure, sure — that's the last person I'd go to.

(Gina and Robbie exit. Maria waits for them to go, then calls out to her mother for help.)

Maria   Mum, Mum!

SCENE TWO

Lights return. Maria and her mother and father are on stage. Her father is reading a newspaper through most of the scene.

Mrs O   What's wrong?

Maria   What's right? There's this girl, Sarah Sockwell, and she's gunna kill me, Mum, all because I let her copy in the exam.

Mrs O   You let her copy and she's still going to kill you? She sounds very hard to please.

Maria   I gave her the wrong answers, okay? Now I'm dead. What should I do? How about I go on a holiday for a while? Maybe I can move to a new school, or you could hire a bodyguard for me. What do you think?

Mrs O   Why didn't you just tell her to get lost?

Maria   Sarah's big — I mean, ginormous! No one tells her to get lost.

Mrs O   You shouldn't let yourself be bossed around, should she, John?

Mr O   *(He doesn't look up from the paper)*   That's right, dear.

Maria   If I'd given her the right answers I wouldn't be in trouble.

Mrs O   You should have just told her you weren't going to let her copy. Right, John?

Mr O   Right, dear.

Maria   Mum, I haven't got a death wish you know.

Mrs O   At least you would have been taking a stand. Isn't that right, John?

Mr O   Quite right, dear.

Maria   Time's running out. Have you got any ideas?

Mrs O   Well, can't you get your friends to help you?

Maria   My friends aren't that stupid.

Mrs O   Then what are you going to do?

Maria   I thought you'd know!

Mrs O   I could write a note to the principal, couldn't I, John?

Mr O   You certainly could, dear.

Maria   Sure. 'Please don't let my little girl get bashed up by that big bully.' If anyone in my group found out I'd be laughed out of school.

Mrs O   Well, you'll just have to face up to her. Won't she, John?

Mr O   You're right, dear.

Maria   Dad! How can you be so heartless?

Mr O   I'm trying to do a crossword here.

Maria   Dad, this is a very serious problem!

Mr O   I know. These cryptic puzzles are tricky.

Maria   Excellent! You haven't even been listening!

Mrs O   Of course he has. Your father always agrees with me — the only way of solving a problem is to stand up to it. Right, dear?

Mr O   Exactly what I said.

Maria   Yeah, right. Thanks anyway.

(Maria addresses the audience.)

Maria   Parents! It's a wonder they survive long enough to have kids — they're not very clever sometimes. Obviously they never knew anyone at school like Sarah Sockwell. Facing up to her is suicide.

Mr O *(He puts the paper down for the first time)* I heard that. As a matter of fact
  I did have someone just like Sarah at school when I was your age — and I had to
  face up to him.

Maria You, Dad? You faced up to a bully? My dad?!

Mr O Certainly did.

Mrs O You didn't tell me this, John.

Maria What happened?

Mr O I got a fat lip and a bloody nose, that's all.

Maria That's all?! Did it hurt?

Mr O I can still remember the pain. It was great!

Maria *(To audience)* Oh no! My father's a masochist!

Mr O I meant that it was a great feeling to know I'd stood up to him.

Mrs O I'm surprised at you, John.

Mr O Sorry, dear.

Mrs O I don't like it when you keep secrets from me.

Mr O Sorry, I just forgot.

Mrs O Well don't do it again.

(Mrs O exits.)

Mr O See, Maria . . . see what happens when you don't take a stand? There comes
  a time when it's too late.

(Blackout.)

SCENE THREE

Maria addresses the audience.

Maria Well, guess what? I took a stand. I met Sarah Sockwell at high noon and I stood
  right up to her and said, 'I believe you wanted to see me.' And even though I was
  shaking I tried not to let her know it. But she didn't hit me after all. She said she
  was letting me off with a warning because she'd had an anonymous phone call to
  say my father was in the Mafia . . . I know it was Kelly that made that phone call
  — but it was my dad who saved me.

Questions

1 Why is Maria chasing Kelly as the play opens?

2 What reason does Kelly give for not being able to join Maria in confronting Sarah
   Sockwell?

3 How did Maria help Kelly to escape a bashing from Sally Rogers?

4 Maria tells us why Sarah Sockwell is going to kill her. What did she do to Sarah
   to make her so angry?

5 Gina and Robbie give two messages from Sarah Sockwell. What are they?

6 What becomes of Maria's attempt to pay off Sarah Sockwell?

7 How does Scene One end?

8 Why is the advice Mrs O gives her daughter rather unhelpful?

9 At first Mr O is unwilling to help his daughter. Why is this?

10 Eventually, how does Mr O help Maria to understand her problem?

11 What lesson from his own schooldays does Mr O have for his daughter?

12 What finally happened when Maria stood up to Sarah Sockwell?

13 What twist occurs in the play's ending?

14 Why do you think the playwright avoided bringing Sarah Sockwell herself into the play?

15 Do you think this is an interesting play? Why or why not?

AGAINST THE ODDS

7

NOVELS

Surviving a Nuclear Attack

When war breaks out, people must prepare for the unthinkable — a nuclear attack! Sarah, her step-mother Veronica, and the two younger children prepare themselves as best they can in their house.

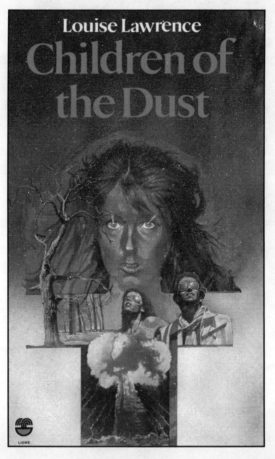

Sarah's whole body was tense and listening. It was very dark in the room but a faint line of sunlight showed through the weave of the blanket at the top of the window. She heard a rumble in the distance, a great wave of sound that came sweeping towards her, engulfing everything in its path, drowning Catherine's cries. Sarah blundered towards the fragile edge of light as the blast struck the house.

Roof tiles smashed and the windows were blown inward. Books and ornaments and light fittings crashed and fell in the upstairs rooms. In the howling darkness the mattress sagged and the bookcase started to topple. The black human shape that was Veronica screamed at her to help. But Sarah was already there, moved by her instinct, exerting force against force. The blanket tore at its nails, came loose at one corner. Heat screamed through the crack. Sarah had one brief glimpse of devastation, a hurricane of tearing trees and whirling leaves, the sky gone dark and lurid with fire, before the wind passed over them and things sank back into stillness.

Catherine was sobbing beneath the table.

Fragments of glass slipped and fell.

The air was stifling.

'Is it over?' Sarah asked.

'That was just the beginning,' Veronica said brutally.

'We don't stand a chance!' Sarah cried.

'There's a torch on the mantelpiece!' Veronica told her. 'And the hammer is beside it. I'll need some nails too. Hurry up!'

Veronica removed the bookcase and nailed the blanket back into place. They had to have something heavier, she said, and between them they managed to lift the settee on top of the sideboard. It was made of leather and horsehair and its carved legs hooked over the back. Sheets and blankets were jammed into the space along the top as the next wave of sound came screaming towards them.

They applied their shoulders, all the strength they had, to hold the settee in place as the bombs fell over Bristol and Cardiff, Cheltenham and Gloucester, and the great winds followed, a roaring tide of heat and darkness that smashed like a gigantic fist against the house. Even through the thickness of the walls Sarah seemed to see it . . . hell-bright hues, impressions of colours that flashed and pulsed, rose and gold and red-vermilion, impaled on her eyes as the wind screamed through the broken upstairs windows and the barricade shuddered. Wave after wave of thundering sound beat at the doors and walls of their sanctuary, until it faded away into silence.

They listened and waited. Buster was howling outside and in the hall the grandfather clock struck four, a silly incongruous sound. It had been a very short war, and they heard nothing more.

'I guess it's over,' Veronica said.

'Bristol?' asked Sarah.

'Everything,' Veronica replied.

Sarah let go. She was weak and shaking. There was a pain in her shoulder where the wooden frame of the settee had cut into her flesh, and her hands hurt so much she could hardly bear it. She sat in the dark on the dining chair, biting her lip.

Veronica switched on the torch.

'Are you all right?'

Sarah wanted to cry, weep like a small child, pretend Veronica was her mother, cling to her for comfort like William and Catherine always did. But she and Veronica had never been close. She was just the woman her father had married, mother of William and Catherine, but nothing to do with Sarah.

'Do you think Daddy's still alive?' she asked.

'If he is,' said Veronica, 'he won't be able to come to us. There's no point in hoping, Sarah. We're on our own.'

from *Children of the Dust* by Louise Lawrence

Reading for Meaning

1 At the beginning of the extract, what tells us that Sarah is expecting something?

2 Is it day or night outside? How do we know?

3 What phrase gives us a clear picture of the strength of the sound made by the first explosion?

4 Why is the darkness described as 'howling'?

5 What does Sarah see outside in her 'brief glimpse of devastation'?

6 Why do you think Catherine has been put beneath the table?

7 Why do they have to replace the bookcase with the settee?

8 What is the purpose of blocking out all that they can?

9 What are the effects of the second group of bombings?

10 What colours does Sarah imagine she can see?

11 Why do these colours seem to fit the experience?

12 '. . . in the hall the grandfather clock struck four . . .' Why does this seem 'a silly incongruous sound'?

13 " 'Bristol?' asked Sarah. 'Everything,' Veronica replied." What does Veronica mean by this answer?

14 How do we know that Sarah has been straining herself to support the settee?

15 Why doesn't Sarah cry and cling to Veronica?

16 Why do you think Sarah asks about her father so soon?

17 In the circumstances, do you think Veronica's answer to Sarah's question about her father is harsh? Why or why not?

18 What do we learn about the characters of Sarah and Veronica in this extract?

Inside the Computer

Space Demons is a computer game with a difference. It seems to be controlled by an evil intelligence, and it holds other surprises.

Full of excitement and anticipation, he began to play the first sequence, releasing the rocket boosters at exactly the right second. As they fell away, he was ready for the asteroid bombardment. The module responded to his deft fingers; his brain and his hands seemed to have become one. Then came the dark shapes and white faces of the space demons, implacable and menacing, but he was too swift for them. They could not touch the module he controlled. Next came the spaceman, and finally, as the magic number flashed up, the gun appeared on the screen. Andrew was impatient to get on to the next vital score, to find out for himself exactly what happened, but he had to control his impatience as skilfully as he controlled the game. He made himself concentrate purely on the task of getting the gun so that he could start to destroy the demons.

Twice he failed. The demons got past his defences, and he felt their gloating triumph as the spacemen were annihilated. His heart lurched, and his breath caught in his throat. A very small part of him was calling out in panic, *Don't go on! Stop before it's too late!*, but he refused to listen to it. Nothing was going to keep him from going on with the game, at least as far as Ben had got, if not further — as far as the game went. He would not turn back or give up. He would master it or bust!

With the third spaceman he concentrated harder than ever. He seemed hardly to exist as Andrew Hayford any more. He was no longer aware of anything but the computer screen and the controls, the spaceman and the demons.

Then suddenly it happened. The right score and the time factor coincided at the precise point. He was no longer controlling the spaceman with the joystick. What he was holding in his hand was the gun. He had done it! He was in the game!

*   *   *

He was a pulsating mass of impulses and reflexes, triggered to respond to the slightest stimulus. A sudden movement, an intimation of light caused him to swing in that direction and let his pent-up energy escape in short bursts towards the source of danger, through his hand, through the gun, and into the demons.

Razor-sharp and laser-clear, his mind had become an integrated part of his whole self. He thought with his whole body, yet his body no longer felt like a thing of flesh and blood and bone, but something more subtle and invulnerable. Mind and body worked together in exquisite harmony. His emotions were no longer conflicting or ambiguous, but clear-cut and strong: he felt excitement in pursuit and pleasure in destruction, but a controlled excitement and a cold pleasure. And when demon after demon exploded around him, filling the darkness with their

moans, he laughed, but the laughter was fierce and cold, too, and came from a place deep inside him he had never known existed.

Something else — a voice — came from that place too. At first he was not sure if it was his own thoughts, or if he could really hear it. 'Welcome,' said the remote voice. It had a tone of respect, almost awe, that Andrew found pleasantly flattering. 'You are a champion. It is good for my children to have someone worthy to contend with. You are an ace. You will master all!'

The words made him laugh in the same fierce, cold way. 'You're not wrong!' he said in his mind. 'I'm going to master this game — and you too, whoever or whatever you are.'

'I am the voice of the program,' it said. 'You can trust me. Don't be frightened.'

'I'm not frightened!' he thought back, and as the gun flashed and flashed, he laughed and laughed.

But his laughter changed to a cry of horror as, too late, he saw a demon get through his defences, and felt the agonising shock of annihilation. Yet even the plunge into non-existence had a kind of despairing exultation about it, as he received in his own self the destruction he had been meting out.

For a split second he thought he had been sent to some place from which there was no return, and then the everyday world came back, and he was sitting again in the chair facing the screen. It had returned to deep blue, and his score flashed across the top: 65 000.

There were no words to express what he felt. He sat speechless, staring at the screen. His body was tingling and shivering, and he could feel blood and adrenalin racing through him. He was amazed, excited and exhilarated all at the same time. He could not believe what had happened. The blue screen in front of him looked so innocent, almost as if it was saying to him, 'Aha! Thought I was weak, didn't you?'

It seemed a tremendous joke. He started laughing with astonishment and release. He laughed and laughed, unable to stop. 'Wow!' he kept saying to himself out loud. 'Wow! This is just fantastic. Far out! Unreal!'

Then it dawned on him that he was ravenously hungry. He felt drained of energy, completely used up. 'I'll play again later,' he thought. 'Right now I must get something to eat. I'm starving. I wonder how long I was playing? I wonder if Dad's home?'

from *Space Demons* by Gillian Rubinstein

Reading for Meaning

1 What does the first sequence on the computer require the player to do?

2 What do the space demons look like?

3 How do we know that Andrew has not played the game at higher levels before?

4 Why is the gun so valuable a prize?

5 What drives him to keep on, even when part of him calls out 'Don't go on!'?

6 What happens when the right score and the time factor coincide?

7 How does Andrew feel after he enters the game and begins to pursue and destroy the demons?

8 What is unusual about the way he laughs as he destroys the demons?

9 How does Andrew react to the voice when he first hears it?

10 What causes his laughter to change to horror?

11 What happens when he is blasted by the demon?

12 There is a moment of horror as Andrew returns to the real world. What fear crosses his mind to cause this?

13 How does Andrew's body react to what has happened as he sits 'speechless, staring at the screen'?

14 What impression does he get from the computer screen?

15 'It seemed a tremendous joke.' What two emotions cause Andrew to laugh?

16 How do we know that being in the computer somehow drained his energy?

17 What happened to his sense of time when he was in the game?

18 What impression of this computer game do you get from the extract?

The Deep Dive

Trapped in an underground lake, Ket and his mates Con and Donny have to undertake a dangerous dive, through a network of water-filled tunnels, to see if they can find a way out.

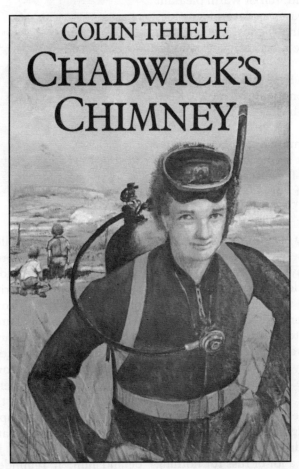

COLIN THIELE
CHADWICK'S CHIMNEY

Ket kept the lamp on the wall of rock as they slowly went down, playing it desperately from side to side in the hope of picking up a tunnel or a passage of some sort. But there was nothing. They were like three underwater blowflies bumbling their noses hopelessly against a concrete wall.

Ket felt the pressure increasing. Five metres, ten metres, fifteen, twenty. The stone barrier seemed to go on endlessly, down and down without hope of change. Thirty metres. They were getting into deep water, as his father had put it — the danger zone.

Pressure on their bodies was growing rapidly, dissolved gases were beginning to accumulate in their blood, the likelihood of disaster was increasing. Forty metres. Behind the burbling noise of the escaping bubbles Ket heard another sound. It seemed to be coming from deep inside his ears, a fast humming and ringing, as if someone had set off an alarm in his head.

Forty-five metres. What an incredible cavern it was. Beside it, Kubla Khan's magic cave would have been a toy. Ket's fear started to leave him and the water began to get thinner, less resistant. Movement was easier, almost like swimming in air. Or so it seemed.

Fifty metres. There was no end to the beautiful underwater lake. It went on and on to the end of the world, full of warm pleasant sounds and simple ease, a place of grottoes and inlets, of lights and shadows, where you could lie down inside a bed of water and go to sleep.

'Keep your head, Ket,' his father's voice said, but it was a long way off now. 'Keep your head in this business. If you don't you're dead.'

He tried to rouse himself and concentrate. The glass in his mask seemed to be distorting the angle of the rock-face because it was bent inwards in a kind of curve.

Fifty-five metres. The distortion was very annoying because it meant that the rocky wall was continually bending out of reach, and Ket had to chase after it with the lamp to keep the light playing on the stone.

Sixty metres. Suddenly the distortion was so great that the wall was actually lying horizontally on the water and Ket had to shine the light upwards to keep it in sight. It stretched away above his head like the roof of an arch. Vaguely Ket realised that the change was not due to distortion at all. It was real.

He wondered whether they were swimming into another big hollow, another blind alley. Actually he didn't care much any more because it all seemed a lot of fuss for nothing and they weren't getting anywhere. Better for him not to bother and just drift along until he went to sleep. He'd almost forgotten about Donny and Con until a tug on the link-line reminded him. He felt faintly annoyed; it was a nuisance to have somebody tied to him like a burden or a weight.

The hollow seemed to go on for a long way — like an entrance hall that had no end. The roof rose and fell, full of knobs and lumps and big limestone excrescences like gargoyles. Ket wondered who on earth would have spent his time carving things like that down here. After a while he couldn't even see

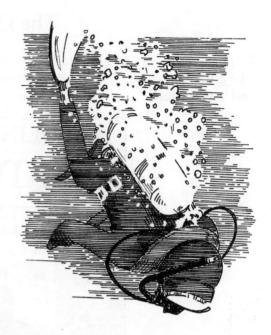

the walls of the hollows anymore; they seemed to have evaporated or melted away in the water to left and right. And then the roof disappeared. It irritated him because he had gone to a lot of trouble trying to keep it within range of his lamp.

He turned the beam upwards trying to find out where the thing had got to, but the lamp was beginning to grow dim and showed nothing but water. There was only one thing to do, it seemed, and that was to chase the roof until he caught up with it again.

He arched upwards and started to rise. As he did so he felt the jerk of Donny's line behind him. It reminded him to be careful just in time, because he had been inclined to forget everything and let his body look after itself, rising faster and faster until it shot up and soared away into space. Then he heard the voice of his father out in the water somewhere warning him — a stern voice saying the same thing over and over again: 'Slow, Ket. Slow, Ket. Slow, slow, slow.'

So they came up slowly, the three of them, like small kraken out of the deep, pausing for what seemed an age, then rising a little, then pausing again. It was a long, long way off, the place they were coming from, and not nearly as pleasant as it had seemed. In fact, it was good to get away from it. They had been hanging about there long enough.

Another rise, another pause, and a rise again. It was taking a lifetime. Pause, rise, pause. Pause, rise, pause. And then, suddenly, Ket's body seemed to take off. For a moment it slid upwards and, without warning, seemed to shoot off into a vacuum. But just as suddenly a force from above stopped it ruthlessly and held it where it was. A great realisation burst over him. He was on the surface. There was nothing above him but air.

He lifted his lamp and held it up hastily . . . The roof of a big cave rose high above his head.

Ket's awareness of everything swept back clearly again and he looked around quickly for Donny and Con. They were just breaking the surface nearby.

from *Chadwick's Chimney* by Colin Thiele

Reading for Meaning

1 What is Ket looking for as he moves the lamp across the rock wall? *a tunnel or a passage*

2 What is the first physical sign indicating that they are going deeper? *pressure on his body dissolved gases were beginning to accumulate*

3 At what depth does the 'danger zone' begin?

4 What two sounds can Ket hear as he reaches forty metres in depth?

5 What is the first sign that the depth is starting to affect Ket's judgement?

6 Why does Ket try to rouse himself and concentrate?

7 At around fifty-five metres the rock wall seems to be bending away from him. What does he think causes this, at first?

8 At what depth does he realise that the rock wall really has flattened out above his head?

9 Why does he feel 'faintly annoyed'?

10 Why is he irritated when the roof disappears?

11 The jerk of Donny's line serves as an important reminder to him. What does it bring back to his mind?

12 Why is his father's voice 'stern' as Ket hears it this second time?

13 Describe how they come back to the surface?

14 As they rise to the surface, their awareness of the place they are coming from changes. How does it change?

15 What is the 'force' that finally stops Ket rising?

16 Where is Ket when he surfaces?

17 What shows us that Ket is thinking clearly again after he has surfaced?

18 From the events of this passage, develop two safety rules that would be important to anyone doing a deep dive.

POETRY

The First Men on Mercury

— We come in peace from the third planet.
Would you take us to your leader?

— Bawr stretter! Bawr. Bawr. Stretterhawl?

— This is a little plastic model
of the solar system, with working parts.
You are here and we are there and we
are now here with you, is this clear?

— Gawl horrop. Bawr. Abawrhannahanna!

— Where we come from is blue and white
with brown, you see we call the brown
here 'land', the blue is 'sea', and the white
is 'clouds' over land and sea, we live
on the surface of the brown land,
all round is sea and clouds. We are 'men'.
Men come —

— Glawp men! Gawrbenner menko. Menhawl?

— Men come in peace from the third planet
which we call 'earth'. We are earthmen.
Take us earthmen to your leader.

— Thmen? Thmen? Bawr. Bawrhossop.
Yuleeda tan hanna. Harrabost yuleeda.

— I am the yuleeda. You see my hands,
we carry no benner, we come in peace.
The spaceways are all stretterhawn.

— Glawn peacemen all horrobhanna tantko!
Tan come at'mstrossop. Glawp yuleeda!

— Atoms are peacegawl in our harraban.
Menbat worrabost from tan hannahanna.

— ou men we know bawrhossoptant. Bawr.
We know yuleeda. Go strawg backspetter quick.

— We cantantabawr, tantingko backspetter now!

— Banghapper now! Yes, third planet back.
Yuleeda will go back blue, white, brown
nowhanna! There is no more talk.

— Gawl han fasthapper?

— No. You must go back to your planet.
Go back in peace, take what you have gained
but quickly.

— Stretterworra gawl, gawl . . .

— Of course, but nothing is ever the same,
now is it? You'll remember Mercury.

Edwin Morgan

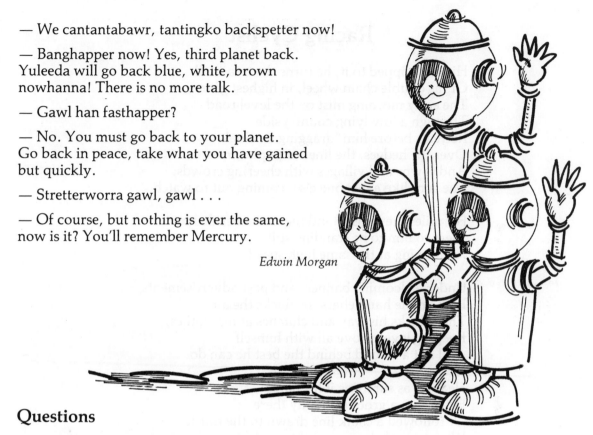

Questions

1 Which planet is the third planet?

2 Although we do not understand their language, the Mercurians ask a question in their first speech. What is the question?

3 Why do the earth people show a model of the solar system to the Mercurians?

4 What is the first word of 'earth' language used by the Mercurians?

5 Why do the visitors repeat that they come 'in peace'? Why is this important?

6 'Yuleeda' is the word created by the Mercurians from which two earth words?

7 When the earthman's speech first begins to be affected by the Mercurian's, which words show the effect?

8 In the next section of the poem the language becomes confused as both parties speak a mixture of languages. What do *you* think is happening here?

9 From your reading of the poem, what do you think 'Banghapper now!' means?

10 Who is in control at the end of the poem?

11 What have the earthmen gained?

12 Why will the earthmen remember Mercury?

13 What did you enjoy about this poem?

Racing Cyclist

His feet clipped to it, he turns the treadmill
Of his double chain wheel, in highest gear.
The early morning mist on the level road
Through a low-lying countryside
Retreats before him, dragging its cloak
Over the hedges, the lines of poplar trees
And towns and villages with cheering crowds,
The sun, like everyone else, coming out to watch.

For miles, he himself and the riders beside him
Seem to him to be standing still,
All moving at the same high speed.

Under welcoming banners and past advertisements,
Low on the handlebars, he ducks the air
That blocks his way and clutches at his clothes,
Keeping level above all with himself
And not a second behind the best he can do.

He rides as surely as if his narrow tyres
Fitted into a groove already there
Or followed a chalk line drawn to the finish
Where people leap up at the roadside,
Beckoning and calling a winner out of the pack.

Stanley Cook

Questions

1 How would you describe what this poem is about?

2 The early morning mist 'retreats' before him. Why is 'retreats' a better word here than 'disappears'?

3 Why do the rider and those beside him 'Seem to him to be standing still'?

4 Why does he ride low on the handlebars?

5 What part of the poem suggests that he is a confident rider?

6 Why do the people 'leap up at the roadside'?

7 From this poem, how does the poet seem to feel about racing cyclists?

8 Did you like this poem? Why, or why not?

But I Didn't

When I got out of bed this morning
I might have tripped and fallen down
The stairs, breaking my neck as I did so
But I didn't,
Going to school
The bus might have crashed
In the morning rain
But it didn't,
There might have been an earthquake
Causing the school to collapse
Before my maths test
But there wasn't,
Eating school dinner
The fish might easily have been poisoned
Leaving me feeling dead
Instead of just sick, as usual,
But it wasn't,
The sweet shop I visited after school
Might have been robbed by men
With sawn-off shotguns
Leaving me wounded
When I became a hero and tried to stop them
But it wasn't,
I might have disturbed a burglar
When I got home
Instead of my mum taking a nap
But I didn't,
Because I don't take chances
Nothing much happens to me
I'm careful never to walk on black lines
Between paving stones
And I always touch my nose and toes
Whenever I see an ambulance,
Being careful can be boring
Tomorrow I might start taking chances
But I won't.

Frank Flynn

The Tunnel

This is the way that I have to go
I've left all my friends behind
Back there, where a faint light glimmers
Round the long tunnel's bend.

I can't see a roof up above me,
I can't find either wall,
My shoes slip on the slimy boulders —
How far is it down, if I fall?

Beneath me the same stream is flowing
That laughed in the fields back there —
Here, it is black, like the leeches and weeds,
And the bats flitting through the dank air.

It's just the same if I shut my eyes:
My companions, all around,
Are trickles, drips, sploshes, sudden *plops*.
Then, a strange, sucking sound.

One shoe's full of the cold dark water,
My hands slither over the stones.
My throat's gone dry, my heart pound-pounds,
but I can only go on —

Till I can see them, they can see me
and again they start to shout,
The rats bite, watch out for the rats.
But now I am almost out.

Dizzy, happy, I blink at the light.
The sun's still shining, the birds still sing.
Someone is patting me on the back —
Now I am one of the gang.

Brian Lee

Questions

1 What is the 'faint light' glimmering behind the boy?

2 What makes the boulders dangerous?

3 What word causes us to picture the stream as friendly when it flowed out in the fields?

4 Identify three unpleasant inhabitants of this tunnel.

5 Explain what is meant by: 'It's just the same if I shut my eyes'.

6 What are the boy's 'companions' in this tunnel?

7 What is going on in the boy's body that shows us he is scared?

8 Why do the other children shout out: *The rats bite, watch out for the rats*?

9 Give two reasons why the boy is 'happy' when he emerges from the tunnel.

10 Why does he 'blink at the light'?

11 Why has the boy gone through the tunnel?

12 What do you like about this poem?

The Cat Came Back

Old Mr Johnson had trouble all his own
He had an old yeller cat who wouldn't leave home
Tried everything he knew to do to keep the cat away
Took him up to Arnhem Land and told him for to stay

But the cat came back
The very next day the old cat came back
Thought he was a goner but the cat came back
'Cos he wouldn't stay away.

On the telegraph pole birds were sitting in a bunch
Saw an even number thought he'd have 'em for his lunch
Climbed softly up the pole till he reached the top
Put his foot upon a 'lectric wire, tied him in a knot.

But the cat came back . . .

They threw him in the kennel where the dog was asleep
And the bones of cats lay piled in a heap
The kennel burst apart and the dog flew out the side
With his ears chewed off and holes in his hide

But the cat came back . . .

They put him in a cotton sack and gave him to a girl
Who was going on a bicycle all around the world
Well over there in China a terrible wreck was found
She's singin' now in Heaven with Angels all round.

But the cat came back . . .

They gave a boy a dollar for to set the cat afloat
He took him up the river in a sack in a boat
Well the fishin' it was fine till the news got around
The boat was missing and the boy was drowned

But the cat came back . . .

They took him to the shop with the butcher not around
Dropped him in the hopper where the meat was ground
The cat disappeared with a blood-curdling shriek,
And the town's mince tasted furry for a week

But the cat came back . . .

Now this cat was a terror and they thought it would be best
To give him to a man who was going out West
Train ran around the curve and it hit a broken rail
Not a blessed soul aboard the train lived to tell the tale

But the cat came back . . .

At last they found a way this cat to really fix
They put him in an orange crate on Highway 66
Come a 20-ton truck with 40-ton load
Scattered pieces of that orange crate a mile down the road

But the cat came back . . .

The farmer on the corner thought he'd shoot the cat on sight
So he loaded up his gun full of nails and dynamite
Hid in the corner till the cat came around
Seven little pieces of that man was all they found

But the cat came back . . .

They put him on a boat bound for Sydney town
Thought with all the rain there he'd surely drown
When the rain came down for the 42nd day
That old darned city just a-floated out the bay

But the cat came back
The very next day the old cat came back
Thought he was a goner but the cat came back
'Cos he wouldn't stay away.

Traditional song

Questions

1 What colour was the cat?

2 Why is Arnhem Land chosen as the place to leave the cat?

3 What caused the cat to be tied in a knot?

4 From the encounter with the dog we learn something new about the cat. What do we learn?

5 '. . . over there in China a terrible wreck was found'. What do you think happened?

6 What caused the train derailment?

7 'Seven little pieces of that man was all they found'. What do you think went wrong?

8 What feature of Sydney's weather is being laughed at in the last verse?

9 What usually happened to people who came into contact with the cat?

10 What seems to be the outstanding characteristic of this cat?

11 How does the writer create the humour in this song?

12 What did you enjoy most about this song?

Better Be Kind to Them Now

A squirrel is digging up the bulbs
In half the time Dad took to bury them.

A small dog is playing football
With a mob of boys. He beats them all,
Scoring goals at both ends.
A kangaroo would kick the boys as well.

Birds are so smart they can drink milk
Without removing the bottle-top.

Cats stay clean, and never have to be
Carried screaming to the bathroom.
They don't get their heads stuck in railings,
They negotiate first with their whiskers.

The gecko walks on the ceiling, and
The cheetah can outrun the Royal Scot.
The lion cures his wounds by licking them,
And the guppy has fifty babies at a go.

The cicada plays the fiddle for hours on end,
And a man-size flea could jump over St Paul's.

If ever these beasts should get together
Then we are done for, children.
I don't much fancy myself as a python's pet,
But it might come to that!

D. J. Enright

Questions

1 In what way is the squirrel apparently better than Dad?

2 How does the small dog show that he is a better footballer than the boys?

3 What two advantages do cats have over humans?

4 The 'Royal Scot' is a train. How is the cheetah superior to it?

5 What is impressive about a flea as far as the poet is concerned?

6 What does the poet seem to be concerned about in the last verse?

7 From your reading of the poem, how does the poet seem to feel about animals in general?

8 Does the poem hold your interest? Why or why not?

WRITING

WRITING FOR A PURPOSE

Whenever people write, they do so for a purpose. For example, when you write a letter to a friend the purpose is just to keep in touch and share what has been happening in your life. Your purpose would be quite different if you were to write a letter to the local Member of Parliament urging support for installing lights at a dangerous pedestrian crossing. You will also be aware that when the purpose changes, your writing style will probably also change. The letter to a friend would be very relaxed, while the letter to the MP would be quite formal, with special attention given to correct punctuation and spelling.

Think for just a moment how your writing style would vary if you were writing for the following purposes:

- to record your day's activities in your personal diary
- to describe a scene for a travel brochure
- to invite someone to a party
- to describe the emotions at a school sporting event to a penfriend
- to write a report for a company on their new brand of dishwashing liquid
- to write a newspaper article about an accident

In all of these writing tasks, and many more, the purpose of the writing would affect the way you wrote.

Now read through the guidelines on the following pages and proceed with each of the writing tasks. In each case, before you begin writing, ask yourself: 'What is my purpose?' and 'How should I write in order to achieve my purpose?'

3 para

ROAD ACCIDENT

Accident Vocabulary

accident	suddenly	cardiac	shriek	onlookers
collision	ambulance	witness	suffered	interview
fracture	tragedy	abrasions	shock	resuscitation

1 Use at least eight of the above words, as you write a three-paragraph story entitled 'Road Accident'. Let the story include details of:

- who was involved
- where they had come from
- where they were going
- how it all finished

2 You were riding your bike nearby at the time and witnessed the accident. Imagine that you are writing a letter to tell a friend what actually happened.

3 The ambulance that arrives to tend the victims has come from Blue Hills Ambulance Station. This ambulance station is currently being inspected for the quality of its service. Imagine that you are the inspector who accompanies the two ambulance officers, and write a one-page report on the efficiency and quality of the service they provide.

4 The police arrive to assist at the scene of the accident, and afterwards interview witnesses to help them with their report. Complete the following script of their conversation, making use of two witnesses. The script could be about one page in length.

Policeman: How did it happen?
Witness 1: . . .

5 A TV crew arrives to do an on-the-spot report for the evening news. What angle will the news item emphasise? — tragedy? fortunate escape? a notoriously dangerous corner? the dangers of drinking and driving? or some other aspect? Write out the three-paragraph news item given by Sandra Delwood. Include a brief interview with a witness.

Sandra: Good evening, viewers. At 2.25 this afternoon . . .

6 Write out a two-paragraph newspaper article on the accident for the local paper.

7 Describe the accident from the point of view of one victim of the accident. Include in your description the person's experience as he or she returns to consciousness in the local hospital. Make the description about three paragraphs in length.

WE'RE HAVING A PARTY

Party Vocabulary

balloons	festive	occasion	celebration
successful	friendship	invitation	stereo
hilarious	barbecue	streamers	informal
guests	serviette	conversation	laughter

Use most of the above words as you write about having a party. Here are your guidelines.

1 Why is the party being held? Where? When? Does it have a theme? After you have decided details, draft out the invitation card you would send to people. Lay out the type and any artwork in an artistic manner on an invitation card.

2 How will you dress for the party? What will you wear? If it is a party with a theme, what costume will you wear? Make a list of things you will need.

3 You have the task of deciding what music to play at the party. Select eight artists or groups whose music you will include. Identify a favourite track for each and give a one-sentence explanation of why you like that particular track.

4 At the party you meet, for the first time, someone you are attracted to. What does he/she look like? Describe, in a letter to a friend, how you start a conversation with this person and your overall impression of his/her personality.

5 Whoops! Suddenly you discover that something important to the party has been completely overlooked. You have to do some quick thinking and take some rapid action. In about a page, tell how you sort things out.

6 During the evening a carload of gate-crashers arrives. Who are they and why don't you want to let them stay? How do you and your friends persuade them to leave?

7 You have the task of making a speech about the guest(s)-of-honour. Write out four paragraphs, or more, telling of your friendship and of the reasons you think they are special.

8 The party is over and the exhausting clean-up is finished. You and some friends are quietly sipping a Coke and talking about the party. Write out your conversation.

You: Wow! I'm glad that clean-up is over. But the party sure was fun!
Friend 1: . . .

9 Write a diary entry about the party. Use at least eight words from the Party Vocabulary box.

LANGUAGE

WORD FAMILIES

Family Forms

Use the correct form of each word in heavy type to complete the sentences below.

Example: Sarah's whole body was **tense** and listening.
The atmosphere was filled with   ....tension.... .

1 Sarah was already there, moved by her **instinct**.
She turned, .instinctly. , in the direction of the sound.

2 Sarah had one brief glimpse of **devastation**.
The explosion .devastated the whole area.

3 Sheets and blankets were jammed into the **space** along the top.
The room was .spacious... and full of light.

4 They **applied** all the strength they had.
It took the .applicat..... of all their strength to hold the settee in place.

5 The wind screamed through the **broken** windows.
'Be careful not to .break....... any of the glassware.'

6 The sound finally faded away into **silence**.
We watched ...silently...... as the planes flew closer.

7 She was **weak** and shaking.
   A sudden ...weakness.... came over her whole body.

8 She sat in the **dark** on the dining room chair.
   All over the city ..darkness.... settled on the smoking ruins.

9 Sarah wanted to cling to her for **comfort**.
   Both decided to dress in the most .comfortable. clothes they could find.

10 Veronica was the woman her father had **married**.
   The marriage....... had been a very happy celebration.

Family Selections

Complete each sentence by selecting the appropriate word from the word family in the box. Each word is to be used only once.

please	pleasure	pleasant	pleasantly	unpleasant

1 Andrew screwed up his face as he tasted the unpleasant... medicine.

2 We were all .pleasantly.... surprised at the way our team played.

3 The waitress did her best to .please...... the rude diner in the restaurant.

4 'It's been a real ..pleasure..... doing business with you!'

5 .Pleasant...... views surrounded the beautiful, coastal resort.

defence	defend	defensive	defensively	defender

1 The demons got past his defence...... and he felt their triumph.

2 Which boat has been chosen as the .defender. of the Cup?

3 'I didn't do it,' he said .defensively.

4 'How can you .defend....... such a cruel action?'

5 The boy's tone sounded defensive. as he tried to explain where the money had come from.

| explode | explosion | explosive | exploded | explosively |

1 Demon after demon *exploded* around him.

2 We kept away because her mother had an *explosive* temper.

3 At the height of the celebration fireworks began to *explode* everywhere.

4 When he pressed his foot on the accelerator the racing car took off *explosively*.

5 'Where were you when the *explosion* occurred?'

Completing the Word Families

Complete the following word families by filling in the blank letters.

1 advertise   advertisem**e n**t   advertis**e**d   advertis**e**r

2 complete   complet**io**n   complet**i n**g   completel**y**

3 glory   glorif**y**   glori**ou**s   gloriousl**y**

4 hope   hop**in**g   hopef**u**l   hopefull**y**

5 horror   horr**if y**   horr**i**ble   horr**i**ff**i**c

6 beauty   beautif**u**l   beautif**u**   beautiful**l l**y

7 satisfy   satisf**a**ct**io**n   satisfact**o r**y   satisf**i e**d

8 signify   signific**e**nc**e**   signif**i c a**nt   signify**i n**g

9 belief   bel**i e v e**   bel**e a**vabl**e**   believ**i n**g

10 pursue   purs**i s**t   purs**u e**d   p**u**rsu**i n**g

11 realise   realis**a t io**n   r**e**alis**e**d   real**i s i n**g

12 anger   angr**y**   angr**i l**y   ang**e r e**d

13 object   object**io**n   obj**e**ct**i n**g   object**i o n**ble

14 purity   pur**i**f**y**   purif**e i**d   purif**i n e**g

15 solid   solid**i**f**y**   solidl**y**   sol**i**dif**i e**d

16 hurry   hurr**i e**d   hurr**i e**dl**y**   hurr**i n e**g

Family Adjectives

Change the words in heavy type into adjectives.

1 An **impatience** move *impatient*

2 a glass of **purity** water *pure*

3 a **menace** look *menacing*

4 a **triumph** cry *triumphant*

5 a **harmony** relationship *harmonious*

6 an **emotion** appeal *emotional*

7 a **strength** hit *strong*

8 a **thoughtfulness** answer *thoughtful / clever*

9 an **awe** sight *awesome*

10 a **worthiness** opponent *worthy*

11 a **fierceness** attack *fierce*

12 a **horror** accident *horrible*

13 a **despair** grab *desperate*

14 an **expression** tone of voice *expressive*

15 an **innocence** mistake *innocent*

16 an **energy** run *energetic*

Family Extensions

Select appropriate words from the box below and change their form to fit the sentences. The first example has been done for you and the first letters have been provided.

inclined	rapidly	disaster	concentrate
annoyed	hopeless	vaguely	distort

1 Ket noticed an ..inclination. to forget everything and just drift.

2 The tug on the line seemed to Ket to be nothing but an a.*nnoyance*

3 They felt trapped but continued to search h.*opelessly*... for some sign of a way through.

4 There was a v.*ague*.......... feeling that the roof of the cavern was rising.

5 Too r.*apid*.......... an ascent could cause one of them to experience 'the bends'.

6 The curve in the rockface at first seemed to be a d.*istortion*.. caused by the glass in his mask. *distortion*

7 The whole experience could have been d.*isastrous*.. if the boys had not been roped together.

8 Each section of the ascent called for Ket's utmost c.*oncentration*... .

GETTING IT RIGHT

DIRECT AND INDIRECT SPEECH

Sentences written in direct speech *express* the actual words spoken. Sentences written in indirect speech *report* the words that were spoken.

Example: Veronica said, 'He won't be able to help us.'   (direct speech)
Veronica said that he would not be able to help them.   (indirect speech)

Note that the change often involves:

- the use of different punctuation
- a change in word order
- a change in the tense of the verb

From Direct to Indirect Speech

The following sentences are in direct speech. Rewrite each of them in indirect speech.

1 Sarah asked, 'Is it over?'

2 Veronica said, 'That was just the beginning.'

3 Sarah shouted, 'We won't stand a chance!'

4 Veronica asked, 'Are you all right?'

5 Sarah asked, 'Do you think Daddy is still alive?'

From Indirect to Direct Speech

The following sentences are in indirect speech. Rewrite each of them in direct speech.

Example: The writer said that he had finished the book.   (indirect speech)
The writer said, 'I have finished the book.'   (direct speech)

1 Veronica replied that it was still too dangerous.

2 Sarah asked if she could go outside.

3 The older woman said to Sarah that she would not leave her.

4 Sarah said that she would be all right if she knew that her father was safe.

5 Veronica instructed Catherine to hide under the table.

DRAMA

It's Not Easy Saving the World, You Know

by Robert Hood

CHARACTERS

Trends-Former Gargelhikspoonwobble
Debbie Raggriter
Hermyonus Wormfeatures
Charlie Wimp
Sharleen Goober
Dr Gorgeous Gung-Ho
Sher Impudence
Hideous Goon
Superhero 1
Superhero 2
Superhero 3 (non-speaking)
Superhero 4
various sleazy-looking characters (non-speaking)
crew (non-speaking)
voice

The Scene: A sleazy bar. There are various sleazy-looking characters sitting around at tables — drinking, gambling and wearing dull clothes that are all alike. One of the sleazy characters is Trends-Former Gargelhikspoonwobble, who looks like an ordinary person, but is in reality an android from the planet Megabucks. He is wearing a dirty greatcoat.

Debbie Raggriter, ace reporter, enters. She is also dressed in dull clothes like the other characters, only less sleazy. She is followed by a disgusting-looking creature called Hermyonus Wormfeatures.

Worm   *(Pointing to Trends-Former Gargelhikspoonwobble)*   That's him, your journalistship.
Debbie   Are you sure?
Worm   No, I'm Hermyonus Wormfeatures.
Debbie   I know that. Don't be stupid!
Worm   Sorry.

Debbie   Well, are you sure?

Worm   That I'm Hermyonus Wormfeatures? Of course I am.

Debbie   *(Frustrated)*   Are you sure that's him!

Worm   Who?

Debbie   Good Grief! Look, it's quite simple. Are you sure that person over there is the hero we're looking for?

Worm   Yep, I'm sure.

Debbie   He doesn't look like he could save 20 cents, let alone the world.

Worm   Nevertheless, that's him.

Debbie   How do you know?

Worm   I have my sources!

Debbie   What sources?

Worm   Oh, there's tomato, worcestershire, tartare, bearnaise, port and onion, asparagus and green ant . . .

Debbie   You drive me crazy, Wormfeatures, you know that?

Worm   Always ready to please, your royal reportership.

(Debbie leaves him with a gesture of disgust and goes to Trends-Former.)

Debbie   Excuse me.

Trend   *(Surprised)*   Arghhh!   *(He drops his glass.)*   Now look what you've made me do. Sneaking up on people like that . . . you could scare a person half to death.

Debbie   Sorry.

Trend   You've made me spill my drink.

Debbie   But the glass was empty.

Trend   Naturally. I never fill it. If I drink, everything spins around and I fall over.

Debbie   You mean you get drunk?

Trend   No. I short-circuit. That's why I never touch the stuff.

Debbie   Short-circuit? You mean, you're a robot? That's great!

Trend   Go away. I'm busy.

Debbie   But I'm a reporter. I smell a story in this.

Trend   That's not a story you can smell, it's my socks. I haven't changed them in over a year and they're drenched in transmission oil.

Debbie   Do you leak?

Trend   That's getting a bit personal, isn't it?

Debbie   Well, what kind of robot are you then? You look so dull and grotty, and robots are usually nice and shiny.

Trend   I'm a Trends-Former.

Debbie   A Trends-Former? Don't you mean a Transformer — one of those androids that can change into a car or plane or a totally impractical gadget for opening jam-jar lids?

Trend   No. I mean Trends-Former. *We* can only change into a new set of clothes.

Debbie   So you're an android version of Clark Kent, eh? A change of clothes in a phone booth and you're ready for action.

Trend   More like an android version of a clothes rack, actually. You see, I'm a trendoid. Trendoids are related to androids, only they're much trendier.

Debbie   But you look so horrible. Why haven't you changed your socks in over a year if you're a trendoid? Aren't trendoids supposed to be snappy dressers?

Trend   I'm too depressed.

Debbie Why are you depressed?

Trend I'm a failure as a trendoid, that's why. Look!

(Trend opens his coat, revealing the worst set of clothes you've ever seen. Nothing matches and all of it is gaudy. There is sudden pandemonium. Charlie Wimp, Sharleen Goober and all the other sleazy characters suddenly jump up, scream and run off.)

Trend I knew something like that'd happen.

Debbie But your clothes are awful, the most gruesome I've ever seen.

Trend Yes, dreadful, aren't they? This is the last thing I changed into and I haven't been able to change out of it. Either my mechanisms are stuck or I've just got no taste.

Debbie Forget it! It doesn't matter.

(Trend collapses sobbing at the table.)

Trend Of course it matters. How can I save the world when I'm dressed so badly?

(Debbie sits by him and tries to comfort him.)

Debbie Look, try to be a man about this . . . oh, sorry. Try to be an android about this. We all have lapses in taste. It's no big deal. Really, um . . . hey, what's your name, anyway? I can't just call you 'What's-'is-name', can I?

Trend My name is . . . *(He breaks down.)* My name is . . . *(He breaks down again.)*

Debbie You can do it.

Trend It's Gargelhikspoonwobble.

Debbie I see. *(Pause)* I think I'll just call you 'What's-'is-name'. Okay? Or 'thingamajig'.

Trend Other trendoids are called Derek or Trevor or Dion or even Trent.

(Trend sobs.)

Debbie   Don't be such a baby, thingamajig. This is your big chance to prove yourself.

Trend   How?

Debbie   My name's Debbie Raggriter and I'm a journalist for the Smarty Pants Radio Network . . .

Trend   What are you doing here?

Worm   *(Appearing from behind her)*   She's looking for a hero.

Trend   Yuck! What's that thing?

Debbie   Wormfeatures.

Trend   I can see that. It's got one of the ugliest faces I've ever seen. But what is it?

Worm   Hermyonus Wormfeatures at your service.

Debbie   He's my informant.

Trend   He looks like something I once stepped in on the planet Puke Minor.

Worm   So that was you, was it? I've still got the treadmarks on my stomach.

Trend   *(To Debbie)*   How did he know I was here?

Worm   I have my sources.

Trend   What sources?

Worm   Oh, there's tomato and white wine special and . . .

Debbie   Shut up, Wormfeatures! You really are too much!

Worm   Okay, okay. Don't lose your cool. It's bad for ratings. You're on air, you know.

Debbie   *(Suddenly panicked)*   Oh, yes. Sorry.   *(She looks straight at the audience as though at a camera and grins.)*   Good evening. This is Debbie Raggriter reporting from a bar somewhere deep in the grotty heart of this city's most seething cesspool of simmering sickness. Braving all dangers and the adulation of ordinary people-in-the-street, I have come here in search of someone who can help us in our most desperate hour of need. Here in this hideous hole of hateful hooliganism I have discovered a hero — an android named . . .   *(To Trend)*   What was your name again?

Trend   *(Grinning into the camera)*   Gargelhikspoonwobble.

Debbie   . . . an android named by my sources as a definite goer when it comes to heroics. Mr Mumble-mumble?   *(She says his name into her hand)*   Can you tell the viewers why you are here in this ghastly place?

Trend   Well, Debbie, some time ago I was hot on the trail of a wicked intergalactic villain. In fact the trail was so hot my radiator boiled and I came to this bar to cool down and have a nice counter-lunch. Unfortunately the barman was very busy and I've been waiting to get served ever since . . .

Debbie   How long have you been here?

Trend   Twenty-five years.

Debbie   That must have been very hard on you.

Trend   Oh, no. I brought a cushion.

Debbie   Could you tell the viewers what you intend to do about the current crisis?

Trend   Crisis? What crisis?

Debbie   You mean you don't know that one of the galaxy's most notorious supervillains and the most evil baddie ever to eat at McDonald's has hatched a perfectly putrid plan of perfidious perplexity and now threatens the planet with utter destruction?

Trend   No, I didn't actually. Tell me about it.

Debbie   Well, it goes like this . . .

(Musical-comedy type music starts.)

Debbie No, no, there's no song!

(Music stops.)

Voice *(Off)* Sorry.

Debbie Through sources of my own . . .

Worm Me. I'm a real busy-body.

Debbie Through sources *of my own* I discovered that a certain evil genius has bought up controlling shares in every clothes company on the face of the Earth. This evil genius, who is not only known as Sher Impudence but is actually named Sher Impudence, has formed all these companies into one company — Dull-Look Pty Ltd — and set them to producing clothes which have two outstanding qualities: they are all exactly alike and they are all really awful in style. Now no one can buy anything except boring clothes — and, moreover, because there are no longer any fashion leaders who are wearing anything except Dull-Look clothes, no one has the imagination to do anything about it — like making their own. The world's morale has completely collapsed. Stars are no longer glamorous, the society pages of the paper are non-existent, yuppies everywhere are starving in their tenements because they don't want to be seen in the streets dressed so badly . . . It's a complete disaster!

Trend I can understand how they feel.

Debbie You must help us, thingy!

Trend But how can I when I'm dressed badly myself? I have no self-confidence. As a hero, I'm a dead loss.

(Suddenly Debbie turns back to the 'camera', producing an advertising pamphlet.)

Debbie   What you need is Superheroes Anonymous — the psychiatric self-help clinic set up by Dr Gorgeous Gung-Ho for underachievers just like you. Superheroes Anonymous is guaranteed to help you with your problem, whatever it may be. On tonight's show we are giving away an absolutely free $10 introductory session with Dr Gung-Ho, and you, whatcha-ma-call-'im, are the lucky winner!

(Sudden enthusiastic applause. The lights fade. During the blackout everyone except Trend leaves. Gung-Ho enters. She is dressed in the same dull clothes as everyone has been wearing and speaks with exaggerated gentleness, preferably in an American accent.)

Gung-Ho   I know it must be very embarrassing for you, Mr . . . what was the name again?
Trend   Gargelhikspoonwobble.
Gung-Ho   Exactly. Well, I'm here to help you.
Trend   But what sort of people come to you for help?
Gung-Ho   Perfectly normal weirdos, I assure you.
Trend   What sort of problems do they have?
Gung-Ho   They're all superheroes who can't cope with saving the world anymore. I'll show you.

(She blows a whistle and four superheroes come on. They stand in a line.)

Some are just plain lazy. Watch!

(She turns to Superhero 1.)

Help! Help! Human life as we know it is doomed. You've got to save the world!
Superhero 1   Okay, okay, I'll save the world. I'll save it for later.
Gung-Ho   *(To Trend)*   Others have just lost the knack.

(She turns to Superhero 2.)

Look, the world is in desperate straits. You've got five minutes to save it!
Superhero 2   *(Eagerly)*   Right! Here's the drill. We synchronise our watches, then we pack a nice lunch, find out what time the first train leaves, put on a clean pair of underpants, feed the cat, leave a note for the milkman, organise a babysitter for the canary, iron the uniforms . . . oh, we'd better take a Vitamin C tablet. You never know what we'll be up against. Then we'll . . . um . . .   *(Pause)*   What did you say needed saving?
Gung-Ho   Never mind.

(She turns to Trend.)

See? Dreadful, isn't it?
Trend   *(Pointing to Superhero 3)*   What about this one?
Gung-Ho   A compulsive.
Trend   A what?

Gung-Ho A compulsive saver. He's saved 87 worlds in the last week alone. Keeps them under his mattress.

Trend That's ridiculous!

Gung-Ho The inhabitants put it a bit more strongly than that. They reckoned none of their worlds needed saving in the first place. Most of them said they'd rather be doomed!

Trend *(Indicating Superhero 4, who is wearing a grey suit and carrying a clip-board and a calculator)* What about this one then?

Gung-Ho Well, you know how superheroes usually have a secret identity — a mild-mannered reporter or a taxi-driver or a football player?

Trend Yeah!

Gung-Ho Well, this one's secret identity is no secret, but no one can find out what sort of superhero he is. Watch!

(She talks to Superhero 4.)

Who are you?

Superhero 4 I'm a shipping clerk. My name's Kent.

Gung-Ho Ah, Shipping Clerk Kent, eh?

Superhero 4 That's right.

Gung-Ho Then you're Superman?

Superhero 4 No. I hate soup. I'm more a toast-and-jammer man.

Gung-Ho The world is about to be destroyed! What are you going to do about it?

(Superhero 4 hands her a piece of paper.)

Superhero 4 Fill out this form in triplicate and I'll see if I can squeeze in your order sometime before next June. If you're in a hurry maybe I can do it in December.

(Gung-Ho blows her whistle and the superheroes trudge off.)

Gung-Ho Pitiful, isn't it?

Trend But do you think you can help *me*?

Gung-Ho Of course. The first thing we'll do is get you a new wardrobe to boost your self-confidence. I've got just the thing here — the very latest from Paris.

(She produces a very dull and boring suit, just like everyone else's. Lights out. When the lights come back on, Trend, Debbie and Worm are back in the bar.)

Trend I don't think I'll take you up on that offer, thanks, Deb.

Debbie Okay. Don't say I didn't try to help. Look, the evil Sher Impudence is going to be here, in this bar, any second now.

Trend How do you know?

Debbie Wormfeatures told me.

Trend How did he know?

Worm I have my sources.

Trend I know, tomato, bearnaise . . .

Worm No, no. The writer. He told me the play was getting too long so he's just gonna whip in the villain so we can get to the Big Confrontation.

(They all face the front and bow.)

Together   All praise to the writer!

(They immediately go back to the way they were.)

Trend   Well, if you're right, Wormfeatures, then this is a chance for me to clear my name.

Debbie   Good idea. Your name wasn't all that clear in the first place.

(Suddenly Sher Impudence and Hideous Goon rush in.)

Sher   The only thing you'll be clearing is out, Gargelhikspoonwobble.

Goon   He could clear our table.

Sher   Shut up, Goon!

(Sher hits Goon.)

Goon   Sorry.

Trend   I knew we'd meet again, Sher Impudence! I tracked you through a thousand galaxies, across a million star-systems, into a billion swamps, down the streets of a zillion cities, along the highways and byways of a . . .

(Pause. He can't think what comes after zillion.)

. . . very large number of . . .

Worm   Places.

Trend   . . .places!

Debbie   *(To 'camera' as on-air news reporter, holding a microphone up to Sher)*
Ms Impudence? Is it true that you've gained control of the clothing industry, thus undermining the self-esteem of everyone on Earth?

Sher   Yes.

Debbie   But how do you find these evil plans affect your own self-esteem?

Sher   They make me feel good.

Debbie   Are you sure?

Sher   *(Annoyed)* No, I'm Sher.

Debbie   How do *you* find these evil plans, Dr Goon?

Goon   Simple. I look under 'Evil Plans' in the Yellow Pages.

Sher   Forget Goon. He's only here to get killed later on. Meanwhile I let him hang around so I've got someone to hit.

(Sher hits Goon.)

Goon   Sorry.

Debbie   Okay, look. How about we just forget the introductions and do the next bit.
I want to get home early to watch *Neighbours*.

Sher   Right.

Trend   Right.

Worm   Right.

Goon   Left.

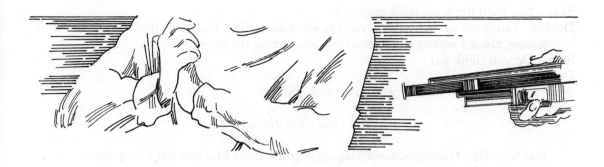

(Trend, Debbie and Worm look puzzled.)

Sher He's ambidextrous.

Trend What *does* happen now?

Worm Sher whips out a weird alien gun and threatens us with annihilation.

(Suddenly Sher whips out a weird alien gun and threatens them.)

Sher This is the end, Gargelhikspoonwobble!

Goon No it's not. It's a weird alien gun.

Sher Shut up, Goon!

(Sher shoots Goon with the gun. He collapses dead.)

Sher Oops.

Trend Curse you, evil villain! This is sheer impudence.

Sher *Sher* Impudence! Get my name right, Gargelhikspoonwobble! I hate it when people get my name wrong!

(Sher shoots Trend. He collapses dead.)

Sher Oops.

Debbie Now look what you've done. You weren't supposed to shoot him.

Sher It was an accident.

Debbie There's still half the play to go and the hero is dead.

Sher Sorry. But I was supposed to shoot somebody, wasn't I? It was in my copy of the script.

Debbie Were you? Who?

Sher I don't know. Him maybe?

(She gestures at Worm and accidentally shoots him. He drops dead.)

Sher Oops.

Debbie We'll just have to make the most of it, I guess.

Sher What'll we do? My next line is 'There's no use trying to escape, Gargelhikspoonwobble. I've got you covered.' I can hardly say that to a dead trendoid, can I?

Debbie We could give the writer a ring.

Sher   No. He'd think we were engaged.

Debbie   I suppose so. Why don't you try something like: 'Ha! Now that What's-'is-name is gone, there's no one left to stop me conquering the universe!'

Sher   Do you think so?

Debbie   Yep.

Sher   Okay. But I'm feeling pretty nervous about it.

(She clears her throat.)

Ha! Now that Hikelspoonwobblegarg is gone, there's no one left to cop me stonkering the universe.

(Pause)

How was that? I was a bit nervous.

Debbie   It was supposed to be 'Stop me conquering', but it'll do. Carry on.

Sher   Okay.   *(She points the gun at Debbie)*   I must do away with you too, Raggriter, because you know the truth. Pay your stares.

Goon   *(From the floor)*   That's 'Say your prayers', I think.

Sher   Shut up! Who asked you?

(She shoots him again.)

Worm   *(Getting up)*   I can't stand any more of this. I wish the secondary characters would come on so we can get to the climax.

(Suddenly Charlie and Sharleen rush in, wearing gaudy clothes identical to those worn by Trend.)

Sher   What does this mean?

Goon   *(From the floor)*   We're getting near the end of the play.

Sher   Shut up, Goon!

(She shoots him.)

Sharleen   How do you like our new threads?

Charlie   Groovy, eh?

Sher   They're appalling. What are you dressed like that for? What have you done with your really tops Dull-Look gear?

Charlie   When we saw that Gargelhikspoonwobble guy's clothes we just decided that Dull-Look was really nowhere.

Sharleen   Yeah. We'll never wear Dull-Look again. And neither will our friends.

Sher   Oh, no. My plan has failed.

Debbie: Yes, Sher. Your plan has failed — thanks to What's-'is-name here. He thought as a Trends-Former he was a wash-out, but when it came to the point he could start a trend as effectively as the next trendoid. Congratulations, thingamajig, wherever you are.

Trend   *(Standing up and shaking hands with her)*   Well, thanks very much, Debbie. I really appreciate everything you've done for me.

Sher   Her? What about me? My whole life's work went down the tubes just so you could win.

Trend   *(Shaking hands)*   Well, thank you too, Sher. I really appreciate what you've done for me.

Goon   *(Standing up)*   What about me? I died so you could be the hero.

Worm   And you trod on me once!

Charlie   And me. Without me, the whole thing would have been a dead loss.

Sharleen   Me too.

Charlie   Yeah. And her.

Other characters: *(From off-stage)*   And us.

(Oscar-night type music swells, a crew member brings on a lectern and attached micro-phone, lights dim, except for a spot on Trend as he comes forward to the lectern.)

Trend   I'd like to thank the director and the crew, as well as all my friends, both here and on the planet Megabucks. I'd also like to thank the audience, without whose patient forebearance none of this would have been possible. I'd like to thank Dr Gung-Ho, whose course I didn't do. I'd also like to thank my parents — the managing directors of the Trends-Former Production House — and everyone who has taken any interest in me. Thank you . . . thank you all.

(Everyone claps, says things like 'well done', 'congratulations' and 'what a great guy'. Trend bows to them and the audience. Lights fade.)

Questions

1 Worm calls Debbie 'your royal reportership'. What quality of Worm's character does this demonstrate?

2 Why does Trend never drink?

3 What is it that causes Trend to be so depressed?

4 How does Debbie's character change when she appears on camera?

5 In a couple of sentences explain the 'evil plot' Sher Impudence has hatched to ruin the world.

6 Why would Superhero 2 never be able to save the world?

7 How *does* Trend end up accidentally saving the world?

8 What ceremony is being made fun of at the end of the play?

9 Comment on the names of the characters in this play. Why have these names been chosen?

10 What techniques did you notice that the playwright used to achieve humour in this play?

THE SEA

8

NOVELS

The Whale

Thirteen-year-old Otter Cannon is living with his uncle, who is the Commandant of the penal colony on Norfolk Island. In this story he experiences the thrills, excitement and horror of harpooning a whale.

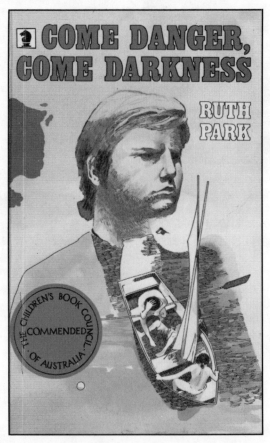

Clouds of seabirds funnelled overhead, their screeching a cover for the sounds of the boats, which with surprising speed overhauled the stragglers in the van of the herd. The majesty of the creatures struck Otter dumb. Right whales were pigmies compared with the vast sperm, but these were the most enormous beasts the boy had ever imagined. Steadily they forged ahead, moving with the regular wheeling motion he had observed from the shore, glistening black backs curving out of the water, massive tail flukes appearing momentarily, and vanishing in a swash of foam.

He could plainly hear the shooshing sound of the blow-holes, and smell the foul blast of warm breath, condensing rapidly to water vapour, that wafted back to them. The other boat was now two hundred metres away, coming up slowly on their starboard.

Not far away he saw a whale's head, an old bull's, marbled with age, water gushing out of the downcurved mouth in torrents. Food, mostly tiny shrimps, was retained behind the black baleen that fringed the animal's jaw. The old bull belched contentedly. He rolled along in leisurely style, for he had not seen the boat.

At a low command from the headsman, the rowers had boated their oars, all except two who used theirs as paddles, quietly stealing up behind the whale. The huge beast heaved over, showing a white patch on his underside, and submerged with a snort.

The headsman nodded to the harpooner who left his oar, bracing his thigh in a crescent cut in the for'ard decking. The harpoon, heavy as it was, seemed but a knitting pin beside the bulk of the whale. Otter had forgotten about Corny Stack, the other boat creeping closer; all he could think of was the immense oval shadow under the water, swimming with seal-like movements, almost serpentine for all its bulk, its short broad flippers moving gracefully. He prodded the steersman's bare shank, pointed.

Like an island emerging from the sea, the whale surfaced, tearing up the water, cascades foaming down its wet-leather flanks. It was over twenty metres long and nearly three metres higher than the men's heads. Its one visible eye, blue with a brown ring, glared in astonishment from that wall of head. Whissssht! The harpooner sent the javelin-like weapon hissing into its flank.

'Socket up!' triumphantly bawled the crew. The harpoon was buried to the tough wooden handle. For an instant there was a splather of pinkish water around the wound.

Agonised, the whale threw itself into a convulsion of foam. The community of Kingston, riding, running, scampering towards Windmill Point, could hear the blows of the tail on the water like cannon shots. The rest of the herd panicked and scattered. Many sounded. Paddy Paul, dumbfounded, saw huge tails and bodies, tall as trees he thought them, upright everywhere, disappearing in clouds of spray. The birds rocketed away, shrieking.

'Stern all!' shouted the headsman, but before the crew could back water, the whale set off for the open sea, with the boat bucking along behind it. Otter was knocked off his feet and floundered amongst the men's knees.

The beast plunged for a moment, then broke water with a smother of white sea that drenched everyone in the boat. Otter was lost in a tangle of legs and oar-handles, but somehow managed to get his arms over the gunwale. He held on like grim death, determined not to miss anything. The confusion in the boat was extreme. One of the rowers began to shout hysterically, but the harpooner gave him a merciless cuff across the face, and whimpering, he bent over his oar again.

Suddenly the whale sounded.

'Hold tight, younker!' warned the headsman, and Otter, breathless, shaking with excitement and fright, held tight. He saw how cleverly the harpoon line ran out freely and swiftly from the two tubs in which it was coiled. It passed around the loggerhead, a strong post projecting through the decking, forward to pass under an iron bar in the bows, so that when the whale ran, the boat would be towed bow first and not overturned.

'Have we lost him?' cried Otter. 'Will he stay down there?'

'He's going deep, no mistake,' said the headsman, 'but he had no time to take in enough air to dally down below.'

The line continued to spin out of the tubs, going so fast that it smoked. The headsman motioned to Otter to pour water on it with the bailer hung nearby. All at once the line ceased to move. The animal was seventy metres down and had nearly run out of air. They waited silently. Otter felt half sick with excitement. He thought he saw a huge shadow underwater; he caught a glimpse of a white throat-patch as the whale twisted in its pain and stupefaction.

Without any warning it rose beneath the boat. It was like an earthquake. The boat was entirely out of the water, sliding help- lessly down the monstrous back as if greased. There was an earsplitting concussion as two of the oars were splintered to kindling wood. Otter was shot out of the boat as if from a sling. In the second that he flew through the air, he heard the lunging tail hammering on the sea, when down he flashed into whirling greenness and bitter cold. His ears roared, his chest clamped tight on whatever air there was in his lungs. He half opened his eyes and saw something like a black tower in the murk. It was the whale standing head- downwards as it smashed with its tail at the boat.

Thanks to Corny Stack, Otter could swim like a seal. He churned away underwater from that incredible sight, saw above him what looked like a sheet of mercury, and flailed up to the surface. The sunlight hit him like a sword. He closed his eyes, treading water, whooping in air, knowing that the boat was shattered to flinders and his com- panions were all dead.

But when he opened his eyes, he saw the craft seventy metres away, still intact; two of the crew were still in the boat, others splash- ing towards it, one man feebly floundering in a circle of blood. But where was the whale?

Otter found himself being dragged into the boat. The harpooner shouted wrathfully at the crew of the other boat, which seemed reluctant to come closer. Indeed there seemed to be a quarrel going on between the young officer who commanded it, and the soldiers and convicts who formed the crew.

The wounded man lay half-conscious in the bottom of the boat. A large splinter from one of the broken oars had pierced his upper

arm. Without a moment's hesitation the headsman put his foot on the man's chest and wrenched out the thin spear of wood. The man shrieked and swooned. The headsman pulled off his neckerchief, pulled it cruelly tight above the wound, and said tersely: 'He'll do.'

Otter took the man's place at the oar. He heard that the whale had sounded again, hanging at forty metres as though sulking. The other boat had now withdrawn some distance away.

'What's amiss with them chicken-livered rogues?'

The headsman angrily bellowed across the water at them, but the argument continued. There was no time to wonder what it was all about, for now the water gurgled and bubbled, the whale was rising, wallowing, for the vast body was wound round and around in the line. It blew once, twice.

'Haul slack.'

Coolly the men hauled in what slack they could, coiling it carefully in the tubs. Now the harpooner went aft to the steering sweep, for it was the headsman's duty to place the killing lance in the quarry. They drew as closely as was safe to the exhausted beast. It was too close for Otter. He felt his blood freeze.

One of the convicts groaned out prayers, not for safety, but that the 'fish' should be got. He was a gaunt ravenous creature; the bones of his back stuck out like knobs.

'Go it, Joe!' shouted the harpooner. The deadly lance, razor sharp, whistled through the air, deep into the vitals of the animal. The whale leaped convulsively, set off trailing the boat at a fantastic speed. But the lance had punctured its lung. It spouted hard, throwing up a spurt of blood as big as a barrel.

Later, when Paddy Paul asked his brother to describe the last flurry of the whale, Otter answered, 'I can't truly remember. There was water going up like fountains, so that I thought we would founder, and then the whale rolling over all of a sudden, and floating.'

Most of all he remembered a vast expanse of poppy-red water, and his resolution that never again would he go whale-hunting.

from *Come Danger, Come Darkness* by Ruth Park

Reading for Meaning

1 How did the seagulls help the boats to approach the whales without being heard?

2 How did Otter react to the sight of the whales?

3 What could Otter hear as the boat came closer to the whale?

4 How do you know that the old bull had not seen the boat?

5 Why had most of the rowers boated their oars?

6 What words can you find that show the whale was huge?

7 What did the rest of the whales do when the old bull had been harpooned?

8 What happened to the birds?

9 What happened to Otter when the whale set off for the open sea?

10 What did the harpooner do to the rower who began to shout hysterically?

11 Why couldn't the whale stay down for a long period?

12 How do you know that the line was going very fast?

13 What happened to the boat when the whale rose beneath it?

14 What happened to Otter?

15 'It was the whale standing head-downwards . . .' What was the whale trying to do?

16 Why was the harpooner shouting wrathfully at the crew of the other boat?

17 What was happening in the other boat?

18 How did the headsman remove the large splinter from the wounded man?

19 Why did Otter feel his blood freeze?

20 Why do you think Otter decided that he would never go whale-hunting again?

The Octopus

Mafatu shows great courage when he enters the domain of the dreaded octopus.

How fantastic was that undersea world! The boy saw branching staghorn corals, as large as trees, through which jellyfishes floated like a film of fog. He saw shoals of tiny mullet, miniature arrowheads — the whole school scarcely larger than a child's hand. A conger eel drew its ugly head back within a shadowy cavern.

Here beside the wall of reef Mafatu's bamboo fish trap hung suspended; before he returned to shore he would empty the trap. It had been undisturbed since the killer shark was killed, and each day had yielded up a good supply of mullet or crayfish or lobsters. Here the wall of living coral descended to the lagoon floor. Its sides were pierced with caves of darkness whose mystery the boy felt no desire to explore. Far below, perhaps forty feet, the sandy floor of the lagoon was clear and green in the dappled light. A parrot fish emerged from the gloom, nibbled at Mafatu's bait, then vanished.

'Aué! These fish must be well fed. My piece of crab meat does not tempt them.'

The boy decided to give it up and content himself with the fish in the bamboo trap. He leaned over the gunwale and pulled it up out of water. Through the openings in the cage he could see three lobsters, blue-green and fat. What luck! But as he dragged the heavy, wet trap over the gunwale, the fibre cord that fastened his knife about his neck caught on an end of bamboo. The trap slipped. The cord snapped. The knife fell into the water.

With dismay the boy watched it descend. It spiralled rapidly, catching the sunlight as it dropped down, down to the sandy bottom. And there it lay, just under the edge of the branching staghorn. Mafatu eyed it uncertainly. His knife — the knife he had laboured so hard to shape . . . He knew what he ought to do: he should dive and retrieve it. To make another knife so fine would take days. Without it he was seriously handicapped. He *must* get his knife! But . . .

The reef-wall looked dark and forbidding in the fading light. Its black holes were the home of the giant *feké* — the octopus . . . The boy drew back in sudden panic. He had never dived as deep as this. It might be even deeper than he thought, for the clarity of the water confused all scale of distance. The knife looked so very near, and yet . . . There it lay, gleaming palely.

The boy gazed down at it with longing. He remembered the morning he had found the whale's skeleton; the first one he had ever seen. Surely Maui, God of the Fishermen, had sent the whale there to die for Mafatu's use! The long hours that had gone into the making of the knife . . . It had saved Uri's life, too. And now Uri, in the bow of the canoe, was looking at his master with eyes so puzzled and true.

Mafatu drew a deep breath. How could be abandon his knife? Would Maui (the thought chilled him) think him a coward? Was he still Mafatu, the Boy Who Was Afraid?

He leaped to his feet, gave a brave hitch to his pareau. Then he was overside in the water. He clung for a moment to the gunwale, breathing deeply. Inhaling, then releasing the air in a long drawn whistle, he prepared his lungs for the pressure of the depths. Many times he had seen the pearl divers do it. In the canoe lay a coral weight fastened to a length of sennit. Mafatu took this weight and held the cord in his toes. With a final deep breath he descended feet-first, allowing the weight to pull him downward. At about twenty feet he released the weight, turned over, and swam for the bottom.

Here the water was cool and green. The sunlight filtered from above in long, oblique bands. Painted fishes fled before him. He saw a giant *pahua*, a clam shell, five feet across and taller than he: its open lips waiting to snap shut upon fish or man. Green fronds waved gently as if in some submarine wind. A shadow moved above the boy's head and he glanced upward in alarm: only a sand shark cruising harmlessly. . . An eel, like a cold waving ribbon, touched his leg and was gone.

The knife — there it lay. How sharp and bright it looked. Now the boy's hands were upon it. He seized it and sprang upward toward the light.

In that second a whiplash shot out from a cavern at his back: a lash like a length of rubber hose. The boy caught the flash of vacuum cups that lined its under surface. Panic stabbed him. The *feké* — the octopus! Another lash whipped forth and encircled his waist. It drew taut. Then the octopus came forth from its den to face and kill its prey.

Mafatu saw a purplish globe of body, eyes baleful and fixed as fate; a parrot-mouth, cruel and beaked, that worked and wobbled. . . Another whiplash encircled the boy's leg. The knife — Desperately Mafatu stabbed for one of the eyes. Then darkness clouded the water as the octopus siphoned out his venom. There in submarine gloom a boy fought for his life with the most dreaded monster of the deep. He could feel the sucking pressure of those terrible tentacles . . . His wind was almost gone.

Blindly Mafatu stabbed again, this time for the other eye. The blow, so wildly driven, went true. The terrible grip relaxed, slacked. The tentacles grew limp. Then Mafatu was springing upward, upward, drawn up toward light and air and life.

When he reached the canoe he had hardly enough strength to cling to the gunwale. But cling he did, his breath coming in tearing gasps. Uri, beside himself, dashed from one end of the canoe to the other, crying piteously. Slowly strength returned to the boy's limbs, warmth to his chilled soul. He dragged himself into the canoe and collapsed on the floor. He lay there, as in a trance, for what seemed an eternity.

The sun had set. Dusk was rising from the surface of the sea. Mafatu struggled upright and peered cautiously over the side of the canoe. The inky water had cleared. Down there, forty feet below, the octopus lay like a broken shadow. The white cups of its tentacles gleamed dully in the watery gloom. With sharkline and hook the boy fished up the *feké*'s body. As he dragged it into the canoe one of the tentacles brushed his ankle. Its touch was clammy and of a deathly chill. Mafatu shuddered and shrank away. He had eaten squid and small octopi ever since he was born, but he knew that he could not have touched a mouthful of this monster. He raised his spear and plunged it again and again into the body of his foe, shouting aloud a savage paean of triumph. A thousand years of warrior-heritage sounded in his cry.

from *The Boy Who Was Afraid* by Armstrong Sperry

Questions

1 Why was the undersea world 'fantastic'?

2 What did Mafatu usually catch in his bamboo fish trap?

3 How did Mafatu come to lose his knife?

4 Where did the knife finally settle?

5 Why did Mafatu feel he must retrieve his knife?

6 Why did Mafatu draw back in sudden panic?

7 What is the meaning of 'the clarity of the water confused all scale of distance'?

8 What had Mafatu made the knife from?

9 How did Mafatu prepare his lungs for the pressure of the depths?

10 Why was the clam shell to be avoided?

11 What did the octopus do after it had attached itself with its tentacles to Mafatu?

12 Why was the octopus horrifying to look at?

13 'The terrible grip relaxed, slacked.' What caused this to happen?

14 What was Uri, the dog, doing when Mafatu was clinging to the gunwale?

15 'Mafatu struggled upright and peered cautiously over the side of the canoe.' What could Mafatu see?

16 How did Mafatu fish up the body of the octopus?

17 How did Mafatu react when one of the tentacles of the dead octopus brushed his ankle?

18 What did Mafatu do after he had dragged the octopus into the canoe?

Surviving the Surf

Even though Johnny is an excellent surfer, he finds himself fighting for his life when he tries to cross the breakers that thunder along the coastline of Australia.

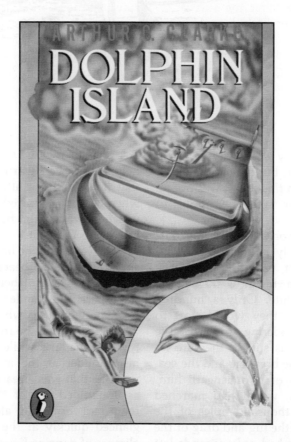

The two dolphins still swam beside him as he paddled towards the shore, kicking the board along with his flippered feet, but there was nothing they could do to help him now. Johnny wondered if, superb swimmers though they were, they could even help themselves in the boiling maelstrom ahead. Dolphins were often stranded on beaches such as this, and he did not want Susie and Sputnik to run that risk.

This looked a good place to go in: the breakers were running parallel to the beach without any confusing cross-patterns of reflected waves. And there were people here, watching the surf from the tops of some low sand dunes. Perhaps they had seen him already; in any case, they would be able to help him to get ashore.

He stood up on the board and waved vigorously — no easy feat on such an unstable platform. Yes, they'd seen him; those distant figures had suddenly become agitated, and several were pointing in his direction.

Then Johnny noticed something that did not make him at all happy. Up there on the dunes were at least a dozen surfboards, some resting on trailers, some stuck upright in the sand. All those boards on land — and not a single one in the sea! Johnny knew, for Mick had told him often enough, that the Australians were the best swimmers and surfers

in the world. There they were, waiting hopefully with all their gear, but they knew better than to try anything in *this* sea. It was not an encouraging sight for someone about to attempt his first shoot.

He paddled slowly forward, and the roaring ahead grew steadily louder. Until now, the waves that swept past him had been smooth and unbroken, but now their crests were flecked with white. Only a hundred yards in front of him they would start to topple and fall thundering towards the beach, but here he was still in the safe no man's land between the breakers and the sea. Somewhere a fathom or two beneath him, the advancing waves, which had marched unhindered across a thousand miles of the open Pacific, first felt the tug and drag of the land. After that, they had only seconds left to live before they crashed in tumultuous ruin upon the beach.

For a long time, Johnny rose and fell at the outer edge of the white water, studying the behaviour of the waves, noting where they began to break, feeling their power without yielding to it. Once or twice he almost launched himself forward, but instinct or caution held him back. He knew — his eyes and ears told him plainly enough — that once he was committed, there would be no second chance.

The people on the beach were becoming more and more excited. Some of them were waving him back, and this struck him as very stupid. Where did they *expect* him to

go? Then he realised that they were trying to help — they were warning him against waves that he should not attempt to catch. Once, when he almost started paddling, the distant watchers waved him frantically onward, but he lost his nerve at the last second. When he saw the wave that he had missed go creaming smoothly up the beach, he knew that he should have taken their advice. They were the experts; they understood this coast. Next time, he would do what they suggested.

He kept the board aimed accurately towards the land while he looked back over his shoulder at the incoming waves. Here was one that was already beginning to break as it humped out of the sea; whitecaps of foam had formed all along its crest. Johnny glanced quickly at the shore and caught a glimpse of dancing figures wildly waving him onward. This was it.

He forgot everything else as he dogpaddled with all his strength, urging the board up to the greatest speed that he could manage. It seemed to respond very sluggishly, so that he was barely crawling along the water. He dared not look back, but he knew that the wave was rising swiftly behind him, for he could hear its roar growing closer and louder every second.

Then it gripped the board, and his furious paddling became as useless as it was unnecessary. He was in the power of an irresistible force, so overwhelming that his puny efforts could neither help nor hinder it. He could only accept it.

His first sensation, when the wave had taken him, was one of surprising calm; the board felt almost as steady as if moving on rails. And though this was surely an illusion, it even seemed to have become quiet, as if he had left the noise and tumult behind. The only sound of which he was really conscious was the seething hiss of the foam as it boiled around him, frothing over his head so that he was completely blinded. He was like a bareback rider on a runaway horse, unable to see anything because its mane was streaming in his face.

The board had been well designed, and Johnny had a good sense of balance; his instincts kept him poised on the wave. Automatically, he moved backward or forward by fractions of an inch, to adjust his trim and to keep the board level, and presently he found that he could see again. The line of foam had retreated amidships; his head and shoulders were clear of the whistling, blinding spray, and only the wind was blowing in his face.

As well it might be, for he was surely moving at thirty or forty miles an hour. Not even Susie or Sputnik — not even Snowy — could match the speed at which he was travelling now. He was balanced on the crest of a wave so enormous that he would not have believed it possible; it made him giddy to look down into the trough beneath.

The beach was scarcely a hundred yards away, and the wave was beginning to curl over, only a few seconds before its final collapse. This, Johnny knew, was the moment of greatest danger. If the wave fell upon him now, it would pound him to pulp against the sea-bed.

Beneath him, he felt the board beginning to seesaw — to tilt nose down in that sickening plunge that would end everything. The wave he was riding was deadlier than any monster of the sea — and immeasurably more powerful. Unless he checked this forward lurch, he would slide down the curving cliff of water, while the unsupported overhang of the wave grew larger and larger, until at last it came crashing down upon him.

With infinite care, he eased his weight back along the board, and the nose slowly lifted. But he dared not move too far back, for he knew that if he did so he would slide off the shoulders of this wave and be left for the one behind to pulverise. He had to keep in exact, precarious balance, on the very peak of this mountain of foam and fury.

The mountain was beginning to sink beneath him, and he sank with it, still holding the board level as it flattened into a hill. Then it was only a mound of moving foam, all its strength stolen from it by the braking action of the beach. Through the now aimless swirl of foam, the board still darted forward, coasting like an arrow under its own momentum. Then there came a sudden jolt, a long snaky slither — and Johnny found himself looking not at moving water but at motionless sand.

At almost the same instant he was grabbed by firm hands and hoisted to his feet. There were voices all around him, but he was still deafened by the roar of the sea and heard only a few scattered phrases like, 'Crazy young fool — lucky to be alive — not one of *our* kids.'

'I'm all right,' he muttered, shaking himself free.

Then he turned back, wondering if he could see any sign of Sputnik and Susie beyond the breakers. But he forgot all about them in that shattering moment of truth.

For the first time, as he stared at the mountainous waves storming and smoking towards him, he saw what he had ridden through. This was something that no man could hope to do twice; he was indeed lucky to be alive.

Then his legs turned to water as the reaction hit him, and he was thankful to sit down, clutching with both hands at the firm, welcoming Australian soil.

from *Dolphin Island* by Arthur C. Clarke

Reading for Meaning

1 'This looked a good place to go in.' Give two reasons why Johnny decided it was a good place to head for shore.

2 How did Johnny know that the people on the sand dunes had seen him wave?

3 'Then Johnny noticed something that did not make him at all happy.' What was this something?

4 What did Johnny know about Australians?

5 Read the paragraph beginning 'He paddled slowly forward . . .' What words describe the sounds made by the surf?

6 In your own words say what 'tumultuous ruin' means.

7 Why did Johnny spend a long time 'at the outer edge of the white water'?

8 What were the waving, excited people on the beach trying to warn him against?

9 What happened to the wave Johnny missed?

10 'Here was one that was already beginning to break . . .' How did Johnny know that this was the right wave?

11 Explain why Johnny didn't need to paddle furiously anymore once his board was in the grip of the wave?

12 What happened to the sounds of the sea when the wave had taken him?

13 What was the only sound he was really conscious of?

14 Give two reasons why Johnny moved backward and forward on his board by fractions of an inch.

15 What great danger threatened Johnny as the wave approached the beach?

16 Why did Johnny have to check the 'forward lurch' of his board?

17 When did Johnny realise he had succeeded in reaching the shore?

18 This passage has an appeal for non-surfers as well as surfers. Why is this?

POETRY

POEMS OF THE SEA

The Song of the Whale

Heaving mountain in the sea,
Whale, I heard you
Grieving.

Great whale, crying for your life,
Crying for your kind, I knew
How we would use
Your dying:

Lipstick for our painted faces,
Polish for our shoes.

Tumbling mountain in the sea,
Whale, I heard you
Calling.

Bird-high notes, keening, soaring:
At their edge a tiny drum
Like a heartbeat.

We would make you
Dumb.

In the forest of the sea,
Whale, I heard you
Singing,

Singing to your kind.
We'll never let you be.
Instead of life we choose

Lipstick for our painted faces,
Polish for our shoes.

Kit Wright

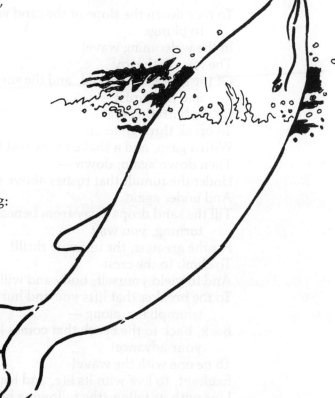

Questions

1 What words in the first verse show that the whale is huge?

2 How does the poet give the impression he is talking directly to the whale?

3 'Crying for your kind'. What is the whale doing?

4 *'Lipstick for our painted faces/Polish for our shoes'*. What is the poet telling us?

5 What is the meaning of 'We would make you/Dumb'?

6 What does the poet mean by 'We'll never let you be'?

7 What is the poet's message to the reader in 'The Song of the Whale'?

8 What are your feelings towards whales?

Surfer

To race down the slope of the sand with a shout, and
    to plunge
In the welcoming wave!
The joy, oh the joy
Of the shock of the cold, and the surge and the pull
    and the thrust
Of the buffeting sea!
To break through to air
With a gasp, and a shake of the wet from your hair,
Then down again, down —
Under the tumult that rushes above you
And under again
Till the sand drops away from beneath you and
    turning, you wait
For the greatest, the ultimate thrill!
To climb to the crest
And to yield yourself, body and will,
To the breaker that lifts you and hurls you,
    triumphant, along —
Back, back to the beach that comes leaping to meet
    your advance!
To be one with the wave!
Exultant, to live with its life, and leaving it
Live with its fellow, the following billow!
For hour after hour, for day after glorious day,
You are fish, you are man, you are thundering
wave,
    you are spray!

Lydia Pender

Beginner's Luck

Well, he had his fibreglass rod
With a fixed spool reel
And monafilament line,
The kind you read about
In the angling magazines
Or stand daydreaming over
In the angling shop
Till the man there wants to know
What it is, if anything,
You're going to buy;

And while he studied
His box of assorted flies
And weights for his float
Of graded size
The brown, red-speckled fish
Lay at anchor
In the shadows of the stream.

And while he watched the eddies
And looked for a likely spot
With overhanging boughs
From where he could ambush
The unsuspecting fish,
I with my bamboo cane
With a worm on a pin
At the end of a piece of string
Was hauling them in.

Stanley Cook

Questions

1 How does the poet give the impression he is talking directly to the reader?

2 What is the poet describing in the first stanza?

3 What was happening while the fisherman was studying 'His box of assorted flies'?

4 What was happening while the fisherman was looking for 'a likely spot'?

5 Why is the poem called 'Beginner's Luck'?

6 How do you think the fisherman with the fibreglass rod would have felt when he saw the poet 'hauling them in'?

7 Did you find this poem humorous or serious? Explain your viewpoint.

8 Why do you think the poet wrote this poem?

Prawning

In the nine o'clock dark we wait for moon-rise
Over the prussian blue lake
That looks like ink
Not water.
Our cold feet walk with a faint
Watery slap
The perimeter of the empty baths
And we mutter about not enough hands
For nets and buckets and swaying lantern.
Watching.
Waiting.
Watching.
The lantern-light draws a perfect circle in the lake
That reveals
A world of palest green
All one colour and shimmering
The sand, the weed, and swaying water.
And held there
Just for an instant
A prawn.
A mere outline
Green as the water.
As we reach for the net
A twitch and it's gone

Catherine Warry

Questions

1 What is happening at the beginning of the poem?

2 What words indicate that it is very dark beside the lake?

3 What word indicates the sound the people are making as they walk along the shore?

4 What complaint do they make as they walk along?

5 'The lantern-light draws a perfect circle in the lake'. What is happening?

6 What does the poet see in the 'world of palest green'?

7 What happens as they reach for the net?

8 What has the poem revealed to you about prawning?

9 What title would you give the poem?

10 Did you enjoy this poem? Why or why not?

The Ships

The little ships
From the harbour sail
Bang in the teeth
Of a southerly gale.

The great white waves
Wash to and fro;
Drum, drum, drum,
Say the engines below.

With their oilskins on
The captains stand;
They drop their nets
Far out from land.

And they bring home,
For you and me,
Snapper and groper
And terakihi.

Then the little ships
At anchor lie,
And the captains' coats
Hang up to dry.

James K. Baxter

Crabs

Crabs, hiders in rock pools,
Scuttling out sideways when nobody's looking,
Ready to pinch an unwary toe.
How do you manage to disappear so completely
Down into the sand with such incredible speed?
If I manage to catch you
Your small beady eyes seem to look up to heaven,
Imploring to be saved from the fishmonger's slab.
All right, do not worry.
I shall let you go,
If only to see your amazing sideways exit.

Katherine Tyrrell

WRITING

DESCRIBING OBJECTS

Looking at an object and then describing it in words is a good test of your writing skills. You must become aware of the details of the object. Observe carefully its shape, size, colour and texture. Think about the impression it makes on you. Have a look now at these descriptions written by famous novelists, Nicholas Monsarrat and John Steinbeck.

THE SHIP

A fighting ship . . . He raised his eyes and looked at *Compass Rose* again. She was odd, definitely odd, even making allowances for her present unfinished state. She was two hundred feet long, broad, chunky, and graceless: designed purely for anti-submarine work, and not much more than a floating platform for depth-charges, she was the prototype of a class of ship which could be produced quickly and cheaply in the future, to meet the urgent demands of convoy escort.

Her mast, contrary to naval practice, was planted right in front of the bridge, and a squat funnel behind it: she had a high fo'c'sle armed with a single four-inch gun, which the senior gunnery rating was at the moment elevating and training. The depth-charge rails aft led over a whaler-type stern. Ericson knew ships, and he could guess how this one was going to behave. She would be hot in summer and cold, wet, and uncomfortable at most other times. She would be a proper devil in any kind of seaway, and in a full Atlantic gale she would be thrown about like a chip of wood. And that was really all you could say about her — except that she was his, and that, whatever her drawbacks and imperfections, he had to get her going and make her work.

from *The Cruel Sea* by Nicholas Monsarrat

THE PEARL

Kino deftly slipped his knife into the edge of the shell. Through the knife he could feel the muscle tighten hard. He worked the blade lever-wise and the closing muscle parted and the shell fell apart. The lip-like flesh writhed up and then subsided. Kino lifted the flesh, and there it lay, the great pearl, perfect as the moon. It captured the light and refined it and gave it back in silver incandescence. It was as large as a seagull's egg. It was the greatest pearl in the world.

from *The Pearl* by John Steinbeck

WHAT IS IT?

This game called *What Is It?* will help develop both your writing and speaking skills. In a paragraph or two, you are to write a description of an object without mentioning its name. You may like to describe one of the objects listed below. When you have finished writing your description, read it out to the rest of the class. If your description has been accurately written, your classmates will be able to identify the object you have described.

- a house
- a golf club
- a pair of scissors
- beachware
- money
- a typewriter
- jewellery
- a toaster

- a boat
- a tennis racquet
- a tool
- a football
- sunglasses
- a gun
- a surfboard
- a paperclip

- clothes
- a watch
- a computer
- spaghetti
- a flower
- a soccer ball
- a skateboard
- a bicycle

- a piece of fruit
- a car
- a pair of shoes
- food
- a piece of furniture
- an iceblock
- a mirror
- an umbrella

LANGUAGE

WORD ORIGINS

Creating Words Using Prefixes

A prefix is a word-part added at the beginning of a word to alter the meaning or make a new word — e.g. **super**vise, **ex**cavate, **tele**vision, **inter**jection, **pre**caution. Many prefixes come from Latin or Greek.

Create words by matching up the prefixes on the left with the endings on the right.

Prefixes	Endings
dia	pone
bene	oxide
post	matic
per	cede
auto	meter
trans	ficial
para	dermic
ex	graph
hypo	hale
pre	continental

Latin Numbers in Our Language

Many of the Latin words for numbers have entered the English language. Here are a few of them.

Unus

Unus is the Latin word meaning 'one'. The box below contains some of the English words derived from *unus*. Select the appropriate English word for each sentence that follows.

universe	united	uniform	unique	union

1 Soldiers tend to look alike because they wear a ...*uniform*... .

2 The workers became as one. They were ...*united*... .

3 The pearl was the one and only of its kind. It was *unique*... .

4 The workers formed a ...*union*... .

5 The ...*universe*... is all space, matter and energy.

Octo

Octo is the Latin word meaning 'eight'. The English words in the box are derived from *octo*. Choose the correct English word for each definition that follows.

octopus   October   octet   octagon

1 This figure has eight angles and eight sides.   *octagon*

2 This was originally the eighth month of the year.   *October*

3 This creature has eight tentacles.   *octopus*

4 This is a group of eight performers.   *octet*

Decem

Decem is the Latin word meaning 'ten'. The English words in the box are derived from *decem*. Choose the correct English word for each definition that follows.

decade   December   decagon   decimated   decimal

1 This month was originally the tenth month of the year: *december*..

2 A .*decagon*. is a ten sided figure.

3 A period of ten years is a .*decade*... .

4 Our currency is referred to as .*decimal*. .

5 The army lost many men. It was .*decagon*..

Find the Word

Listed in the table below are ten Latin words, their English meanings and the English words derived from them. Study the table carefully.

Latin Word	English Meaning	English Derivations
audio	I hear	audience, audible, audition, auditorium
pes (pedis)	a foot	centipede, pedestrian, pedal, biped
flos (floris)	a flower	floral, florist, flora
manus	a hand	manipulate, manuscript, manual, manufacture
dens	a tooth	dentist, dental, denture, trident
aqua	water	aquarium, aqualung, aquatic, aqueduct
porto	I carry	porter, portable, transport, export, import
annus	a year	annual, anniversary, annuity
magnus	great	magnify, magnificent, magnitude
mare	the sea	marine, submarine, maritime, mariner

Now select the appropriate word from the 'English Derivations' column for each of the following definitions.

1 a person who sells flowers *(flos)*   florist

2 a place where fish are kept *(aqua)*   aquarium

3 a person who looks after your teeth *(dens)*   dentist

4 a person who carries your luggage *(porto)*   portor

5 able to be heard *(audio)*   audible

6 the plants of a specific region *(flos)*   flora

7 a room where an audience sits *(audio)*   auditorium

8 a ship that can operate underwater *(mare)*   submarine

9 the yearly return of the date of an event *(annus)*   anni annivesary

10 a person who walks on foot *(pes)*   bipedrion

11 made or worked by hand *(manus)*

12 a set of artificial teeth *(dens)*   denture

13 using a lens to increase the apparent size of an object *(magnus)*   magnify

14 a lever operated by the foot *(pes)*   pedal

15 an apparatus for breathing underwater *(aqua)*   aqualung

INTERESTING ORIGINS

Read about the origins of the following words and answer the questions.

TEDDY BEARS

Former US President Theodore Roosevelt, whose nickname was Teddy, was invited on a hunting trip in Mississippi in 1903. His host, wishing to ensure that the President bagged something, caught and stunned a small bear and left it in a prearranged spot. Roosevelt, however, discovered the trick and would have nothing to do with it. When the story emerged, the *Washington Post* published a cartoon of the scene and toy manufacturers immediately renamed their line in stuffed bears as 'teddy bears'.

Questions

1 What was the nickname of President Theodore Roosevelt?

2 What did President Roosevelt's host do on the hunting trip?

3 What did the *Washington Post* do when the story emerged?

4 How did toy manufacturers cause the term 'teddy bear' to be used?

BARBER

The Latin for a beard is *barba* and the adjective, bearded, is *barbatus*; Roman citizens preferred to be cleanshaven and the barbershop/stall was quite common.

As they already possessed the tools, sharp instruments and cups, barbers, who were also surgeons and dentists from the Middle Ages, added blood-letting to their range of services and hung their bloody rags to dry on a pole outside their premises. The red-striped pole remains the barbers' trademark to this day.

Questions

1 What is the Latin word for a beard?

2 Why were barbershops common in Rome?

3 Why were barbers able to add blood-letting to their range of services?

4 What is the origin of the red-striped pole of the barber's shop?

POSTMAN

The postman began as a dispatch rider and the term 'Post' referred originally, in the most literal sense, to fixed posts where fresh relay horses were tethered (posted) so that royal messages could get from point A to point B on the king's service. The term 'riding post' was used to describe this service. Many post-roads are still to be found throughout Europe.

In the 17th century private citizens and trade guilds were permitted to use this royal amenity, for a fee of course. Later still 'common carriers', continuing to use the old term 'post', delivered dispatches etc.

In 1861 the 'penny post' was introduced in England. It was an immediate success.

'Mail' referred to the container for the documents that were conveyed by post and comes to us from the French *malle* which means a bag, pack or wallet.

Questions

1 What did a postman do originally?

2 How did the word 'post' become part of the postman's name?

3 How did the word 'mail' come about?

GETTING IT RIGHT

USING PREPOSITIONS

Prepositions appear in most of your sentences. Here are some commonly used prepositions: by, with, from, for, under, over, above, beneath, across, through, into, during, among, between.

Complete these sentences by inserting the correct preposition from those given in the brackets.

1 The teacher was angry ...*with*..... the student.   (with, by)

2 The explorers were suffering ...*from*...... exhaustion.   (about, from)

3 The books were divided ...*between*.. the two boys.   (between, into)

4 The professional golfer depended ...*on*.......... his coach for help.   (at, on)

5 The criminal was ashamed ...*of*........... his past.   (of, from)

6 The archer aimed ....*at*.......... the target.   (at, during)

7 The student apologised ......*to*........ the teacher.   (against, to)

8 The patient complained ......*of*.......... dizziness.   (at, of)

9 Your opinion differs ...*from*..... mine.   (about, from)

10 Our garden is free ......*from*.... weeds.   (through, from)

11 The girl had been inspired ....*by*....... the music.   (by, along)

12 We were disgusted .....*with*.... his behaviour.   (with, from)

DRAMA

ACT-OUTS

Arrange yourselves in groups of five or six. After your group has chosen one of these situations to act out, have one member of the group read the story aloud. Allocate a part to each member of the group, then act out the situation, improvising as the story develops. Some groups may prefer to write the dialogue first and then act from a completed script.

THE RAFT

A plane crashes in the Pacific Ocean during the Second World War. The survivors manage to scramble onto a raft. They soon realise that they will have a hard time ahead of them and may never be rescued. The water around them is shark-infested and their food supply, with strict rationing, will only last fifteen days. The hot sun and turbulent sea are other problems they will have to face. Act out this situation.

CHARACTERS

Nurse Carruthers   Captain John Whittaker   Margaret Johnson
Ingrid Burden   Joseph Bond   David Gordon

THE ALIENS

Creatures from another planet suddenly enter the Cameron home. The family is terrified at first, but when the creatures explain their reason for being on earth, the Camerons are able to adjust to the arrival of the visitors.

CHARACTERS

Aliens	**Debbie Cameron** (twelve years old)
Mr Cameron	**John Cameron** (fourteen years old)
Mrs Cameron	**Jip** (the family dog)

YEAR 7

The teachers of a Year 8 class have arranged a meeting to discuss the problems they are experiencing with the class. Some teachers are very unhappy about the behaviour of certain students. Their comments about these students are not always flattering.

CHARACTERS

English teacher   Maths teacher
History teacher   Geography teacher
Science teacher   other teachers

ACKNOWLEDGEMENTS

The authors and publishers are grateful to the following for permission to reproduce copyright material:

Poetry and prose
Angus and Robertson Publishers for the extract from *Does This School Have Capital Punishment?* by Nat Hentoff © Nat Hentoff, for 'Surfer' by Lydia Pender from *Morning Magpie* © Lydia Pender, 1984, and for the extract from *Josh* by Ivan Southall © Ivan Southall, 1971; Mrs J. C. Baxter for 'The Ships' by James K. Baxter; The Bodley Head for the extract from *Children of the Dust* by Louise Lawrence, for the extract from *The Animal, The Vegetable and John D. Jones* by Betsy Byars, for the extract from *The Glory Girl* by Betsy Byars, for the extract from *The Boy Who Was Afraid* by Armstrong Sperry, and for the extract from *The TV Kid* by Betsy Byars; Campbell Thomson & McLaughlin Limited (Authors Agents) and Mrs Ann Monsarrat for the extract from *The Cruel Sea* by Nicholas Monsarrat, copyright © Nicholas Monsarrat, Cassell/ Penguin; Carcanet Press Limited for 'The First Men on Mercury' from *Poems of Thirty Years* by Edwin Morgan; Bill Condon for his plays *The Dicey Brothers* and *Facing Sarah Sockwell*; Stanley Cook for his poems 'Beginner's Luck' and 'Racing Cyclist'; Curtis Brown Australia Pty Ltd for the extract from *Come Danger, Come Darkness* by Ruth Park; David Higham Associates Limited for the extract from *Dolphin Island* by A. C. Clarke; Faber and Faber Limited for 'My Uncle Mick' from *Meet the Folks* by Ted Hughes, and for the extract from *The Turbulent Term of Tyke Tyler* by Gene Kemp; Eric Finney for his poem 'Sarky Devil'; The Five Mile Press for 'A recipe for a pudding' from *Outback Cooking in the Camp Oven* by Jack and Reg Absalom; Hodder & Stoughton Limited for the extract from *On My Honour* by Marion Dane Bauer; Julie Holder for her poems 'Hannibal the Snail' and 'The Loner'; Robert Hood for his play *It's Not Easy Saving the World, You Know*; Houghton Mifflin Australia for 'Susannah Potts', 'The Road to Glamour', 'a.m. p.m.', and 'Friends' from *Snakes and Ladders* by Robin Klein; J. M. Dent & Sons for the extract from *Quite Early One Morning* by Dylan Thomas; Methuen London for the extracts from *The Secret Diary of Adrian Mole Aged 13¾* by Sue Townsend, and for the extract from *I Am David* by Ann Holm; Omnibus Books for the extract from *Space Demons* by Gillian Rubinstein; Oxford University Press for the extract from *The Demon Headmaster* by Gillian Cross (1982), for 'Crabs' by Katherine Tyrrell (11 lines), from *Thoughtshapes* by Barry Maybury (1972), for the extract from *The Diary of a Teenage Health Freak* by Aidan Macfarlane and Ann McPherson (1987), for 'Road Up' (16 lines) by Norman Nicholson from *The Candy Floss Tree*: poems by Gerda Mayer, Frank Flynn, and Norman Nicholson (1984), and for 'But I Didn't' (36 lines) by Frank Flynn from *The Candy Floss Tree*: poems by Gerda Mayer, Frank Flynn, and Norman Nicholson (1984); Penguin Books Australia Ltd for the extract from *Unreal!* by Paul Jennings; Penguin Books Ltd for 'Cousin Lesley's See-Through Stomach' from *Gargling with Jelly* by Brian Patten (Kestrel Books, 1985) copyright © Brian Patten, 1985, for 'The Tunnel' from *Late Home* by Brian Lee (Kestrel Books, 1976) copyright © Brian Lee, 1976, and for 'The Song of the Whale' from *Hot Dog and Other Poems* by Kit Wright (Kestrel Books, 1981) copyright © Kit Wright, 1981, p. 17; Pixel Publishing for the extract from *Ratbags and Rascals* by Robin Klein; Rogers,

Coleridge & White Ltd, Literary Agency for 'Street Boy', 'Friday Morning Last Two Lessons is Games Day' and 'The Building Site' by Gareth Owen © Gareth Owen; Maureen Stewart for her play *Cinderfella and the Ugly Misters*; Victor Gollancz Ltd for the extract from *The Great Gilly Hopkins* by Katherine Paterson, for the extract from *Z for Zachariah* by Robert C. O'Brien, and for the extract from *The Outsiders* by S. E. Hinton; Walter McVitty Books for the extract from *So Much to Tell You* by John Marsden; William Heinemann Ltd for the extract from *The Pearl* by John Steinbeck; Raymond Williams for his poem 'Old Johnny Armstrong'.

Advertisements, photographs, book covers and cartoons
The Age for the photograph on pp. 242–3; Antarctic Division for the photograph on p. 106; Auspac Media for the Garfield and Peanuts cartoons on pp. 23, 59, 101, Copyright United Media Syndicate; Andrew Chapman for the photographs on pp. 38–9, 96, 186; Collins Publishers for the covers on pp. 80, 110, 202; Conquest Sports Pty Ltd for the advertisement on p. 149; Malcolm Cross for the photographs on pp. 75, 141, 187; Diogenes Designs Limited for the Footrot Flats cartoon on p. 101; Gaffney International Licensing Pty Ltd for the Hagar the Horrible cartoon on p. 23, copyright 1984 King Features Inc. World rights reserved; Hanimex Pty Ltd for the illustrations, script and photographs on pp. 152–5; James Hardie Building Products Pty Limited for the advertisement on p. 143; Manly Daily for the photograph on p. 131; Methuen London for the cover on p. 76 from *The Secret Diary of Adrian Mole Aged 13¾* by Sue Townsend, illustrated by Caroline Holden; Northside Productions for the photograph on p. 25 (bottom); Omnibus Books for the cover on p. 205; Oxford University Press for the cover on p. 46 from *The Demon Headmaster* by Gillian Cross 1982, © Gary Rees 1982; Pan Books London for the covers on pp. 85, 168, 171; Penguin Books Australia Ltd for the cover on p. 2; Penguin Books Ltd for the covers on pp. 6, 43, 113, 116, 164, 251; Pixel Publishing for the cover on p. 9; Repco Cycles for the advertisement on pp. 146–7; Salisbury for the Snake cartoon on p. 226; Stock Photos for the photographs on pp. 25 (top), 58, 108–9, 188, 200–1, 224, 261; Toyota for the advertisement on p. 145; Victorian Police Force for the photograph on p. 222; Westpac Banking Corporation for the radio advertisement on p. 157; Wildlight/Carolyn Jones for the photograph on pp. 162–3; Wildlight/Philip Quirk for the photograph on p. 24; World Wildlife Fund for the advertisement on p. 150.

While every care has been taken to trace and acknowledge copyright, the publishers tender their apologies for any accidental infringement where copyright has proved untraceable. They would be pleased to come to a suitable arrangement with the rightful owner in each case.

Edited by Vivienne Perham
Illustrated by Carol Pelham-Thorman
Cover design and photograph by Jan Schmoeger